Evaluating Adam Smith

Adam Smith is well recognised as the forefather of modern economics and his success can be attributed not only to what he wrote but also for his use of the language. In this new book, Willie Henderson shows how Smith engaged creatively in writing about the economy and analyses the extent to which he tried to ensure that the reader is drawn into the text and informed by it.

The book demonstrates methods of undertaking analysis in ways that are helpful to new researchers on the works of Adam Smith. *Evaluating Adam Smith* sets Smith's work in the cultural context of the eighteenth century and explores the lexical and conceptual inter-relations between Smith and the sources he consulted. Issues explored include Smith's use of irony and his work in the context of wealth, virtue and happiness as presented in the *Moral Sentiments* and the *Wealth of Nations*.

This study employs the literary techniques of close reading and close textual analysis and applies them to sustained passages of Smith's writing.

Willie Henderson was until recently Professor of Continuing Education/Director of the Centre for Lifelong Learning at the University of Birmingham, UK. In February 2006 he took up the post of Director of the Alworth Institute, University of Minnesota Duluth in the United States of America.

Routledge Studies in the History of Economics

Evaluating Adam Smith

Creating the wealth of nations

Willie Henderson

Routledge
Taylor & Francis Group

LONDON AND NEW YORK

First published 2006
by Routledge
2 Park Square, Milton Park, Abingdon, Oxon, OX14 4RN

Simultaneously published in the USA and Canada
by Routledge
270 Madison Ave, New York NY 10016

Routledge is an imprint of the Taylor & Francis Group, an informa business

Transferred to Digital Printing 2009

© 2006 Willie Henderson

Typeset in Times New Roman by
Newgen Imaging Systems (P) Ltd, Chennai, India

British Library Cataloguing in Publication Data
A catalogue record for this book is available from the British Library

Library of Congress Cataloging in Publication Data
A catalog record for this book has been requested

ISBN10: 0–415–33668–6 (hbk)
ISBN10: 0–415–49412–5 (pbk)

ISBN13: 978–0–415–33668–0 (hbk)
ISBN13: 978–0–415–49412–0 (pbk)

To Angus

Contents

Preface

Although the essays presented in this volume are focused on a variety of topics they are untied by the notion of 'reading Smith'. The title, *Evaluating Adam Smith: Creating the Wealth of Nations*, contains a deliberate pun. The suggested images are those of creating the wealth of nations through understanding and possibly applying Smith's content and of shaping the work itself. It asks us, if we take the notion of the *Wealth of Nations* as a text seriously, to look chiefly at the 'how' of Smith's work. This implies an examination of the means whereby he encoded and hence developed ideas on wealth creation and the dynamics of economic life. It implies that Smith did more than write about the contemporary economy as a matter of factual observation suggesting rather the creation as an act of systematic and literary imagination, a prospective economy, one functioning under the notion of a 'system of natural liberty' and its associated motivational drives in 'every man' (human nature in general) and its related propensities and ambitions. One significant idea behind the present work is that of 'Reading Smith Writing', an idea derived from a book by Kemple published some years ago and entitled 'Reading Marx Writing'. Kemple's work locates Marx writing in the context of the literary culture of his day. I have not attempted this in the sense that I have not looked for parallels in the sort of English literature that Smith had access to except in passing or in relation to Smith's sense of irony. I am interested in making as explicit as I can, within a small compass, the marriage between content and the means Smith chose to convey that content to his readers (real or imagined).

It is commonplace in writing on the *Wealth of Nations* that Smith was a great synthesiser who made it easy for his readers (most of the time) to read his vision of an economic and social world driven by principles of 'natural liberty'. Many commentators on Smith, from Dugald Stewart to the present time, have drawn attention to aspects of Smith's writing. Stewart acknowledges the way in which Smith exercises caution in presenting major elements of his argument, a concern analysed in this work in terms of 'hedging' and 'hedging strategies'. Schumpeter puts the success of the *Wealth of Nations* to the simplicity and even to the looseness of his writing. Looseness allows others to 'read in' ideas from their own concerns as well as creating opportunities for later writers to contest Smith's work in matters of detail. The notion that Smith leads his readers gently on in elegant eighteenth-century prose is repeated in more recent works. So there seems to be a general consensus amongst those interested in the history of economic thought that Smith's long-term success with the *Wealth of Nations* owes something to the persuasive nature of the text and the way or ways in which the economy and the notion of predictable patterns in economic life are created by Smith through writing.

There may well be a general agreement, but this agreement is not necessarily backed by a detailed analysis of Smith as a maker and shaper, through text, of an economic world. The 'system of natural liberty' was not a simple representation of the economic world in which Smith lived. Rather it was essentially constructed as a coherent and imaginative challenge to a world that he viewed as made up of feudal remnants and outmoded mercantile policies. Of course, there are many ways of making an analysis of Smith, and historians of economic thought are quite properly concerned with the analysis of concepts. This work focuses on the analysis of Smith's ways of writing economics and on reading strategies that help reveal aspects of the writing such as text patterns, hedging, the use of narrative and the use of metaphor and irony. Although it has similar concerns as those of Vivienne Brown, the approach is not rooted in any particular theory of text or of literary criticism but in the pragmatic analyses of text based loosely on applied linguistics, rhetorical analysis and reading methods. My aim is to illustrate a variety of methods and approaches. Although there is an influence from McCloskey's work on economic rhetoric and earlier works by Shell on *The Economy of Literature* (1978) and by Heinzelman on the *Economics of the Imagination* (1980), ways of reading are drawn also from applied linguistics. Essays published here are not concerned with philosophies of interpretation, that is the big methodological questions of interpretation, though the work is informed by notions of hermeneutics based on Ricoeur. Rather they are all concerned with applying and hence exemplifying method, that is particular and contextualised ways of investigating economics writing based on a way or ways of reading and of undertaking text analysis. In this respect, it also draws upon a literature on economics writing that continues to grow around the notion of 'literary economics' (Henderson, 1995) and the 'new economic criticism' (Woodmansee and Osteen, 1999) on the one hand, and work that has its origins in applied linguistics and its approach to economics writing, including issues around text-patterning and genre analysis. Research students, wishing to further their understanding of issues such as 'narrative in social science' more widely than can be illustrated here, may wish to consult Barbara Czarniawska's *Narratives in Social Science Research* (Sage Publications, 2004).

In some respects the output of the analyses conducted parallel insights developed in Fleischacker's first chapter 'Literary Method' in his *On Adam Smith's Wealth of Nations* (Fleischacker, 2004). I only discovered this book a few weeks before sending this volume to press and time has not allowed a full reflection on the implications, though I have made one or two minor adjustments in the text to recognise the links with his work. Clearly, and unwittingly, we have been moving along parallel tracks.

Is this of interest to historians of economic thought and to intellectual historians more broadly? The quality of Smith's writing as economics writing has been an issue. Schumpeter, who blows hot and cold about Smith, felt that Smith's rhetorical success was based on his capacity to keep the conversation within the range of his least able readers as well as on his capacity to keep the reader involved. Smith's loose writing was, according to Schumpeter, part of his success. In a more recent scholarship, Copley has talked of Smith's 'strategic imprecisions', the division of labour being apparently advantageous in terms of productivity, and so to be recommended, but culturally a disadvantage (Copley, 1995, 18). Fleishchacker sees Smith as a 'refined eighteenth-century belles-letterist' (Fleischacker, 2004, 3). This puts Smith's ambitions as a writer close to those of his friend and sparring partner David Hume and re-establishes a link between Smith's *Lectures on Rhetoric and Belles Lettres*, and his writing on social and economic themes. The belles-letterist notions of the eighteenth century fell into disfavour in the nineteenth century and Hume's style became suspect, 'tainted with an element of popularisation' (Box, 1990, 6). Smith's original audience was composed of very young students and there is an element of 'popularisation' in his writing. If we are to understand 'irony' in the *Wealth of Nations* one may as well read what Smith says about ridicule in his lectures. Smith's aspirations are implicitly recognised by modern-day writers' use of the compact and highly visual aphorisms that are lifted from Smith's writing, like cherries plucked out of a bun, to make modern-day points. Smith, if Schumpeter's judgement is correct, is essentially engaged in the creation of a popular text, one suitable for polite conversation in fashionable society. Oscar Wilde, in the latter part of the nineteenth century, was to satirise the extent to which political economy had become the object of fashionable education.

Smith is recognised, also, as having achieved a 'synthesis' but more is required to understand how that synthesis is achieved in writing. Furthermore, since the rediscovery of the 'rhetoric' of economics, largely thanks to the work of McCloskey, it is now understood that 'style' is not simply 'mere style'. There is more going on in the creation of Smith's text than issues around developing a 'nice' style. Smith looks at both sides of an issue motivated by an understanding of what we may call 'rhetoric properly understood', hedges his claims and works to make economic thought the subject of 'polite conversation' in much the same way as David Hume did in his essays on economic and political topics and in the tradition of writing established by Shaftsbury and developed by the writers in the *Spectator*. Smith would have agreed with Hume's somewhat (perhaps) pointed judgement that 'Learning has been a great Loser by being shut up in Colleges and Cells, and secluded from the world and good Company' (EMPLit, 534–35). The historical Smith invested a great deal of effort into drafting and redrafting the *Wealth of Nations* into a form that was suitable for publication as a text for the general eighteenth-century reader. A systematic thesis that is accessible and reader-transforming is something that needs to be worked and reworked as a literary product. What the collection of essays published here try to do is to provide insight into the way or ways Smith wrote about 'the economy' (even if the idea of an economy as a system somehow distinct from the social and political came much later) and the theories that he devised to illustrate actual or possible ways individuals within an economy could or should work to create wealth and justice. Smith's writing may look simple but that simplicity was only achieved by careful consideration. Putting views before the public implied, given the sense of the belles-letterist tradition, shaping textual elements and details to appeal, as Box says, in *The Susasive Art of David Hume* (1990), of Hume's writing, to 'the concerns of a sensible man of the world'. Smith would have wished to influence opinion and so needed to work within the cultural assumptions of his first and intended readers. Smith does just that and as a result, his is writing that does not draw attention to itself as writing.

The approach taken here is to treat the text as a worked product and to put elements of the writing under close scrutiny in terms of micro-analysis of passages or features of the text. I have only imperfectly achieved the vision that motivated the analysis. It is not a definitive work but an introductory one. The aim is to illustrate ways of reading or of undertaking an analysis of Smith's writing that can be usefully used by researchers to further their various interests in the study of Smith's intellectual output. It is addressed to those coming new to the systematic study of intellectual history in general but in particular to those interested in the history of economic thought. It treats Smith's writing as an artefact and attempts to explore what contribution the study of Smith's writing as writing can make to our understanding of Smith's text and of its economic purposes. It is not a cultural analysis of Smith's works though cultural themes, such as politeness or Smith's influence on the development of the novel, his use of irony, or of sentimentalism to secure emotional appeal, are illustrated. Its main aim is to raise issues concerning the constructed nature of Smith's writing, the efforts that he made to persuade. The collection illustrates ways of engaging in the analysis of Smith's writing in the hope that the illustrations will assist younger researchers to engage productively in direct reading of Smith's works.

My direct interest in Smith is recent, though I was first introduced, many years ago, to Smith as an undergraduate student at Glasgow under the guidance of Andrew Skinner. I still retain a strong impression of his lectures over a distance of nearly forty years! My interest in economics as discourse is much more longstanding and has its origins in experiences as a young lecturer in Ghana where my students were studying economics through the medium of a second language. Further experiences in Birmingham awakened my understanding that some students find the language of economics difficult. I became aware of metaphor, of the issues around the use of 'if/then' language in positive economics, of the behaviour of verbs and the sometimes awkward use of English in simple economic model building and gradually, of 'problem–solution' text patterns in stretches of introductory economic analysis. In this I was helped by applied linguists working in the University of Birmingham at the time (Tim Jones and Tony Dudley-Evans in particular). More or less at the same time, Deirdre McCloskey was awaking the wider profession to its rhetoric, its particular way of arguing inscribe in writing. It was only then a matter of time before I moved to applying insights from this 'literary' or 'text analysis' approach away from modern-day economics writing to texts in the history of economic thought or in the related field of the history of economics education. The works in this volume owe much in their approach to insights gathered over the years in thinking about what is to 'understand' economics or rather 'economics writing'. I am less familiar, though rapidly becoming more familiar, with the vast secondary literature on Smith. I have tried, however, to link in a number of ways the analysis made here, where appropriate, with some issues found in the established literature. What the works published here (in the main) do is help the reader refocus on the text as a cultural artefact. It attempts to look directly at the text (whilst being aware of the intellectual difficulties involved in such a task). Smith's writing is worth reading and reflecting upon as a literary artefact, and understanding the micro-construction of the text helps provide insight into its higher level preoccupations.

Acknowledgements

I owe thanks to a number of people. Roger Backhouse, Elsa Braekkan Payne, Vivienne Brown, Tricia Cusack, Martin Hewings, Alison Johnson, Ann Lewis, Warren Samuels and Sebastian Mitchell have provided comments and conversations, as have Maureen Bell, Susan Hunston, and many others that have influenced in some form or another what is published here. I am grateful to Suganthi Jones and to Ramesh Krishnamurthy for advice on making the analysis of 'hedging'. Routledge is thanked for permission to republish 'A very cautious, or a very polite, Dr. Smith? Hedging in the *Wealth of Nations*' from *The Adam Smith Review* (editor Vivienne Brown, 2004), Volume 1, pages 60–81 and 'How does Smith achieve a synthesis in writing? Evidence from his analysis of the propensity to truck, barter and exchange' from *Essays on the History of Economics* (eds W. J. Samuels, W. Henderson, K. D. Johnson and M. Johnson, 2004), pages 72–89. I wish to thank the University of Birmingham Press for permission to republish 'Exemplification Strategy in Adam Smith's *Wealth of Nations*' from *Academic Writing in Context: Implications and Applications* (editor Martin Hewings, 2001), pages 150–168. Errors discovered in the first publication have been amended.

Abbreviations

ECHU *Enquiry Concerning Human Understanding* (David Hume)
LJ *Lectures on Jurisprudence*
LRBL *Lectures on Rhetoric and Belles Lettres*
MS *The Theory of Moral Sentiments*
THN *Treatise of Human Nature* (David Hume)
WN Inquiry into the Nature and Causes of the *Wealth of Nations*. Unless it says otherwise, references to the *Wealth of Nations*, and to other works by Adam Smith, will be to the Glasgow Edition of the *Works and Correspondence of Adam Smith*.

1 Reading the *Wealth of Nations* and Smith's other writings

Introduction

There is a huge and international scholarly industry devoted to interpreting Adam Smith. Hardly a week goes by without some new publication on Smith's economics writings. Even to raise the question 'Why read Smith?' would seem to be redundant, and certainly those scholars engaged in reading primary and secondary literature on Smith, and in the creation of new literature, in order to further the academic conversation, are not usually explicitly engaged in such a question. The products of this industry are to be found in intellectual histories, in discussion by economists, philosophers, economic historians, political scientists, those interested in the historical development of Scotland, those interested in the cultural impact of the Scottish Enlightenment and many other disciplinary and interdisciplinary contexts. Whilst there is a great diversity of scholarship, it is also possible to detect, for example, an emerging theme in the current literature that refocuses on the *Wealth of Nations* as an Enlightenment text, part of the outcome of Scottish Enlightenment thinking and linked to the European Enlightenment by common themes, philosophical inclinations and direct engagement (say) with the Physiocrats of France or the continental natural law tradition. So the question 'Why read Smith?' is implicit in the scholarly exercise, and tends to become explicit, in some form or related form such as 'What to read for in reading Smith?' especially at periods when key questions change or old questions are refocused. The questions may not be put in either such formal or such general terms but may nevertheless be readily seen to have a connection with such more general questions.

The products are not uncontested. Not everyone likes the periodisation of Scottish history that the notion of the Scottish Enlightenment suggests, or the reemphasis on the cultural significance of the *Wealth of Nations* as an Enlightenment text (Moore, 1990, 38). Periodisation, and its associated nationalisation, can isolate and may have a tendency to distort. In earlier times those who are now identified as the Scottish Enlightenment were generally known as 'the Scotch Philosophers', the term Scottish Enlightenment did not gain currency until the early years of the twentieth century (Stewart, 1990, 3). There is not so much difference between the phrase 'the Scottish Enlightenment' and 'the Enlightenment in Scotland', yet the sense of who belongs to what and where could be seen as very different. The latter formulation also suggests a coherent European movement and this too may be subject to question.

Even this shorthand form of talking covers individual intellectual projects, disputes and different contexts and may suggest a unity both within and beyond Scotland that on further investigation may not be justified (Brown, 1996, 2). Hume, for example, whom most would consider pre-eminent amongst the group, could also be considered as someone slightly apart, not a member of any University where theological conformity was an expectation, and pursuing, through his religious scepticism, and his notion of justice as a 'negative virtue', a path of his own. Adam Smith's 'theories of justice as a negative virtue', sets him apart, with Hume, some of whose views Smith shared, from 'their contemporaries' (Haakonssen, 1990, 61). The 'mainstream' with respect to moral philosophy, according to Haakonssen, is rather the 'cognitivist and realist tradition' that goes from Hutcheson through Reid and 'on to Dugald Stewart'. The outcome of Hume and Smith's approach is that the notion of 'the common good' beyond the principles of negative justice cannot be secured by law but by political expediency (Haakonssen, 1990, 85). Hume and Smith were also concerned about 'obedience to government' as another 'artificial virtue' (Whelan, 1985, 6). Principles are then replaced by empirical investigation. Danford argues that to see Hume as a figure of the Enlightenment is to distort Hume's work for Hume, who has been described as 'a conservative rationalist', and put limits on modernity (Danford, 1990, 25; Watkins, 1951, vii). Of course, there is a question here about what 'Enlightenment' means for us, as well as what 'Enlightenment' or 'Aufklärung' meant for the eighteenth century. An ambiguity in Hume, also found strongly in Smith, concerns whether that which is 'natural' is inevitable. Smith spots a gap with respect to agricultural development, analysed here in Chapter 7, between what is 'natural' and what is found in history (Wood, 1994, 125). Smith, in the context of sectoral development uses what is 'natural' to judge what is found in history. What may unite the Scottish approach, even given the differences, is a stress on the essential sociability of human nature and hence on links between values, human emotions (human nature) and economic and political life.

There are, however, also valid reasons for the notion of a 'period'. It helps to locate the activity in time and to form a stable basis from which to grow a consistent and sustained conversation around themes, texts and problems of scholarship. It provides an economical shorthand for a set of complex ideas. On the other hand, periodisation can exclude, and in the case of the Enlightenment in Scotland set, those designated by convention as the principal actors apart from their contemporaries. Thinkers not located within Universities may be overlooked in favour of the better-known. Periodisation can lead to ways of talking that by repetition become clichéd and unhelpful, such as the identification of Francis Hutcheson, Smith's 'never to be forgotten' teacher, as 'the father of the Scottish Enlightenment', a product of periodisation thinking, which can cloud as much as it can reveal. Playing around with the paternal metaphor, which is used also to fix Smith in relation to the development of formal economics, can very quickly lead to silliness. Do Hutcheson's concerns and his relationship with Smith make

Hutcheson a part of the Enlightenment in Scotland or a precursor? In British terms it would not make sense to exclude him. And are his colleagues and immediate predecessors, such as Gershom Carmichael at Glasgow and Walter Scott at Edinburgh, to be included or excluded from the generative process, and if they are to be included, in what sort of capacity or role? (Emerson, 1990, 18–19; Moore and Silverthorne, 1983, 73 and 87). The point is that there are continuities as well as discontinuities in the intellectual climate of the eighteenth century, some of which reach back into the intellectual and political conditions of the seventeenth, including the development of natural law, thinking and the assimilation of the implications of Newtonianism into the University curriculum. The aim remained, within the Scottish Universities, to instill 'principles of virtue and good citizenship within a general context of piety' (Stewart, 1996, 274). In this respect, Stoicism recommended itself for study as it was 'morally attractive' and at the same time did 'not endanger the faith' (Stewart, 1996, 276). Jones, however, traces out how this tradition was modified as the century progresses by the growing reputation of Scottish institutions for 'pedagogic efficiency' and the economic and market consequences for academic staff (Jones, 1983, 116).

Periodisation suggests specific and fenced-off questions such as 'What was the Enlightenment in Scotland?', 'When did it start?' and 'When did it end?'. These have their uses but are likely to work best when the questions and the answers are seen as problematic. If we hold, with Griswold and Herman, that the modern world, with all its benefits and faults, is the (unintended) product of Enlightenment thinkers such as Smith, then periodisation becomes problematic (Griswold, 1999; Herman, 2003). Herman points out that the influence of the 'Scottish Philosophers' lasted, though 'in retreat', in the American Higher Education system until the retirement of James McCosh (Herman, 2003, 375). The question, 'When did it end'? is transformed, by this insight into 'Has it ended?'. A problem then becomes determining the sense in which is has or has not ended. If it has ended then Smith's work becomes grounded in the cultural assumptions and understanding of the period.

However, Smith's analytical insights into commercial society and the way that commercial society operates, albeit shaped in terms of Enlightenment concerns, have a significance that go beyond his own historical context. The Enlightenment may have ended, but some of their works still have a modern-day impact beyond the academy. Few economists call upon the Physiocrats to contribute to the appeal of an argument to a modern audience, but an article in *Newsweek* in 1996 calls Adam Smith 'a man of our time' (Samuelson, 1996, 63). The author argues, drawing upon Muller's work on Smith that Smith 'tried to balance the government and the market' (Muller, 1993). The journalist (who shares a name with a famous economist) also makes it clear the he has not read the whole of the *Wealth of Nations*, rather relying, for an appreciation of the work as a whole, on Muller as an informed secondary source. Smith's thinking was concerned with the functioning of a 'decent society' and could inform, according to Samuelson, modern-day debates between American liberals and conservatives on the appropriate role of the market and of government.

Newsweek is not alone in using Smith to make a case. In the mid-1970s, Margaret Thatcher linked her drive for economic reform to 'Adam Smith' whom she saw, in Copley's words, as having 'heralded the end of the straitjacket of feudalism and released all the innate energy of private initiative' (Copley, 1995, 2). Copley's summarisation does not overly distort Smith's views on feudal society. A recent work by Rothschild has tried to revive the understanding that Smith was also concerned about the well-being of the poor, a point appreciated, according to Rothschild, by Malthus in the early part of the nineteenth century (Rothschild, 2001, 62).

Turning to Smith continues. In making a case for globalisation, say, it is possible to reach back to Smith to make a supportive argument in simple terms. The *Economist* newspaper on 27 September 2001 published an article on 'Globalisation and its critics', evaluating the positive and negative aspects of rapidly developing international trade. No matter how significant Smith's predecessors are for the development of Smith's thought, it is Smith, rather than Hutcheson or Galiani or even Hume (the odd mention in the context of monetarism in the 1970s and 1980s), who is quoted in the journalistic press. One of the sub-headings, entitled, 'Good old invisible hand', in the article under reference, drew readers' attention to Smith's notion that individuals choose 'what serves their own interests', and 'society as a whole prospers and advances – spontaneously, not by design of any person or government' (Economist.com, accessed 6 September 2004). This assumes that in waving the 'invisible hand' we are certain of the meaning that can be attached to it. Possible meanings, with respect to Smith's use of the term, to be considered and evaluated are the 'invisible hand' as metaphor, irony, situated irony, synechdoche (with respect to the Deity), a notion predictive of 'general equilibrium theory' and the implications of these alternative views. Rothschild reviews the notion against a backcloth of 'invisible hands' in the literature of the day, including the dagger wielded by an invisible hand in *Macbeth* (Rothschild, 2001, 5 and 119). It may be surprising that so many figures of speech are listed with respect to the interpretation of the 'invisible hand'. Smith as a writer produces many sentences of phrases that are short, pithy and memorable. Aphorisms for Smith are often quoted but rarely recognised as such and their availability for integration into a persuasive argument and familiarity are reasons why they are so used. Notions such as 'the invisible hand' or 'nobody ever saw a dog make a fair and deliberate exchange of one bone for another with another dog' summarise a whole set of ideas in a neat and transportable way (*WN*, I.ii.2).

More recent editions of the *Economist*, in the context of discussing globalisation, also make direct reference to Smith. In the context of the Hayek Memorial Lecture, sponsored by the Institute of Economic Affairs, in 2004, Martin Wolf quotes once from Smith at the start and refers to him once in the opening moves of the lecture. Wolf is a neo-liberal financial writer and the institutional context is that of the free market. Wolf's theme curiously parallels Smith's notion of the individual drive to self-betterment and the capacities of government to frustrate that drive by inappropriate policies (Wolf, 2004). Smith continues, then, to have currency beyond the academic world where there is a desire to find a means of gaining political leverage on the ongoing and necessarily political discussion about what (so-called) free markets can do best and what governments can best do. Smith thought that issues of policy in commercial society needed to be evaluated and discussed and would not have been surprised by the continuation of the debate. Whilst Smith's writing needs to be understood in the historical context, to avoid simply picking cherries out of a bun, some analytical aspects continue to have modern-day relevance, including direct political relevance. Whilst it is true to say that Hume and Rousseau still have cultural relevance, their works do not have direct political relevance in the same manner as Smith's.[1] As a text, the *Wealth of Nations* is still being read, albeit selectively, and quoted and Smith's ideas are still being fought over. Rees-Mogg writing in the *Times* newspaper suggested that the cardinals, portrayed as likely to be under the influence of socialist thought, in considering the appointment of a new Pope should inform themselves of Smith's ideas on the best way to help the poor (Rees-Mogg, *Times*, 11 April 2005). This is an interesting new twist on the notion of the 'bible of capitalism'.

Hutcheson, Smith's teacher at Glasgow, of Scottish descent, was born in Ireland, and whilst he shaped, directly, a more liberal approach to the curriculum and to the education of the clergy, others in Scotland and beyond helped shape both the context and the content of philosophical thinking in Scotland, including English and continental thinkers. Indeed it has been argued that the reform of Scottish University education, a consequence of the impact of the Glorious Revolution on Scottish political and social life, made a key contribution to the development of the Enlightenment in Scotland (Jones, 1983). Many of the significant figures were University professors, with Hume as the great exception and in contrast to the location of much of Enlightenment thinking elsewhere in Europe. The Enlightenment in Scotland therefore drew upon a teaching and spoken tradition, developed within the Universities that drew upon the continental natural law theories, as well as on the implications of Newtonian and (even) Baconian science and (perhaps significantly in Adam Smith's case) Bacon's sense of the inter-relatedness of knowledge. Hume can be seen as working with tools supplied by the 'natural law tradition' as a synthesis taught within Scottish Universities and using elements to establish a new understanding of institutions and social relations (Westerman, 1994, 84). Smith, who shares much with Hume, especially the notion of the significance of history, 'customs and manners' for social evolution, must also have changed the expected emphasis of the tradition. The Enlightenment in Scotland was also the product of significant English political and social, as well as international, influences. To a list of names such as Pufendorf, Grotius, Hutcheson, Locke, Mandeville and Hume must be added, when thinking about Smith, Montesquieu and the French *philosophes*, and, according to Force, Rousseau (Force, 2003, 4). Developing Locke and writing against Hobbes was a source of intellectual stimulation. The balance from within Scotland, from England and from the continent shifts with new perspectives.

The parental metaphor, on the other hand, a metaphor that also links the past with the present through some form of family resemblance, can lead to possibly trivial metaphorical extensions, such as the identification of Edgeworth, Marcet and Martineau, and, more recently, other women economists, as 'Adam Smith's daughters' (Polkinghorn and Thomson, 1998). This is a product of the idea of Smith as the 'father of modern economics' and hence of the idea that economics subsequent to Smith has what can be called a 'family resemblance' to Smith. Generative metaphors seem to recur when a search for the 'origins' of modern economics is engaged with. Skinner reports that Hume's essays were identified by the first significant biographer of Hume, John Hill Burton, as 'the cradle of economics' (Skinner, 1993, 222).

The notion of 'Adam Smith's daughters', however awkward or inappropriate the title may appear, essentially secures legitimacy for a set of writing that was seen, at the time of publication of the first book with this as its title, as being outside the canon and thus excluded from the history of economic thought, considered as the development of economic doctrine or analysis. The notion of 'family resemblance' amongst the ideas, suggests some sort of genetic continuity (as a metaphor). It also suggests 'patriarchy' and therefore an approach to the group of nineteenth century women writers that does not necessarily fit comfortably with today's feminist approaches to women in economics, however much the notion of patriarchal complicity may apply to (say) Maria Edgeworth. McCloskey talks of 'the grandsons of Adam Smith', an idea that expresses not only a family connection but also a degree of difference, and if we push the metaphor there ought to be another set of grandparents, though searching for them is a matter of choice rather than a necessary implication of explicating the metaphor (a metaphor normally suppresses some aspects of the source: the vicious circle of poverty, for example, has direction but no area). Stigler argues that the 'correct way of reading Adam Smith is the correct way to read the forthcoming issues of a professional journal' (Stigler, 1982, 110). This would seem to imply that Smith either works in modern terms or he does not work at all. It would be a view that Brown, or Rothschild, concerned with taking Smith as a 'whole' and reading it within its historical context, would reject (Brown, 1998; Rothschild, 2001). For Stigler, as for Schumpeter before him, what is important is the history of economic analysis as opposed to wider intellectual history (Schumpeter, 1954, 38). This view does however have the merit that it suggests – that a reading of the *Wealth of Nations* undertaken today is not a historic reading of a new text but a contemporary reading of an old one. Whilst we can work towards some understanding of what it might have been to read the *Wealth of Nations* when it was new (to borrow a phrase from Rothschild), the experience of such a reading is not directly available. Such readings can only be recovered through studying the incorporation of the outcome of such readings in other contexts. How, when reading the *Wealth of Nations* at this distance, can we be certain of the significance of what is written in an eighteenth century context? Stigler's position removes both the valid and invalid in Smith from its historical context and in its attempts to deproblematise the reading of Smith would, on reflection, merely problematise it further. We need to keep in mind

Ricoeur's notion that a significant text is both 'universal' and 'contingent', and hence both familiar and, as the past is a foreign country, alien (Ricoeur, 1976, 31).

Whether or not economics has a useful history, the *Wealth of Nations* and its subsequent interpretations certainly have. Smith's work when it was first published was noticed and discussed, according to Teichgraeber, but it did not have a huge and immediate impact on the ways in which policy was thought about or the way in which an international economy could be supposed to work in ideal or any other terms (Teichgraeber, 1987). Rashid points out that by 1815, Smith out-competed other writers including Sir James Steuart (Rashid, 1982, 80). Whilst Smith's book was given a 'warm reception' by reviewers, Smith's influence on economic and policy discussion built up gradually as a result of engagement by others, directly and indirectly, in the changed context of the late eighteenth and early nineteenth century (Teichgraeber, 1987, 341). Ricoeur reminds us that, 'it is the response of the audience which makes the text important' (Ricoeur, 1976, 31). The notion that Smith's sales represent a 'modest achievement' has recently been challenged by Sher (2004, 18) who holds that the work ought to be compared with the success or otherwise of similar works if we are to correctly estimate the extent and significance of Smith's readership in his lifetime. Sher's conclusion is that 'the *WN* achieved greater commercial success during the last quarter of the eighteenth century than any other comparable work' (Sher, 2004, 24). This success in publishing terms provided a basis in familiarity on which early nineteenth century authors could build.

The topic of the Corn Laws and Free Trade was a specific focus for the first readers who tended otherwise to ignore wider issues or to be put off by what they saw as the works' 'scale and complexity' (Teichgraeber, 1987, 340). Indeed the perception that political economy was difficult and that it is worked through a complex and specialised vocabulary, created a space for the work of Marcet, Martineau, Millicent Fawcett and others, including the writers of dictionaries of economics, in the nineteenth century. The *Edinburgh Review* extended over time the issues raised by reading Smith, and contributors, such as Horner, worked to maintain Smith's reputation even when disagreeing with Smith on particular points, as did McCulloch (Chitnis, 1986, 118). Schumpter is clear that whilst Ricardo was a 'serious check' in many respects to Smith, 'most economists were not quite up to Ricardo', and so in the first half of the nineteenth century Smith was 'invested with the "insignia" of founder' (Schumpeter, 1954, 194).

We need to heighten our sympathetic understanding of Smith as an Enlightenment philosopher who happened to be interested in economics because he was also interested in human nature. We also need to heighten our understanding that what is available in a text is influenced by the context that readers bring to it. Different contexts sustain different readings, and it is only if a work is read, to paraphrase Teichgraeber and Ricoeur, that it has any significance, historical or otherwise. Smith continued to be read avidly well into the nineteenth century, McCulloch's edited second edition of the *Wealth of Nations* was still available in the 1860s. The relationships between the status and significance of the *Wealth of Nations* and the multiple ways it has been read over time as problems and contexts change is itself complex. The nineteenth century narrowed what was seen as potentially available in Smith, and that narrowing enshrined in Mill's *Principles* against which John Ruskin reacted vigorously (Henderson, 2000; Tribe, 1995, 28). Ruskin, though targeting Mill, mistakenly (though there may be an element of dissembling for I am not certain that Ruskin fully stated his debt to eighteenth-century thinking on the question of 'sympathy' and 'virtue' in his socio-economic criticism) traced the source back to Smith. There is, of course, no single correct interpretation. It was only in the latter part of the twentieth century that Smith's intellectual output, including the *Wealth of Nations*, came to be seen as concerning a complex of analytical and social concerns including 'customs and manners' relating to economic life including ethics ('virtue'), law and government, issues concerning the cohesion of society including 'sympathy'. The pluralistic notion of histories of economic thought, with many ancestors and many interpretative orientations requiring negotiation, rather than the monopolistic notion of 'the' history of economic thought, is a more appealing contemporary proposition.

Such reactions are part of what makes academic discussion interesting. Interpretation and systems of interpretation, hermeneutics and a variety of related methods of analysis, offer an alternative to science as a basis for thinking about texts and social life as text. One reason for reading Smith, then, is that others are also reading him, or at least, reading commentaries on him. This is a justification at a general cultural level. Smith is seen by many still to have significance for the way in which we think about the modern world, a world that some would have it, has been shaped by aspects of Enlightenment thought, in particular the thought of Smith, Hume, Robertson, Ferguson and Smith's student John Millar and so on. Herman's view is that it was essentially the Scots who invented 'the modern world' (Herman, 2003). This case may be over stated, but there is little doubt that in academic subject terms, political economy (Smith), politics (Hume), sociology (Ferguson) and the systematic study of English literature (Smith and Blair) were brought into being as new and specialised disciplines as the result of the work of the 'Scotch philosophers'. Political economy had an Edinburgh dimension into the nineteenth century that goes from Smith through Dugald Stewart to Lauderdale, McCulloch, Brougham and James Mill.

This general cultural significance, manipulated by the followers of Smith, necessary also for the impact of the *Wealth of Nations* over time, came about because ideas from the *Wealth of Nations* worked its way onto society by a variety of means. In Smith's case it is relative easy to illustrate the cultural influences, within Britain, that flow from his work. Smith influenced Dugald Stewart. Stewart taught Walter Scott, who can be seen as a 'conservative rationalist' somewhat in the manner of Hume, his romanticism notwithstanding (Forbes, 1953–1954, 20). Scott, also an avid reader of the *Edinburgh Review*, read *Castle Rackrent* (published in 1800) by Maria Edgeworth, the daughter of a Lunar Society member (a club of enlightened thinkers, many of who had Scottish connections through their education and experience), Richard Loval Edgeworth, who presented Maria with a copy of the *Wealth of Nations* when she left school and returned to Ireland (Butler, 1992, 28). Ideas derived from reading Smith and Hume, on the nature of rent, on the exchanges in trade that go beyond the direct exchange of commodities, on 'customs and manners', and the links between law, social organisation and behaviour, are used as one basis for Edgeworth's novel of regional customs and manners, *Castle Rackrent*, being another for her detailed knowledge of Irish life. The novel inspired Scott who had drunk deep of the cup of philosophical history, to produce fiction on the customs and manners of Scotland, contrasting cultural and economic conditions in the different context of Highlands and Lowlands and, indeed, Scotland and England. *Waverley* is a prime example. Smith's influence over the novel had begun, though it may be wrong to suggest that Scott was either directly indebted or uniquely indebted to Smith; any influence was more likely indirect and through Stewart. Scott was a friend of Adam Ferguson to whom he was directly indebted for the philosophical elements of what has been called his 'grand sociological display' (Forbes, 1953–1954, 23 and 31), and it is important too to recognise that Scott was influenced also by Hume and Hume's insight, noted by MacQueen as part of the intellectual origins of the historical novel, that 'differences of mental habit exist among nations and between historical epochs, even in the same nation' (MacQueen, 1989, 31). The notion of social progress informs alike the work of Smith, of Ferguson, of Stewart, of Hume and of Scott. *Castle Rackrent* and Maria Edgeworth's adaptation of economic stories, from the *Wealth of Nations*, for children inspired Jane Marcet and Harriet Martineau, and they in turn inspired other fictional works raising socio-economic concerns. Ricouer's notion that a 'work creates its public' and 'enlarges the circle of communication and properly initiates new modes of communication' is exemplified in the various ways in which the *Wealth of Nations* was read as a jumping off point for new works, both fictional and systematic (Ricoeur, 1976, 31).

Both Smith and Hume reflect upon 'customs and manners' in the sense both of laws and institutions and of particular situated behaviour. Smith influenced Robert Burns directly with respect to the implications of the 'impartial spectator' ('o wad some power the gift tae ge'us' is a direct translation of a sentence in *Moral Sentiments* into Scott's) and indirectly through his views on the vanity of the rich and the potential moral virtue of the poor, though the influences here will be multiple. It is interesting to note that Smith is interpreted in France by J-B Say, according to Whatmore, as an advocate of 'Republican manners', again evidence that those passages in *Moral Sentiments* and *Wealth of Nations* that dealt with 'customs and manners', and Smith's assumptions about the economic and intellectual capacities of 'every man', struck a cultural chord elsewhere. French political economy, where it was influenced by J-B Say, who also worked up Smith's 'rudimentary equilibrium theory', developed along different lines from that of the tradition established by Ricardo and Ricardo's interpreters (Schumpeter, 1954, 189; Whatmore, 2000). On the whole, however, the nineteenth century stripped questions of virtue and civilisation out of much formal writing on political economy and especially out of any popular discussion of the subject, despite the protestations of Carlyle and Ruskin.

This influence of Smith's work developed in the early years of the nineteenth century thanks to other writers such as Maria Edgeworth, Jane Marcet, Harriet

Martineau and the socio-economic writers of the Victorian period including the challenge from Charles Dickens. Dickens, according to Bernard Shaw, was Marx 'by another name' but this does not in itself suggest any influence (either direct or indirect) from Smith's ideas as Smith got to alienation (the downside of the division of labour) before Marx. Before the development of formal economic thinking, economic ideas and comments on economic life were carried through poems and stories. Mandeville's poem (barely that) *The Grumbling Hive*, was a work that told a specific and highly critical tale of the role of prudence and virtue in economic life. Mandeville wrote the poem before he wrote the discursive and influential work that later accompanied it. But there were critical poems with economic themes long before Mandeville. Moore's *Utopia* reflects upon economic motivation and economic changes in Tudor England, even if the story is set in a fictional location. In uniting story with analysis, Smith was not therefore original. His way of uniting economic phenomena with human reason and human sentiment (the whole of human nature) primarily in the *Moral Sentiments* but also in the textual detail of the *Wealth of Nations* provided others, such as Maria Edgeworth, Harriet Martineau and even much later in the nineteenth century, Millicent Garrett Fawcett with a rich source of educational literary continuations.

The interpenetration of stories and economics writing continued after the development of formal economics but with a few exceptions (such as the not-quite fictional character, Robinson Crusoe, who moved from real-life to story to textbook to potential real-life implications through the application of economic theory) the links have gone from economics to novels and literature rather than the other way round. Even Smith incorporates the notion of shipwreck into his discussion of 'occupation', that is the taking possession of the free gifts of nature, into his *Lectures on Jurisprudence*: 'If a number of persons were shipwrecked on a desart island their first sustenance would be from the fruits which the soil naturally produced, and the wild beasts which they could kill' (*LJ*, B 150). The story is contained within a discussion of the significance of the stadial theory for the development of legal concepts of ownership (where the 'spectator', unqualified in the version available) is introduced as part of the argument for possession and subsequently by inheritance. Isolation of a community on an unoccupied island makes illustration of key points easier. Stories written by Martineau and Millicent Garrett Fawcett make use of isolation to simplify economic concepts, to specify 'universal' truths as well as to distinguish the real from the purely monetary. Although these stories involve communities and therefore in that sense do not relate directly to Robinson Crusoe, the story lines (e.g. the nature of gold as wealth or the establishment of the inventory of resources rescued from the isolation event) exhibit some similarities.

Defoe's *Robinson Crusoe* taught economic lessons, though this may not have been Defoe's purpose in writing the novel, in the nature of resources (the inventory of potential resources salvaged from the wreck; the inadequacy of gold in Crusoe's immediate context; the transformation of labour into capital) and these lessons, mixed with Smith, turn up in very similar form in Harriet Martineau's and Millicent Garret Fawcett's economic lessons crafted as stories. Indeed, even

John Ruskin in the mid-nineteenth century uses two stranded sailors to simplify his economic analysis of the nature of money. Smith's notion of 'the division of labour' and of the impact of work on skills and mental agility, both positive and negative, and his view of situated motivation, all percolated into popular literature.

One of the reasons that Smith's economics writing readily influenced literature is that both *Moral Sentiments* and the *Wealth of Nations* can be seen, in part if not as a whole, as satires on human behaviour and ambition. In the *Wealth of Nations*, Smith's targets are the greed of merchants and the consumption patterns of the aristocrats. Satire is strongly in evidence in the *Moral Sentiments*, where irony, ridicule, paradox and sentimental narratives, aspects of literature analysed by Smith in his *Lectures on Rhetoric and Belles Lettres*, are all used to construct and evaluate economic agency. This is explored in Chapter 3. Rothschild, has recently stressed and tracked the role that sentiments play in the *Wealth of Nations*, thus bringing the reading of the two texts back into a close relationship. This whilst newly focused on the *Wealth of Nations* is not in itself a new notion. Dwyer had earlier pointed to the 'primary role that human emotions played in individual motivation and social organisation' for Smith in particular and the Scottish Enlightenment more widely (Dwyer, 1998, 1). On such understandings it becomes easier to see how Maria Edgeworth's comic novel, with its unreliable narrator (a very partial spectator), its preoccupation with rent, the economic and sometimes unethical behaviour, and economic understanding and misunderstanding of the Rackrents, *Castle Rackrent*, can be read as an Enlightenment, or more specifically a Smithian tale.

There is probably no single, summative account available of Smith's impact on the novel and so no single source for the fictionally situated 'readings' of Smith in the nineteenth century as far as other writers are concerned. Dwyer's analysis of the role of passions in Smith and others in the Enlightenment in Scotland provides a sense of the cultural impact of Smith and others through the idea of a 'polity' created by 'small-scale sympathetic exchanges' and hence an impact on literature of the day (Dwyer, 1998, 9).

Furthermore, Stewart influenced Thomas Carlyle, and Carlyle, particularly through the development of Smith's insight that education should be used for social and cultural purposes to offset the negative effects of the division of labour, influenced John Ruskin. This became known as the 'Adam Smith doctrine', an idea that holds that education be kept as general as it can be for as long as it can and one that led to the development of an educational system in Scotland differing from that of England, which became, following Joseph Priestley, more technically and narrowly based (Davie, 1973). Stewart influenced Carlyle and Carlyle influenced Ruskin (Henderson, 2000). Ruskin thought of Smith as the 'blackest devil' and so seemed to have been unaware of the 'Adam Smith doctrine', but his analysis of the down-side of mid-Victorian capitalism, his concept of education for working men to offset the narrowing of spirit that mechanised work produces, his choice of educational means to achieve this (science and art) and even his concept of political economy as 'the science of the legislature' owes more, perhaps, to Smith than Ruskin was prepared to admit.

Given the idea that these too represent responses to reading Smith, interpretations sometimes cast in the form of 'continuations' of Smith's ideas, particularly by women economics educators working through story formats derived from a mixture of Smith, economic writers contemporary with them, and (say) Daniel Defoe's *Robinson Crusoe*. Smith's *Wealth of Nations* makes use of lists to organise and systematise knowledge and stories (such as the story of the division of labour 'in a tribe'), and both the lists and the stories were available to fictional writers for recontextualising. One way of looking at the relationship is through the literary convention of 'continuations' (Henderson, 1995). Whilst it is easy to identify textually lists and stories (though some stories contain mini-lists) it is more difficult to determine whether or not they carry a different functional significance. Economists still tell stories but their stories are increasingly formal, built around models that serve to plot key events in a sequence of analyses. A methodological approach to 'literary economics' or to its American version, 'the new economic criticism', capable of tracing the development and making an analysis of economic ideas in literary contexts, is still developing.

A general cultural significance, though interesting, is inadequate to explain the continued interest in Smith as an economist. There is also a history of 'economic' interpretation going back to the writings of Karl Marx, John Stuart Mill, David Ricardo, Jean-Baptise Say, Dugald Stewart (whose account of Smith's economic significance was written in 1799) and of many other authors both major and minor. Stewart, who knew Smith, is now seen as someone who focused on the analytical aspects of Smith and rescued his reputation from possible attacks from those that opposed the French Revolution (Rothschild, 2001, 58). Ricardo developed his interest in political economy as a result of reading Smith, though there was a substantial gap, according to Winch, between his reading of the *Wealth of Nations* in 1799 and his first publications ('three letters to the *Morning Chronicle* on the price of gold in 1809') (Schumpeter, 1954, 472; Winch, 1973, v). Ricardo, who provided intellectual leadership to a significant group of economics writers, including Jane Marcet further narrowed the subject matter, contested much of Smith's views, and wrote in the context of British problems at the time. J-B Say reviewed Smith's work within the context of the aftermath of the Revolution and took political economy in France down a path that was different from what developed in Britain out of Ricardo's work (Whatmore, 2000). In Germany, a considered set of responses to the *Wealth of Nations* did not appear until 1796 (Tribe, 1995, 31). Tribe considers Smith's style, as did early German commentators on Smith, but concludes that German readings were carried out in a German cultural context that laid more emphasis on 'government than on the autonomy of free subjects'. A serious reading of Smith's ideas took place within a ' "reduction" of the text' (Tribe, 1995, 35).

In addition, in Britain, and also in France, Spain and elsewhere, dictionaries of economics set out profiles, in the nineteenth century, of earlier thought and served as repositories of the intellectual history of economics before the emergence of more formal and worked-up historical and intellectual analysis. Smith's work is written into theirs either by absorption or by criticism and evaluation. Indeed

Schumpeter, who blows hot and cold on the subject of Smith's contribution to the development of economic analysis, is of the view that this 'type of leadership' was achieved by Smith because of the strengths, 'weaknesses' and 'the very looseness' of his arguments (Schumpeter, 1954, 189). More recently Tribe has talked of Smith's 'diffuse principles' and of 'the sometimes rambling text' as features that early readers had to be helped, through translation and summarisation, to overcome (Tribe, 1995, 28 and 31).

Historians of economic thought also read Smith's work because later economists wrote his work into theirs. In this sense Smith's *Wealth of Nations* is a key canonical text. He is still mentioned by writers of modern day textbooks as a source of relevant economic ideas ('a classic'), perhaps in line with the issue of intellectual paternity. Treatment of Smith in this context varies, though it is usually summarily and sometimes, in an attempt to reach student readers, over-simplified (references, say, to the 'invisible hand' or Smith's rules of taxation) and possibly slightly dismissive ('old Adam Smith') (Swailes, 1993, 226). As has already been mentioned, current affairs and economically informed journalistic writing, such as found in the *Economist*, or *Newsweek*, still call upon Smith's name and concepts derived from Smith to make a case for liberal capitalism. Smith has a currency in the modern world that is not readily available to other eighteenth-century writing.

As a result of Ricardo taking issue with some of Smith's conclusion, or of Say taking a stand on Smith's arguments and conclusions, different from Ricardo, of the development of Marx's notion of alienation from Smith's views on the negative features of the division of labour, Smith is written into later economic thought. Mill found Smith 'in many parts obsolete, and in all, imperfect' but, at the same time, accepted that the *Wealth of Nations* set a standard in its 'object and general conception' for his own *Principles* (Evensky, 2003, 1–2; Mill, 1848, xxvii). This process of reference and incorporation continues. Economic theorists such as George Stigler and Garry Becker, in exploring the 'first principles' of the subject, resort, according to Force, to Smith's writing as part of the way in which they place the discipline (Force, 2003). This view is one that Force in his writing intends to disrupt. Donald Winch is clear that the modern-day economist may imaginatively construct Smith and his writing in ways that are historically inappropriate. Lubasz goes so far as to claim that those who in the late twentieth century claimed Smith as their intellectual mentor 'have never read the *Wealth of Nations*' (Lubasz, 1995, 48). Given such views, historically minded and curious people are bound, therefore, to ask questions such as 'Are the various interpretations of Smith's economic ideas justified or not?' This becomes a concern, in principle at least, for what is historically constrained and culturally specific in Smith and what can be taken as analytical or scientific and so universal or timeless. However, the specific cultural context of given readings will always have to be reflected upon.

The range of potential questions is, of course, huge, and is no longer constrained by either what subsequent economists made of his work or fixed views as to the nature of the economics canon but arise out of the twists and turns of scholarship and exegesis. Is Smith the hero of the right, in the guise of 'patron saint of capitalism', source of the 'bible of capitalism' as the Adam Smith Institute would probably have it, an author who built economic behaviour on the sole principle of self-interest? Is he, in common with the French Enlightenment, a critic of society, friend of the poor and critic of the *ancien régime* and who stands therefore, if we can use the term prior to the French Revolution, on the left? Putting the question this way is to use Revolutionary (right and left are terms derived from the seating arrangements in the National Assembly) terminology to ask questions about Smith that could not have been asked in this way in 1776. Or were his concerns to construct an economic order that related to human nature but in which rhetoric supported by reason could be used to find a basis for a harmonious as well as prosperous society? Do we read the *Wealth of Nations* through the *Moral Sentiments* or against it? Present day readings suggest 'through' but this has not always been the case. Social and historical circumstances and conceptualised intellectual concerns alter readings.

Rothschild's *Economic Sentiments* raises some of these questions directly as does Whatmore's work on J-B Say. Smith certainly used terms, such as 'liberty', and recommended policies, such as potential efficiency gains to be made by sale of Crown Lands and the breaking up of other landed monopolies, that in the light of the French Revolution could be considered radical and even dangerous. According to Rothschild, Stewart's memoir provides a conservative view of Smith for political reasons. Stewart wanted to save Smith's work from the consequences of a conservative reaction that influenced knowledge and knowledge production (see later). It would seem that given ambiguities in the *Wealth of Nations*, political interpretations of Smith are inevitable. The question of Smith's 'stance' is of some interest beyond academia because free-market economists use his name symbolically as well as practically (in the sense of clarifying contemporary issues). Detecting Smith's stance requires detailed and sophisticated readings. It is certainly the case that the debate as to what is best done by markets and what is best done by the state is a long one and one that is not essentially capable of a final resolution in purely 'scientific' terms. Where the line between government action and markets is drawn will be partly determined by theoretical insight as well as historical experience and partly by the political *Zeitgeist* prevailing at a given time. The idea of privatisation started as a minor and somewhat experimental policy in the United Kingdom and became transformed, by ideological manipulation and distanciation, into a global movement, backed by politicians such as Margaret Thatcher and, elsewhere, Ronald Regan, that became almost synonymous with the idea of democracy. Smith constructed and explored a system of natural liberty but this in itself did not eliminate the state from action with respect to economic life, nor does it mean that his theoretical system equates directly with the nineteenth-century interpretations of laissez-faire. If we hold that the modern world was essentially created, for good or ill, by Enlightenment thinkers such as Smith, then it would seem to be a matter of some significance that we take the trouble (some of us at least) to understand what such writers argued, particularly with respect to economics.

Answering the question of Smith's stance on the poor, for example, is one that has recently been explored. Rothschild touches upon the issue in her analysis of the changing contexts of reading Smith before, during and after the French Revolution and points to Dugald Stewart's desire to preserve the scientific aspects of Smith from potentially contentious elements in his social thinking (Rothschild, 2001). Stressing the scientific nature of Smith's arguments meant that other aspects were suppressed. It is hard for us to imagine the ways in which even 'hard' scientific subjects, such as chemistry and natural philosophy, were reclaimed for (natural) religion or for conservatism (with a small 'c') in the era of the revolutionary and Napoleonic wars. Margaret Bryan, who published her *Lectures on Natural Philosophy* in 1806, includes a quote from Rowe on her title page, 'God speaks through all and is in all things found' and includes pious statements before each scientific lesson. The *Encyclopaedia Britannica* came to see the French Enlightenment as a source of the French Revolution and the disorder that it set loose, so the *philosophes* and literature sympathetic to them were under suspicion. The cultural context for knowledge in Britain itself was changed by the course of the Revolution in France.

Purpose and methods

What has been developed thus far is a variety of contexts or points of view from which or through which it is possible to read Smith. The works presented in this monograph are not primarily concerned with evaluating historical or current themes in the interpretation of Smith's writings on economic and related topics. This may appear surprising given that the message thus far has been about questions and approaches to Smith's work. The aim has been to show how contexts make particular readings or sets of readings possible and also constrain them. The emphasis here is on the word 'primarily'. Nor are they concerned primarily with assisting the reader to read other scholarly works (though enhanced capacities in this respect will be, I hope, an outcome of reading the chapters that follow). The aim is to assist the reader read Smith's economics writing through initial and direct engagement with his texts. In other words to help readers develop capacities to make a direct, critical reading of Smith, based on an engagement with the text through the use of forms of text or discourse analysis. The aims imply a reflection upon ways of reading and ways of undertaking textual analysis.

This is not easy and the volume is not entitled, *How to read*, if I can borrow a phrase from Richards, for that implies reading better perhaps than I do (Richards, 1991, 65). Richards was very aware that neither 'linguistic theory' nor fine 'distinctions' necessarily help to produce such analytical readings that develop understanding. Strengthening our ability to 'read' is, according to Richards, a matter of 'experience'. Richards appreciates the ambiguity of such a word and the difficulties that we have in understanding how it is that two people may achieve the same reading experience, but one may profit from it and the other may not. Richards recommends a reflective, monitored, self-questioning approach to potentially difficult reading that we really care about understanding.

There are other, more philosophically based, explorations of reading and, whilst reference will be made to ways of approaching textual exploration and negotiation that are hermeneutically based, or indirectly related, the thrust of this work is not to explore philosophical ideas about reading and interpretation, though the work produced here is hermeneutically informed, as it were. Rather, the aim is to demonstrate practical ways of approaching textual analysis, and in this case of the economic writings of Adam Smith, some of which will be based upon specific 'methods', whilst others will be eclectic and pragmatic in nature or composition. As specific readings are often guided or driven by questions, either explicit or implicit, the use of general questions, already introduced above, will continue to be developed in what follows. Links will be made from these general questions to specific topics explored later in the collection.

There is no single section that deals directly with hermeneutics as a philosophically inspired methodology. Hermeneutics is a process of understanding a text that first arose out of a Christian tradition of biblical interpretation. Some biblical passages can be accepted more or less at face value, others, such as the parables, for example, need to be interpreted, and the meanings derived from the bible are not fixed and secure for all time but vary according to historical experience or insight. Hermeneutics is concerned with the meaning of a text (rather than with its truth value) and with exposing the unanalysed assumptions on which it is built or the lack of reflection associated with established interpretations. The hermeneutic circle as a basis for thinking about meaning suggests that texts can be read and reread and what will be seen in them will change as a result of reconsideration. To understand a text is an ongoing task but in moving towards understanding we need to consider the parts in relation to the whole and the whole in relation to the parts. Where do we stop if the understanding produced becomes unstable? To some extent we are not free to make any meaning. We are constrained by the text itself and we are constrained by the acceptability of a given interpretation, within a range of interpretations, by negotiation with others as part of the exercise of scholarship. What follows is hermeneutically-informed rather than the product of hermeneutics as it is currently understood.

The essays published and republished in the rest of this collection illustrate possible readings that engage with the text through a variety of methods. Here, the target texts are texts produced by Adam Smith (in the case of *Lectures on Jurisprudence* it would be appropriate to say 'in some sense' as the resultant text is transcribed from student notes) especially where Smith engages in creating texts of some economic significance. Passages, either long or short, from Smith, will be analysed, and, like Richards, in one sense at least, through exploring techniques in relation to texts. But there is a paradox, for reading is not about reproducing the text, but understanding it and using that understanding for other purposes. In understanding a text, we change it as our own experience and knowledge interacts with what is written. As academics or potential academics we read in order to teach or more specifically to write, so we read not essentially to reproduce but to transform, based on the understanding achieved and the purposes being pursued. Active readings create meanings and so transform how texts can be understood. The philosophical problem with respect to interpretation is analysed by Weinsheimer in his hermeneutical exploration of Swift's *Tale of a Tub*, used in

Chapter 3 to develop insight into Smith's notion of interpretation (Weinsheimer, 1993, 14–15). Here the aim is for a process of critical reading, by identified methods, to lead to increased knowledge of the writing either on a personal basis, or when reported and incorporated into further academic work, on a collective basis.

Although I hope that this is itself a scholarly work, target readers are not primarily the scholarly community currently engaged in interpreting Smith's output. There will be such readers but this work is not specifically constructed with them in mind. Rather it focuses on: any final year undergraduates studying the history of economic thought or related topics within the wider context of the history of ideas; those interested in rhetoric and communication; those developing post-graduate students wishing to embark on research in the history of economic thought, particularly, but not exclusively on Smith and those working on literary economics or in cultural studies and interested in how economic ideas become incorporated in the novelistic literature of a given time. It is not primarily about historical approaches and contexts (though these will be given some considera-tion) but about literary, or perhaps more fully rhetorical approaches, based upon notions of reading a text. It aims to treat Smith's writing, the *Wealth of Nations* in particular as a literary document, a combination of narrative and analysis, available for literary analysis or some form of discourse analysis (the two are not necessarily the same), a written text devoted to the development of theoretical and practical ideas about economic life and its management. The various chapters aim to illustrate what it is to engage in reading Smith, in describing his writing and making judgements about the persuasive power of his writing. It takes a rhetorical approach but one that is grounded in reading and in text analysis, eclectically considered. It demonstrates approaches to textual analysis around Smith's writing. It helps demonstrate skills that are potentially helpful to those interested in Smith and in histories of economic thought, and related intellectual histories.

This does not mean that historical and current themes in the interpretation of Smith will be ignored but simply means that they are not central to the work. It is not possible to ignore other interpretations or to clear them entirely from the mind. All readings are located in overt prior experience and covert and unconsidered pre-suppositions. Indeed the chapter on Smith's 'propensities' is directly related to an issue raised by other scholars as is the chapter on hedging. These are the issues of potential plagiarism in the first example and of 'politeness' in the second. The notion of intertextuality, already acknowledged, must act against this conceit. The fact that Smith was once viewed as 'the father of modern economics' or that his works have long been held to be a 'synthesis' continues to shape either wittingly or unwittingly ways of approaching the texts. What is being referred to by this metaphor is essentially 'economic science at the moment of its coming into being' (Force, 2003, 5). We can accept this formulation or contest it by thinking of a series of events, rather than one act of paternity, that can be taken as bringing the modern notion of economics into being. This liberates both the subjects of history or histories and the ways in which subsequent events are narrated (histories of economic thought rather than the history of economic thought). The notion of Smith as 'father of modern economics' gives rise to an enduring tradition of secondary study that has tried to relate modern economic concepts such as human capital to ideas formed in the *Wealth of Nations*. It would seem reasonable that if we accept the image of Smith as 'father of modern economics' to establish links between hints made in Smith's writing (discovered retrospectively) and modern-day approaches to theoretical developments in the subject. If the initial conceptualisation is challenged then whilst this does not invalidate such searches, it will tend to deemphasise the activity. The image of Smith and his works that economists have today probably have 'little to do with the founding father of their discipline' (Force, 2003, 4; Winch, 1978). It is currently frowned upon, according to Force, to read past writing as 'foreshadowing the present' (Force, 2003, 4). But as mentioned above this calls for a differentiation between what is culturally and historically constrained and what is 'universal' in Smith's writing and concept development, for there are those convinced of the universal qualities inherent in the work. Whatever Force's views, mainstream economists continue to see some validity in quoting Smith when the chosen quote suits their purposes.

Similarly, the notion of 'synthesis' can be a productive way of thinking out textual explorations. Schumpeter makes great play of Smith's abilities in this respect, writing of Smith that his 'mental stature was up to mastering the unwieldy material that followed from many sources and to subjecting it, with a strong hand, to the rule of a small number of coherent principles' (Schumpeter, 1954, 185). An added advantage, according to Schumpeter, in the same passage, is that Smith 'never moved above the heads of even the dullest readers'. Schumpeter is unambiguous in his belief that Smith's success was not primarily analytical but rhetorical and owes it to the fact that he spent time building a synthesis.

A series of questions can be asked that derive from the 'synthesis' insight such as, the most obvious one, 'Is it a synthesis?' Answering this question would entail making some judgements about what is filtered out of past literature and what, if anything, is new in the *Wealth of Nations*, and indeed, what we take a synthesis to be. Synthesis is usually taken, following Bloom's taxonomy, as a higher-level intellectual skill. A work of synthesis carries with it an expectation that it is, by drawing together various ideas developed piecemeal in other texts into a new work, exhibiting a greater degree of conceptual unity (say) than that found elsewhere. Thus we have Schumpeter's judgement that all economics writing before Smith leads up to the *Wealth of Nations*, and all writing after Smith leads away from the *Wealth of Nations* (Schumpeter, 1954). But it ought to be clear that any such text will deal in ideas, concepts and points of view that will be a combination of already established or given and those that are in some sense new. A successful synthesis produces a new text that is both reliant upon, and independent of, its predecessors. Such reliance and independence will be found in the subject matter and in ways in which the subject matter is expressed through language. All of this is amongst that which is implied by the notion of a 'synthesis'.

A related question must then follow: 'What sources are drawn upon to achieve the synthesis?' This is essentially a question posed by the editors of the Glasgow Edition of Smith's works in which a great deal of scholarly activity focused on linking, through footnotes, texts prior to Smith that put forward ideas that Smith called upon or was aware of. This is an historical method to which textual analysis can also be applied. But the shift in perspective away from Smith's *Wealth of Nations* as a foundation text in economics and towards Smith as a generator of an Enlightenment text reveals new areas in which it is necessary to consider as contributing to the synthesis. Force has raised this, if only by implication, as an issue when he reads both the *Moral Sentiments* and the *Wealth of Nations* through Mandeville and Rousseau and, indeed, by reading each off against the other two. Force thus adding another 'triangle' of interests and synthesis to the Hume–Steuart–Smith 'triangle'. The metaphor ('triangle') found in established literature, establishes both relationships and boundaries and we must be wary of the implications of fixity rather than of fluidity (Omori, 2003,103). What we find in a text will vary as the point of view and the experience of the reader shifts. Smith, for example, is seen, along with his contemporaries, as concerned with the relationship between wealth and virtue. Smith holds, in *Moral Sentiments*, that the social group from which he came, the middle and professional ranks of society, had the potential to achieve both, through prudence, deferred gratification and the avoidance of luxury and licentiousness. Here is Daniel Defoe, writing in *Robinson Crusoe* (1719), more than a generation earlier, on the same lines:[2]

> [B]ut that the middle station had fewest disasters, and was not exposed to so many vicissitudes as the higher or lower part of mankind; nay, they were not subjected to so many distempers and uneasiness, either of body or mind, as those were who, by vicious living, luxury, and extravagancies on the one hand, or by labour, want of necessaries, and mean or insufficient diet on the other hand, bring distempers upon themselves by the natural consequences of their way of living; that the middle station of life was calculated for all kinds of vertues and all kinds of enjoyments; that peace and plenty were the hand-maids of a middle fortune; that temperance, moderation, quietness, health, society, all agreeable diversions, and all desirable pleasures, were the blessings attending the middle stations of life.
>
> (Defoe [1719], 1965, 28)

It is not being suggested, here, that *Robinson Crusoe* as a text made any direct contribution to the development of either *Moral Sentiments* or the *Wealth of Nations*. It is simply that there are other texts and other contexts in which ideas, such as the possibility of wealth and virtue coinciding in the manners and customs of the middling classes, circulate and so some wider cultural influences that can not easily be made explicit. The sentiments expressed by Crusoe's father (above) illustrate the self-regarding nature of this class and are essentially out of the same stable as those on which Smith can be explicitly shown to draw upon.

Any study of synthesis must have an element that identifies and assesses sources and so this, in turn, provides another question: 'How close is Smith to the sources?' 'Does he borrow and if he does borrow, how does he borrow and how does he acknowledge?' There has been some speculation in the literature that

Smith may have been too close to his sources, and this literature needs to be evaluated textually. It is easy to imagine that a host of related questions spin out of the initiating questions including exploring eighteenth century conventions on plagiarism, paraphrasing and referencing living and dead authors. Mediaeval scholars, such as Thomas Aquinas, borrowed freely from other earlier texts. Conventions on what we would call 'plagiarism' are not constant. We also now understand that the more we read, the more we absorb other people's writing, so that there is an inescapable element of commonality between what is produced and the multitude of sources consulted or simply read in the past. The scholarly culture in the Middle Ages was one of elaborating on texts, layering and improving them. Conventions in the eighteenth century though different from those of the mediaeval period, are not our conventions. References to others were expected, though in the case of living authors often indirectly by textual implication. It is as well for us to recall that 'ideas are never the product of solitary individuals but of persons in dialogue with others . . . ' (O'Banion, 1992, xvii). There is therefore an additional question that grows out of all that have been set out here, and that is 'if Smith did synthesise, how is that synthesis achieved as writing?' This is a question that calls for direct textual comparison and analysis, as well as for an understanding of the conventions. Researching this issue fully would probably require the development of a significant eighteenth-century corpus and exploration of it by means of computational linguistics.

A work may very well be a work of synthesis, but for a synthesis to be successful it must also be persuasive. Much has recently been written in economics about what economists find persuasive (McCloskey). There is little doubt that the *Wealth of Nations* was and is a persuasive text, if it were not it would simply be an historical curiosity rather than something that is still resorted to. Schumpeter draws attention to the efforts that Smith makes to gently lead his readers down the road that he wishes them to take. Smith's success, in terms of Schumpeter's understating, is essentially founded upon rhetoric. One of the principle concerns of this work will be to illustrate in a variety of contexts, derived mainly but not solely from the *Wealth of Nations*, the ways in which Smith keeps the readers engaged and entertained, whilst developing an imaginary world based upon 'natural liberty'.

If we hold a text to be persuasive, then this suggests the question of the means whereby readers are persuaded by the work. This introduces the notion of rhetoric. As a work on political economy, it calls upon argument and sets standards (observation; examples; logical implications and sequencing of inter-connected ideas; analytical content formulated in universal or 'scientific' terms) for the evaluation of ideas and arguments. However long-winded Smith's writing of political economy may appear to twenty-first-century eyes, he invested significant literary resources in sequencing, in creating opportunities for repetition, in holding ideas together through sustained chains of reason and provided the reader with the means of integration both in the details of the writing and at the 'macro' level. Smith was very anxious to explain, and his demonstrations (examples, stories) and lists together illustrate the reasoned and literary/scientific aspect of the work. So too do the textual patterns revealed in his writing. Smith, particularly in book one, resorts to a limited range of textual patterns to carry his carefully exemplified and carefully hedged arguments though he varies the way in which readers experience them (see Chapter 5).

But there is more to Smith than this and this 'more' is sometimes recognised as a puzzle: 'What sort of text did Smith think he was producing?' A question in this form suggests a focus on '*intentio lectoris*' or the author's intentions. If the author is present in the text, for example where the text is 'author-saturated' rather than 'author-evacuated' it may be possible to arrive relatively easily at the author's intentions (Geertz, 1988, 3). We may not be able to answer, that question, unless Smith evaluates his own authorial stance, but may be able to answer, on the basis of textual evidence, what kind of text the *Wealth of Nations* can currently be evaluated as. Most readings are not concerned with establishing 'what as historical fact was going on in an author's mind' when the work was written (Richards, 1991, 65). We read, normally, to be challenged and to understand. Established literature recognises both explicitly and by default that the *Wealth of Nations* as a literary artefact is complex. Historically it has been implicitly recognised by the fact that economists have tended to pay greater attention to books one and two than to the rest of the work. Later in this present work, 'lists' and 'stories' will be analysed in an attempt to show other ways in which the *Wealth of Nations* is a mixed genre and that this reflects Smith's belief that both reason and the passion need to be engaged in order to persuade readers of the validity of the points that he wishes to make. Smith himself, in the *Wealth of Nations*, makes use of those 'small-scale sympathetic exchanges' that Dyer, confirmed indirectly by Rothschild, has drawn attention to. We know that Smith admired Rousseau's ability to appeal both to reason and sentiment, and there is every reason to believe that Smith also knew that to engage an audience he needed also to entertain them. And if the notion of story is raised, the issue of types of story (satire has already been mentioned) can also be legitimately explored.

Furthermore, Smith analysed the world in which he lived and viewed it, and encouraged his readers to view it, through economic eyes, in terms of the division of labour, the division of capital, the extent of the market and so on, though he did not lose sight of notions of virtue. The 'spectator' metaphor is developed in the *Moral Sentiments* but it makes appearances, explicitly as well as implicitly, also in the *Lectures on Jurisprudence* and in *Wealth of Nations*. Smith's spectator is originally all too human but in the course of the *Moral Sentiments* it is transformed into an ideal. Not all spectatorship is of the ideal type. By building upon the notion of spectatorship, he changed the readers' relationship with the everyday world of common experience. By participating in his observations, they saw the world through his terms. He also created through the imagination another related world, that of the 'system of natural liberty'. His book is one where conceptualisation imagined the world of the system of natural liberty. The actual world, the world of the Britain of his day, as he conceptualised it, was riddled with the remnants of feudalism (constructed in the *Wealth of Nations* as indentured labour; slavery; needlessly long apprenticeships; aristocratic manners and consumption patterns in the form of unproductive labour; landed monopolies) and mercantile monopoly practices. The 'system of natural liberty' disclosed another possible world, a world that challenged feudal remnants as well as mercantilist commercial policy and established aristocratic behaviours. Smith's 'proposed world', to borrow and indeed slightly change, a term from Ricoeur (Ricoeur, 1981, 143), is a mixture of fact, of interpretation (of the actual world) and aspiration. In this respect Smith's text is 'world disclosing' and 'revealing' and hence fitting Habermas's view on the 'literary/rhetorical' text. This is one way to try and conceptualise the 'given/new' relationship in Smith. He could be seen as creating a possible world that was, as yet, largely a world of the imagination, even if that world were constructed analytically on notions such as the division of labour, the extent of the market and so on. It is legitimate to read in order to discover the literary devices that Smith employs to fix this world, to clothe it in possibilities through exemplification and people it in realist terms.

Smith's writing disclosed such a world but also assisted the development of a way of talking about such a world in theoretical terms, in which unintended consequences of economic action becomes significant. Smith's 'invisible hand' metaphor has tended to be treated in isolation, (though not by Force and Rothschild, though each in differing ways), but there is an array of language in the *Wealth of Nations* that stressed 'unintended' outcomes either directly (as in his view of the long-term impact of the propensity in human nature to trade) or though the verb forms chosen (commerce spreading itself along the banks of navigable rivers). There is a need here to avoid trivialising the insights. It is the stuff of economic analysis that policy actions have unintended as well as intended outcomes. This is not a context for reading Smith. What is significant for Smith is the notion that human nature either intends the general good (through choice and discussion) or a personal good (through looking after one's interests) but either way the general good is served. In *Moral Sentiments* he creates, through narrative, a rich satire on the ambition for riches and power. Economic agents are duped by nature into thinking that possessions can lead to a life of ease and happiness when in reality, as opposed to in the imagination, wealth is also burdensome. The spectator is duped, according to Smith, for in the face of decline, illness and death, unease returns to haunt the imagination. Whilst it may be destructive of individual well-being, it is essential that the delusion be maintained for the general good. Smith sees nature's irony and explicates it but knows that his work is in vane as it is a necessary part of the human condition that we are duped. So there is some reason for reading Smith's later writing through his views on rhetoric and persuasion. In addition, Smith gave reason and speech as an aspect of the 'propensity to truck, barter and exchange'. According to Griswold, Smith's insight is that 'Life in a market society is an ongoing exercise in rhetoric' (Griswold, 1999, 297). Reading, constructed hermeneutically, is also based on negotiation and exchange.

Rorty also helps us think about rhetoric in this context. His is the notion of stable and routinised science as opposed to unstable science working towards a new paradigm. Once the new paradigm is in place, order and routine are restored.

Smith's new view is the notion of 'natural liberty'. The economic success of such a system is based upon human propensities (available to 'every man' – Smith's principal economic agent) for self-betterment through the propensity to truck barter and exchange, through learning based on situation and interests and the resultant short-term and accumulate long-term unintended consequences of such improving action on the world. This system of the imagination became what John Ruskin saw in the middle of the nineteenth century as the distorted demon of 'laissez-faire', a principle of action shorn of Smith's notion of the need for reasonable behaviour that is capable of avoiding monopolisation and alienation. If we admit Rousseau as influencing Smith, and Mandeville's influence on both of them, and accept the role of 'virtue' and 'sentiment' in the *Wealth of Nations*, in the manner of Rothschild and Force, then Ruskin in the middle of the nineteenth century, and even if he did not know it or was unwilling to admit it, may not be seen as such a wild card in his arguments against what Classical Economics, in his eyes, seemed to have become, an overly narrow discourse stripped of human sympathy.

The set of questions and ideas set out above suggests that the questions themselves, the processes engaged in and the potential answers are unproblematic, though this is not necessarily the case. The questions have not been asked necessarily in order or with full awareness of the relationship of one to another. They have been posed here as a means of illustrating how one concern leads to another. At the same time, if the insight of hermeneutics and the related notion of inter-textuality – the idea, essentially, that one conversation always implies another held in a different time or place or text – there may be influences that come from (say) an ongoing historical discussion and from elements in that discussion that are part of the common currency. The ideas that may be incorporated into a new text, such as Smith's *Wealth of Nations*, as it was being first written, may not come simply from a given source but through a tradition of interpretation and discussion, or in Smith's case, of teaching and being taught.

Thus, for example, questions concerning the relationship between human nature and economic life were part of an on-going discussion throughout the eighteenth century, with extended links with seventeenth-century discussions. What, for example, is the relationship between human nature, property and justice or between human nature, changing historical circumstances and economic motivation? These are questions that were discussed by Locke, Mandeville, Hutcheson, Hume and Smith and many others, at that time. Hume is of particular importance here, for he focused on human nature itself, essentially removing discussion about possible links between human and divine nature. For Hume, human reason was not subordinated to God. Human nature is a given and the important thing for Hume, and hence also for Smith, is to take the given and examine the consequences.

But elements appropriate to the discussion of human nature, including self-interest, were discussed by others, including, in the thirteenth century, Thomas Aquinas and his predecessors back to Aristotle. The question is not only a common one, but also assumes that we are clear about 'human nature' itself. A dividing line that Hume essentially helped to draw between earlier and more modern discussions is the recognition that it is possible to discuss human nature without also discussing divine nature. If we think of humankind as 'made in the image of God' and 'reason' as a specific link between human nature and divine nature – a view that goes back at least as far as Aquinas – then the discussion of what it is to be human can all too readily be compounded with God's purposes for human kind. If we start with human nature, suppress the 'divine' link, as Hume did, and focus on consequences rather than causes, then a new world of implications can be explored (Stroud, 1977, 11). Start with human nature and through experimentation (introspection) and observation trace out implications in terms of institutional arrangements (justice and property), sentiments (social bonds and morality) and economic and other motivations (self-interest and benevolence). This was Hume's intellectual project and it may have become that too of Adam Smith.

Just as we talk of 'alienated labour' without necessarily specifically mentioning Marx, who put the concept into socio-economic discussion, so Smith talks of 'propensities' in human nature without any necessary direct reference to any previous discussion or source. If we were to take terms associated with 'propensity' such as 'human nature', 'natural passion' (key to 'every man' as the prime economic mover) and investigate them in Smith and related works upon which he drew, it is likely that we will find not only a sharing of concepts but also a sharing of semantic sequences (i.e. the repetition of words with a similar meaning of the main concept in a common pattern of sequencing) across texts.[3] Terms, like coins, circulate, 'held' by a given individual, within a set of institutional arrangements, at one time but by many individuals over time. A study of sources cannot always help to pinpoint inter-textual links. There are questions concerning the possibilities of a tradition of analysis (passed on through teachers or public discussion in clubs and social gatherings) or of a cultural orientation that it not necessarily transparent in texts or of 'half-forgotten influences' or of 'the spirit of the times'.

In this work, attention will be paid to Smith's writing primarily as writing and to reading as a 'commonplace' experience that needs to be examined and reflected upon (Tordov, 1990, 39). The notion of looking at Smith's writing as writing may not be an entirely transparent statement. What does it mean? What follows in this monograph is not primarily focused upon Smith as an economist (even Smith's writings on political economy involve philosophical, political and cultural concerns that go well beyond the concerns of modern day economists) but on Smith as a writer, a producer of texts that contemporary and subsequent readers have taken to be 'economic' or related in some way to 'economics'. Smith's text endures, partly for reasons of historical 'inertia': there is a body of scholarship that focuses on the texts and where a battle of interpretation and reinterpretation takes place so that even if Smith were to become of less direct significance to the modern world, the scholarly discussion continues, as a focus on its own concerns. But it also endures because of the meanings that are potentially and actually available in the text. Smith's analysis of commercial society still has relevance in the professional sense that economists still refer to his work and in the rhetorical sense that (say) a newspaper such as the *Economist* calls upon familiar images, such as the 'invisible hand' to make points about the essential nature of the liberal economy. The richness of Smith's writings is itself evidenced by the range of interpretations and criticisms that they give rise to. The concern here is with Smith's writing as writing, albeit economic writing. This is a study that is text-based rather than interpretation-based. It is not about encouraging an involvement with secondary literature on Smith nor is it, primarily, a review of ways in which that literature has dealt with Smith and his ideas. It is about reading Smith writing on economics and related topics, about puzzling out how Smith argues in writing and why he argues the way he does, using the writing as evidence.

2 How does Smith achieve a synthesis in writing?

Evidence from his analysis of the propensity to truck, barter and exchange[1]

What is striking about chapter two of book one of the *Wealth of Nations* is that the format and content of the argument are very similar to (say) arguments presented by David Hume in both the *Treatise* and the *Inquiry*. Start with human nature; link human nature to all aspects of human behaviour; compare, using examples, human nature to animal nature, looking at similarities and differences, and reach conclusions about human relations and human institutions. With respect to Hume's work, his conclusions concern property, justice and morality. With respect to Smith's second chapter the conclusions relate to the respective role of benevolence and self-interest, contracts, class structure, genius and the impact of the division of labour. So in exploring the implications of the human propensity to 'truck, barter and exchange', is it possible to look at processes in the text to reach conclusions about Smith's writing as a combination of the familiar and new? Can we look at the product and reach conclusions about the writing process? Can we, in any sense, watch Smith writing?

In a general sense, the form of Smith's argument, that is, its structure and moves, is one that would have been familiar to an educated eighteenth-century reader. Whilst there are some advantages in interpretation in isolating Smith's chapter, by close reading, a richer investigation would be that of interpretation based upon sources. Or, to put the problem another way, Smith's chapter is an outcome of a longer eighteenth-century discussion of the relationship between human nature and the economy. This is, of course, what is implied by synthesis. To Hume, as a model for a form of argument, we can add texts by Mandeville and Hutcheson, for example, and, no doubt, many others.

It is a long-established commonplace in studies of Smith that the *Wealth of Nations* is a work of synthesis (Roll, 1942, 148; Schumpeter, 1954, 18; Skinner, 1979; Stewart, 1980 [1794], 320). In this view, the work finds its strength not in the originality of the many principles expounded within it but in the way that the various parts are brought together into a relationship with each other, and, though this is not often stated quite so clearly, with Smith's target reader. In other words, the strength of the text is to be found in its composition its rhetoric and also in its familiarity (Schumpeter, 1954). Much scholarly attention has been given to the synthesis of theoretical ideas but comparatively little has been given to Smith's writing as writing. One exception is Brown's reading of Smith's works in which the issue of intertextuality is a basis for the analysis (Brown, 1994, 3, 5).

There has been discussion, also, of Smith's writing as evidencing plagiarism – a charge that ignores Schumpeter's caveat that 'no charge of plagiarism can be made against Smith or on his behalf against others' (Rashid, 1990, 1992; Rothbard, 1995a, 435; Schumpeter, 1954, 185).[2] Although Rashid's charge of plagiarism was challenged, robustly (Ahiakpor, 1992) the initial debate was confused.[3] It needed a clearer understanding that ideas can be borrowed without incurring the charge of plagiarism but words cannot be borrowed in the same way. Paraphrases, saying the same thing but in different ways, are part of the writing process and distinguished from plagiarism by the fact that different words, and altered purposes, are involved; that is, there are issues of context and objectives. In addition, issues of plagiarism have to do with words internal to one text in relation to words internal to another. Matters outside the text such as biographical information are irrelevant. Evidence is primarily textual (though there are, in modern-day discussions, issues of intent). Ahiakpor implicitly understood this point when he called for detailed textual exemplification from Rashid, a request that does not seem to have been met (Ahiakpor, 1992, 171).

Ahiakpor's defense of Smith with respect to the charge of plagiarism continued in his response to Rothbard's views, published later, on Smith's alleged plagiarism. Ahiakpor quotes, in support of his skepticism, 'Cannan's view of Smith's acknowledgements' (Ahiakpor, 1999, 380). But, despite this defence, detailed analysis of Smith's writing, in relation to possible sources, is still required. Furthermore, an acceptable analysis would need to accommodate old and new rhetoric. From classical rhetoric the notion of 'transformative imitation' (*imitatio*) may be relevant. From the modern, 'intertextuality', the location of texts in the spirit of a particular time, is also relevant when considering Smith or any other author's writing. This approach accepts, as does that of Dooley, that the continuity of discussion is significant: 'As Smith followed Hutcheson, so Hutcheson followed those that went before him' (Dooley, 2003, 1).

Whilst there has been much written on Smith's work as a work of (economic) synthesis, the question of how Smith achieved this synthesis in writing has tended to be sidestepped. Can we trace out how this synthesis is achieved in writing? Can we establish a sense of what is given in the resulting text and what is new? This is a bigger question and it is within this context that the question 'What are we to make of Smith's propensity?' is to be addressed.

In what follows, close attention is given to Smith's writing in the second chapter of book one of the *Wealth of Nations*. The evidence is not thematic but based upon the comparison of passages with earlier writers. We are still interpreting and the attention is still focused on 'truck, barter and exchange', but the attempt is to dig over Smith's sources and so understand Smith's argument as an eighteenth-century argument, complete with characteristic moves and common lexical elements that he then bends to his own uses. The article does not always present essentially new ideas, for it restates some already established links between Smith's text and those of other writers, for example, in the annotations provided in the Glasgow Edition of the *Wealth of Nations*. The paper does not re-produce influences already noted if there is nothing to add. Rather it illustrates, at the level of a given chapter, paragraph or phrase, the sense in which Smith's writing is a synthesis.

The wider literature and chapter two

Chapter two has rarely been subjected to close analysis, and, as far as I can establish, nor to any sustained studies of relationships with other texts. The Glasgow Edition of the *Wealth of Nations* sets out sources in the footnotes and comments on them. These do not cover all aspects of Smith's sources for the chapter. How could they? A basic insight of intertextuality is that all texts are made up, knowingly or unknowingly, of shreds of other texts and although the comments are extensive, there is always more that can be said. Furthermore, Smith's notion of the origins of the propensity to truck, barter and exchange is not given a lot of analytical attention in the secondary literature, whilst other details in the chapter (e.g. Smith's controversial notion of genius) have been given some attention.

Survey of written work in the history of economic thought, on the propensities, has not yielded much in terms of detailed analysis – the treatment has been variable – and this has promoted new work. Rothbard, for example, is critical of Smith's notion of propensities (Rothbard locates motivation for exchange in the fact that each party benefits) and provides, essentially, a historical account: 'But Smith unfortunately shifts the main focus from mutual benefit to an allegedly irrational and innate "propensity to truck, barter and exchange," as if human beings were lemmings determined by forces external to their chosen purposes' (Rothbard, 1995a, 441–442). This and explanations like it overlook the fact that Smith was operating, as we shall see, within an established discourse structure. Evensky, who has made detailed analyses of several of Smith's strategic chapters, has not paid, as far as I can establish, detailed attention to book one, chapter two. In a recent paper, however, he has shown the role of chapter two in the development of Smith's fuller 'moral philosophical vision'. Essentially Evensky illustrates how Smith develops 'a compelling story' about social evolution based upon the division of labour and its consequences over time for productivity, inventiveness and social and economic divisions (Evensky, 2003, 6–9). This 'compelling story' is composed partly of elements found in the works of earlier writers.

The reading that is presented here is built around the question 'How does Smith achieve a synthesis in writing?' It is not a search for origins as such – even though some parallel passages are established – but a means of illustrating an approach to understanding Smith's writing that goes beyond simple categorisation in terms of this or that source.

An analysis based primarily upon some of Hume's writing

Smith's text:

> Whether this propensity be one of those original principles in human nature, of which no further account can be given; or whether, as seems more probable, it be the necessary consequence of the faculties of reason or speech, it belongs not to our present subject to inquire.
>
> (*WN*, I.ii.2)

Hume's text:

> Its effects are everywhere conspicuous; but as to its causes, they are mostly unknown, and must be resolv'd into *original* qualities of human nature, which I pretend not to explain. Nothing is more requisite for a true philosopher, than to restrain the intemperate desire for searching into causes, and having establish'd any doctrine upon a sufficient number of experiments, rest contented with that, when he sees a farther examination would lead him in to obscure and uncertain speculations. In that case his enquiry wou'd be much better employ'd in examining the effects than the causes of his principle.
>
> (*Treatise*, 13)

And elsewhere:

> We must...glean up our experiments in this science from a cautious observation of human life, and take them as they appear in the common course of the world, by men's behaviour in company, in affairs, and in their pleasures.
>
> (*Treatise*, xxiii)

So what we have in chapter two is a form of argument that follows Hume in the sense that human nature is a given. We do not know why it is the way it is: that part of nature is shrouded in darkness, as it were. It is foolish to speculate, that is not the road to knowledge. Focus on the consequences of human nature, for these can be discovered experimentally through observation and experience. Notice too that not only is the form of argument similar to that of Hume, so too is a detail of the language: 'original qualities of human nature' (Hume); 'original principles of human nature' (Smith, though the phrase used to translate Grotius in a recent modern translation is 'the first principles of nature' (Grotius, 1964 [1625]) so that although the investigation of the synthesis here is limited, it must be understood as yet more complex); 'they are mostly unknown'; 'no further account can be given' (Smith, though this is closer in phrasing to Hutcheson); 'I pretend not to explain' (Hume); 'it belongs not to our present subject to inquire' (Smith). This insight does more: it places the idea of unintended consequences in a philosophical context. If the consequences were intended there has to be some thing or someone (God) who intends: this sort of investigation is ruled out by Hume's method. It is pointless to speculate, for such speculations are not based upon observation and experience. Another implication of the unintended consequences is that human society progresses as human needs develop, that is, that there is a human propensity for action in the world. The text signals, here and elsewhere, through notions of unintended consequences, an evolutionary approach to society. Hume, of course, in the *Treatise*, saw justice, arising out of common adjustments to self-love, as 'advantageous to the public; tho' it be not intended for that purpose by the inventors' (*Treatise*, 529). Unintended consequences abound; they are part of a wider discourse.

This progressive discovery of human possibilities, and of what is advantageous and what is not, is also in line with the natural law tradition as initiated much earlier by Grotius and expounded by Pufendorf (Buckle, 1991, 67). It is also in keeping with Adam Ferguson: 'Man, like other animals, has certain instinctive propensities, which, prior to the perception of pleasure or pain, or prior to the experience of what is pernicious or useful, lead him to perform many functions of nature relative to himself and his fellow creatures' (Ferguson, 1966 [1767], 10–11).[4] Hutcheson too talks about 'propensity' in relation to 'those "springs of action"' which do not presuppose antecedent opinions of good or evil in their objects' (Jensen, 1971, 12). Smith also held (*WN*, 540) that humans exhibit 'a natural effort which every man is continually making to better his own condition'. He does not use the term propensity for this potentially powerful 'natural effort' but it is clearly meant to be such. The phrase 'natural disposition' is how Smith refers in the *Lectures on Jurisprudence* to what later becomes 'propensity' in the *Wealth of Nations* (*LJ*, vi, 44). Statements about propensities and dispositions are part of a wider discursive practice.

It would seem that in writing this passage, Smith had Hume's recommendation for the experimental (scientific) study of society in mind. That he does not specifically say so is probably partly due to eighteenth-century convention and partly due to his understanding of his target audience. Smith assumes that his intended reader has knowledge of current philosophical discussions. This is taken as a given. Of course, it is possible to dig much deeper. For a deeper understanding of Smith's 'propensity', there is always Aquinas and the notion of 'natural inclination' to turn to. A target audience for his published work is, accordingly, people that would have some knowledge of Hume and of relevant writings prior to Hume, such as Hutcheson, Locke, and Grotius and so on, back to mediaeval conceptions of the natural law. But Smith tells us none of this directly: *imitatio* suggests that 'the structure and language of an old text may help introduce radically new ideas' (Leff, 1997, 201, 203). Some of this will be in the *Zeitgeist*. Some of this will be derived from the general intellectual character of the times (*Zeitgeist*) rather than simply from particular texts. If we accept the idea of intertextuality, two related texts (say) may contain common elements derived from an ongoing intellectual conversation informed by the general climate of opinion and by common assumptions and vocabularies.

Smith's text:

> as seems more probably, it be the necessary consequence of reason and speech.
>
> (*WN*, I.ii.2)

Hume's text:

> Men are superior to beasts principally by the superiority of their reason; and they are the degrees of the same faculty, which set such an infinite difference between one man and another.
>
> (*Treatise*, 610)

Grotius's text:

> The mature man in fact has...an impelling desire for society, for the gratification of which he alone among animals possesses a special instrument, speech.
>
> (Grotius, 1964 [1625] (*DJBP*), Prol. 7)

The emphasis of the second part of the quote from Hume is mine. Given how Smith develops his text, it is significant that, as will be seen later, he does not share Hume's view in this respect. Hume influenced Smith's thought, though does not mean that Smith swallowed Hume's ideas whole. Smith's argument is original in many respects and that also needs to be kept in mind. That Grotius identifies the social significance of speech and its consequence, a desire for social order, underscores Smith's concerns, as do the views of Hutcheson, about the sociability of human nature. Smith's 'reason' suggests that as progress takes place, instinct ('propensity') gives way to reason for this too is part of human nature. Linking the propensity to speech stresses that the propensity be linked to sociability. The word is loaded, of course – especially when combined with trade and the property that trade implies – with, for example, notions in Grotius and Locke concerning (self-) 'Preservation' and hence acting according to our nature and following the dictates of self-love (Buckle, 1991, passim). This strengthens the role of the propensity with respect to self-interest.

Smith's text:

> Two greyhounds, in running down the same hare, have sometimes the appearance of acting in some sort of concert. Each turns her towards his companion, or endeavours to intercept her when his companion turns her towards himself. This, however, is not the effect of any contract, but of the accidental concurrence of their passions in the same object at that particular time.
>
> (*WN*, I.ii.2)

Hume's text:

> An old greyhound will trust the more fatiguing part of the chace to the younger, and will place himself so as to meet the hare in her doubles; nor are the conjectures, which he forms on this occasion, found in any thing but his observation and experience.
>
> (*ECHU*, section ix, 83)

Pufendorf's text:

> From this state it follows that man should recognize and worship his Author, and marvel at all His works; and also pass his life in a very different manner from the brutes. Hence this state is contrasted with the life and condition of the brutes.
>
> (*De Officio*, II.2.1)

The Glasgow Edition makes no mention of this link between Smith and Hume at this point. Again, the form and content of the argument are close to that of Hume though the context is different. Both writers appreciate the need for exemplifications that will make issues clear for the reader. Both settle on the hunting of hares with greyhounds. Smith writes in terms of the accidental concurrence of the passion of each dog.[5] Hume writes in terms of the experience and observation of the 'old' dog: ultimately Hume did not use reason as a distinctive attribute of humans. Hume does not accept any sharp distinction between the human and animal in this respect (Buckle, 2001, 231). That two greyhounds and a hare are chosen for the exemplification suggests, not simply that the example would have been understood by the target readers but that Smith had Hume in mind when writing this section. The dog in both cases is male and the hunted animal female. It is likely that the dog in the chase would be male and that the female for the hare is suggested by the need to contrast the pronouns. But then again, the sexual imagery may be culturally telling. Smith's point is one about 'contract'. This evidence would suggest that Smith knew Hume's writings in detail and that in thinking about the relationship between economics and human nature, he would turn, in his writing, to Hume.

It is not suggested that the quote from Pufendorf is directly relevant. It does however illustrate that the contrast between human nature and brutish nature is fundamental, even if in some later discussion animal and human nature share some elements. Pufendorf builds his ideas upon Grotius, and so a cumulative discussion becomes part of intellectual life. Economy is organised, and social, and fundamentally linked to human nature. It is useful to keep in mind that, according to Buckle, the Scottish Enlightenment read Locke as having a significant relationship with the thinking of Grotius and Pufendorf and that Hutcheson's predecessor at Glasgow, Gershom Carmichael, worked Pufendorf into Scottish moral philosophy (Buckle, 1991, 193). Hutcheson himself tells us as much, referring, in his *Short Introduction to Moral Philosophy*, to his sources in the ideas of Cicero, Aristotle, Pufendorf and Carmichael (Dooley, 2003, 2). Given Smith's early biography, it is not surprising that he synthesised his own thinking through exploration of earlier writers whose acquaintance he made by studying at Glasgow. Smith benefited accordingly from these teachings in an already synthesised form.

Smith's text:

> Each turns her towards his companion, or endeavours to intercept her when his companion turns her towards himself. This is, however, not the effect of any contract, but of the accidental concurrence of their passions in the same object at that particular time.
>
> (*WN*, I.ii.2)

Hume's text:

> Thus animals have little or no sense of virtue and vice; they quickly lose sight of the relations of blood; and are incapable of that of right or property.
>
> (*Treatise*, 326)

Hume's text:

> And that all contracts and promises ought carefully to be fulfilled, in order to secure mutual trust and confidence, by which the general *interest* of mankind is so much promoted?
>
> Examine the writers on the laws of nature; and you will always find, that, whatever principles they set out with, they are sure to terminate here at last, and to assign, as the ultimate reason for every rule that they establish, the convenience and necessities of mankind.
>
> *(ECPM*, 195)

Smith is of the same opinion as Hume concerning 'right or property'. His context is the propensity to 'truck, barter and exchange'. When exchanges take place, essentially what are exchanged are property rights. But in the example of the greyhound and the hare, the chase is instinctual, it is not based upon discussion and bargaining, there is no operating propensity based upon reason and speech, though the notion of experience is not necessarily ruled out. In this context, contract is about agreements to exchange, either implicit or explicit. The links are between property and contract, that is, between creating, exchanging and maintaining. Smith's animals are also (largely) Hume's animals, as we might expect, though Smith's poor are not Hume's poor. Smith terminates his chapter with the bringing together of difference and specialisations for the benefit of society as a whole. The overall structure of Smith's chapter is in conformity with a style of argument shared with others, especially Hume. The context of his writing includes some of the sustained intellectual arguments of his day and with respect to his reader, he takes this as a given.

Smith's text:

> Nobody ever saw one animal by its gestures and natural cries signify to another, this is mine, that yours; I am willing to give this for that.
>
> *(WN*, I.ii.2)

Hume's text:

> What other reason, indeed, could writers ever give, why this must be *mine* and that *yours*; since uninstructed nature, surely never made any such distinction?
>
> *(ECPM*, 195)

Again, although the sentence and the context are not identical, there is a close affinity between what Smith writes and what Hume writes. Smith's words could be seen as a (very loose) paraphrase of Hume's, though this is a view that requires some justification. In both, the reader is expected to agree with what is on offer. This expectation is carried in the opening phrases: 'Nobody ever saw' (Smith) and 'What other reason indeed, could writers ever give' (Hume). Smith's use of 'mine' and 'yours' (located centrally in both sentences) and the setting of his animal episode in what is, in effect, 'uninstructed nature' ('gestures and natural cries') suggest, again, that at this point in his writing, he had Hume in mind. Even if the relationship between this sample of Smith and the sample from Hume is not a directly corresponding one (though I think that it is), this would still be information relevant to understanding the way or ways in which Smith achieves synthesis in his writing. Smith's sentence is not strictly a paraphrase of Hume – it is certainly not plagiarism – but it is close both in meaning and in structure. Both are drawing upon juridical vocabulary and distinctions made, concerning 'meum and tuum', in Roman Law, the system to which Scottish thinkers turned to 'fill in the gaps in their own law' (Herman, 2001, 84). Smith writes out similar ideas to Hume – as a man of his time – but the ideas are transformed, characteristically for this chapter, into dramatic narrative.

An analysis based upon some of Mandeville's writing

Mandeville's influence on the *Wealth of Nations* and on Smith's understanding of the division of labour has long been recognised. We know that Smith came to Mandeville through Hutcheson and Hume and directly by his own reading. It is also recognised that 'one of the most famous passages of the *Wealth of Nations* that about the labourer's coat is largely a paraphrase of the *Fable*' (Kaye, in Mandeville, 1924, cxxxv). The phrase, 'the division of labour', given pride of place in the opening sentence of chapter two, is Mandeville's (Kaye, in Mandeville, 1924, cxxxv). Hume had also talked of the 'partition of employments' and Hutcheson, earlier, had referred to the idea – again this topic was one that was part of an ongoing discussion (Herman, 2001, 200). Dooley traces origins in the work of Petty and in Plato's *Republic* (Dooley, 2003, 3). It is significant that Kaye uses the term 'paraphrase' even though he makes no analysis of its linguistic elements. What else is there around that suggests Smith had Mandeville in mind as he wrote?

Smith's text:

> It is the necessary, though very slow and gradual consequence of a certain propensity in human nature which has in view no such extensive utility; the propensity to truck, barter and exchange one thing for another.
>
> (*WN*, I.ii.1)

Mandeville's text:

> Cleo. But it is a great while, before that Nature can be rightly understood; and it is the Work of Ages to find out the true Use of the Passions, and to raise a Politician, that can make every Frailty of the members, add Strength to the whole Body, and by dexterous Management turn *private Vices into public Benefits*.
>
> (*Sixth Dialogue*, 1924 [1732], vol. ii, 319)

An aim is to show how Smith's second chapter is constructed as an eighteenth-century argument. Smith does not share Mandeville's views on 'Management'. But he shares the notion that establishing the outcome of human nature is a slow process. It is 'the Work of Ages to find out the true Use of the Passions' (Mandeville). Smith's statement is 'It is the necessary consequence, though very slow and gradual'. Elsewhere Mandeville demonstrates the evolutionary significance of 'Experience' (Mandeville, 1924 [1732], 171). Smith has not identified the exchanging of goods and services as a 'passion' but rather as an orientation, a 'propensity', though any distinction between a 'passion' and a 'propensity' is not explicitly made. However it may be implicit in the reference to 'reason and speech'. For Hume, reason is a means of achieving ends that 'passions' set. A propensity, linked to reason and speech, would not have the force of passion but would rather be a means of channelling 'passion' into productive activity, by reason and discussion. The coexistence of 'Deliberative and non-deliberative elements', with respect to motivation in Smith, is an aspect noted by Oakley (Oakley, 1994, 79–80). Hume's views, in attenuated form, can be traced back through Hutcheson and even to Aristotle (Buckle, 1991, 63). This is what it is to write as a contribution to a developing analysis.

It is, nonetheless, the 'Work of Ages' before that propensity is manifest in highly specialised economic activity. In this sense Smith echoes Mandeville's notion of historical evolution and in this sense too Mandeville inspired Smith, an insight, with respect to the division of labour, supported by Dugald Stewart (Kaye, in Mandeville, 1924, cxxxv). He also seems to share Mandeville's view that 'What belongs to our Nature, all Men may justly be said to have actually or virtually in them at their Birth' (Mandeville, *Third Dialogue*, 1924 [1732], 121). But he does not seem to share Mandeville's view that 'All Passions and Instinct in general were given to all Animals for some wise End', for Smith writes that human nature 'has in view no such extensive utility' and, as someone interested in Hume's philosophy, Smith is unlikely to make any arguments about the origin of human nature. So whilst there are some things that are the same and said in related ways, with respect to Mandeville's writing, other elements are carefully avoided. Smith (elsewhere) acknowledges Mandeville as having 'original' ideas (*EPS*, 250).

Smith's texts:

> But man has almost constant occasion for the help of his brethren, and it is in vain for him to expect it from their benevolence only.
>
> It is not from the benevolence of the butcher, the brewer, or the baker, that we expect our dinner, but from their regard to their own interest. We address ourselves, not to their humanity but to their self-love; and never talk to them of our necessities but of their advantages.
>
> (*WN*, I.ii.2)

Mandeville's text:

> (On money)
> How to get these Services perform'd by others, when we have Occasion for them, is the grand and almost constant Sollicitude in Life of every individual

Person. To expect, that others should serve us for nothing, is unreasonable; therefore all Commerce, that Men can have together, must be a continual bartering of one thing for another. The Seller, who transfers the Property of a Thing, has his own Interest as much at Heart as the Buyer who purchases the Property; and, if you want or like a thing, the Owner of it, whatever Stock or Provision he may have of the same, or how greatly soever you stand in need of it, will never part with it, but for a Consideration, which he likes better, than he does the thing you want.

Which way shall I persuade a Man to serve me, when the Service, I can repay him in, is such that he does not want or care for?

(*Sixth Dialogue*, 1924 [1732], vol. ii, 349)

The two extracts from Smith and the longer extract from Mandeville are set in different contexts but Mandeville rehearses the issues – in a different context from Smith – which Smith treats in his famous aphorism. Smith did not arrive at his aphorism without effort. An earlier reference is less dramatic:

When you apply to a brewer or butcher for beer or for beef, you do not explain to him how much you stand in need of these, but how much it would be your [*sic*] interest to allow you to have them for a certain price. You do not address his humanity but his self-love.

(*LJ*, vi. 46)

Revisions made for publication in the *Wealth of Nations* successfully add to the dramatic force of the statement. It is transformed from a commonplace to an aphorism. Note also that Smith is concerned about what Hutcheson called 'springs to action' but Smith assumes pre-existing knowledge: the term 'benevolence' is not explained but taken as given or already understood.

Whilst there are common themes in the writings of the two authors, here, there is, neither common language nor common context. Both share the notion however that there is a power to persuade, located in self-interest. Both, interestingly, are written from the point of view of the agent and not of the social critic.[6] Smith's aphorism is, in words, entirely his own, but if we were to treat it fully we could trace a line of development back through Hutcheson to Shaftesbury. Shaftesbury, according to Miller, conceptualised 'a balance of selfish and benevolent feelings within human nature' such that, quoting Shaftesbury, 'the private interest and good of everyone...works towards the general good' (Miller, 1995, 49; Shaftesbury, 1964, vol. 1, 336 and 338). Again, the issue of benevolence versus self-love is a concept that is repeatedly reflected upon, prior to the publication of the *Wealth of Nations*. Throughout the eighteenth century 'benevolence' versus self-love was part of the discourse and located both within and beyond texts. Smith does not deny benevolence, simply records that it is not a strong enough motive in commercial transactions.

Smith, the storyteller, also borrows from Mandeville. We have already mentioned the labourer's coat from chapter one. Smith makes use of Mandeville when telling his tale of how the division of labour comes to be established as the norm in a developing community.

Smith's text:

> As it is by treaty, by barter, and by purchase, that we obtain from one another the greater part of those mutual good offices which we stand in need of, so it is this same trucking disposition which originally gives occasion to the division of labour. In a tribe of hunters or shepherds a particular person makes bows and arrows . . .
>
> (*WN*, I.ii.3)

Mandeville's text:

> Cleo. Man, as I have hinted before, naturally loves to imitate what he sees others do, which is the reason that Savage people all do the same thing: This hinders them from meliorating their Condition, though they are always wishing for it: But if one will wholly apply himself to making Bows and Arrows, whilst another provides Food, a third builds Huts, a fourth makes Garments, and a fifth Utensils, they not only become useful to one another, but the Callings and Employments themselves will in the same Number of Years receive much greater Improvements, than if all had been promiscuously follow'd by every one of the Five.
>
> (Mandeville, 1924, vol. ii, 284)

Smith's passage is too long to reproduce here, besides which it is well known. The two passages are available in the Glasgow Edition but no analysis is made there of them (Mandeville's version of the spread of the division of labour is reproduced in the Glasgow Edition at I.ii.3, 27, in footnote 8). What is striking about Smith's narrative episode is that its main dramatic elements are structured according to Mandeville's text. Smith writes of four people: the arrow maker, the hut maker, the brazier and the tanner (who makes clothes), whereas Mandeville writes explicitly of five. The 'food' maker is implied, however, in Smith's text, for the arrow maker 'frequently exchanges' the arrows 'for cattle or venison'. The 'smith or brazier' is the equivalent of the one who makes 'Utensils'. Smith has modelled the five elements of his writing here directly on Mandeville.

This insight need not be used to do Smith down: Smith does not use Mandeville's words, or at least not in the development of the narrative – the attributes of 'the Savage', such as bows and arrows, may well be conventional – nor even Mandeville's theory.[7] The developmental context of the tale is different from that of Mandeville in that the analysis is consistently focused upon propositions that are broadly theoretical. Smith is, again, expanding a narrative and making it work within the context of a developing and consistently worked argument. Mandeville's context is (initially) that of imitation, and Smith's is that of the propensity ('this same trucking disposition'). Mandeville opens his passage with: 'But if one will'. There is no theory grounding this change, indeed the general principle of imitation acts against it. Smith develops Mandeville's short six-line illustration into a story of social evolution based on an operating principle, linked to self-interest – the propensity to truck, barter and exchange. This is seen even more transparently in the *Lectures on Jurisprudence* where Smith introduces a short passage, parallel in spirit to the passage in the *Wealth of Nations*, on 'A savage who supports himself by hunting' with 'This bartering and trucking spirit is the cause of the separation of trades and the improvements in the arts' (*LJ*, 348, 47). The relationship with Mandeville's example becomes thus more complex as the text in the *Wealth of Nations* is adapted also from Smith's prior writing. The relevant textual process is that of paraphrasing though the results move the (final) new text beyond mere paraphrasing, as there is a theory-based, and extensive, creative element in Smith's writing that is absent from Mandeville's original. Smith's story is placed within a systematic account of socio-economic development and this systematic element is lacking in Mandeville.

Smith's text:

> The difference of natural talents in different men is, in reality, much less than we are aware of; and the very different genius which appears to distinguish men of different professions, when grown up to maturity, is not upon many occasions so much the cause, as the effect of the division of labour.
>
> (*WN*, I.ii.4)

Mandeville's text:

> Human Nature is every where the same: Genius, Wit and Natural Parts are always sharpened by Application, and may be much improv'd in the Practice of the meanest Villany, as they can in the Exercise of Industry or the most Heroic Virtue.
>
> (*An Essay on Charity and Charity Schools*, 1924 [1732], vol. i, 275)

The Glasgow Edition makes no reference to this link between Mandeville's thought and Smith's writing, at this point, but when it is taken together with Mandeville's view on schooling and that the 'Brain of a Child, newly born is a Charte Blanche' (Mandeville, *Fourth Dialogue*, 1924 [1732], 168), then Smith's writing is here, again, synthesising many elements that would have been familiar to eighteenth-century readers. The two excerpts (above) seem to be saying the same thing in different words; that is, the themes are similar though the details of the language completely different. The Glasgow Edition at this point in the text points to extensive passages in Hume. The whole passage on nature and nurture is interwoven with ideas from other writers such as Hume.

So what do we make of Smith's 'propensity' and can we watch Smith writing?

Smith's 'propensity' is located in Humean, and pre-Humean, ideas about human nature and the link between nature and economy. In this sense it is a familiar starting point, a means to get into the matter at hand which is that of setting a framework for the development of society through a cumulative process of experiment and conversation: trucking, bartering and exchanging are social activities aided by speech. It acknowledges Smith's debt to Hume generally and specifically with respect to links between 'property' and human nature, essential foundations for specialisation and exchange. But the influences on his writing are also multiple. Smith was a man of his time and he was writing in the context of a developing eighteenth-century argument – about links between human nature and economic activity – some of which had already become part of a synthesised, standard body of shared knowledge and were not therefore located in any specific text.

What also emerges, from this analysis, is a sense of how Smith achieved a synthesis in writing. The product, that is, chapter two and its outcomes, is unique to Smith, even if strongly influenced by others, and his text is carefully constructed to show how individual specialisation and interest are inevitably and usefully bound together as a contribution to the whole. But the process is one in which elements of earlier eighteenth-century thinking, including terminology (lexis), and expectations about moves in the argument (comparisons of human and animal nature), are drawn together to produce a new text. Smith's writing is located in a series of eighteenth-century discussions and any one element in the text may draw from a number of sources – Mandeville, Hutcheson and Hume being the most easily recognisable. A methodological basis for the construction of the chapter is based upon Hume's ideas concerning observation and experience. In other words the chapter is partly constructed around Hume's interpretation of Newtonian methods ('experimentalism', rejection of *a priori* principles and the practice of simplicity in explanation) as applied to the study of human nature and society, an interpretation that Smith also set out for himself (*LRBL*, 145–146; see Buckle, 1991, 237; Smith, 1983).[8] That this is all packed into two short episodes should not give any cause for concern; Smith's target reader was expected to have recognised the argument. It is a decision made, by the author, between what needs to be said (i.e. about what is new) and what can be taken as given (Coulthard, 1994, 4–5). The contrast made between human nature and animal nature is textually informed by Hume, but there is also a smattering of Mandeville and no doubt many others. The location of economic life in human nature is informed by details of the writings of Hume, Hutcheson and Mandeville, but those details are carefully adapted to Smith's purpose. Suggestions of plagiarism, on the evidence supplied here, seem misguided. Even though the evidence presented here is not drawn from areas directly relating to either Rashid's or Rothbard's discussion, the method used here needs to be applied to the episodes referred to in those articles. On the basis of what has been demonstrated here, Ahiakpor's skepticism of Rothbard's claims seems justifiable.

Smith's notion of a 'propensity in human nature' is his way of linking to the ongoing eighteenth-century discussion of the ways in which economic life is related to human nature. He does not explicitly say that what is traded is property, that is, the product of individual human effort. Neither does Smith explicitly say, in his opening moves, that human nature is social and that there is no state of nature in the sense contrived by Hobbes. There are implications that follow from what he does say. Trade implies others. Speech implies others. Property implies product and producers (others) since such rights are social and based upon constraints. A 'propensity to truck, barter and exchange' implies a human nature that is purposive and active in the world and that results, in contradistinction to animals, in patterns of living that are subject to significant change over time. Human society is located in a human energy to transform materials and relationships. And by identifying the link between human nature and economic life, in the way that he does, Smith has a sure foundation (we are talking of the eighteenth century) for unintended consequences and for his use of 'every man' (i.e. human nature is consistent) as an economic agent, later in his work. Indeed unintended consequences in this view come out as very significant and even if the 'invisible hand' is used ironically later in the work, it is still contained within the notion of human nature. Not only that but the invisible hand is textually realised elsewhere in the *Wealth of Nations* by the development of language that removes the actor.

But can we really watch him writing? Well, yes, but only in a very general sense. He is clear about his target reader: from the evidence presented here, the target reader knew something of Hume, Hutcheson and of Mandeville, for example. He did not need to spell everything out for them: the target reader was already engaged in a conversation about the origins of social and economic life. Was it one target reader or a set of target readers? Smith is consistent in his theoretical arguments, in this chapter, but the argument is shaped by a variety of different means, though narrative predominates. This suggests that he may have had more than one target reader in mind: the message is consistent but the means of achieving it textually are varied by genre, that is, logical and story-based. The target reader helps an author define the writing and the writing then defines the audience. Actual readers were more or less similar to target reader(s), or struggled to become his target reader, and familiar with the cultural context, and, therefore were unlikely to be surprised by (say) the comparison of human nature and animal nature. Indeed, once human nature was mentioned, the comparison would be expected. If animals are constantly engaged in reproducing the same and humans engaged in change and exchange (i.e. engaged in a set of changing relationships with each other and, so, if the implications of the narrative of the 'tribal society' are followed through, with nature) then the eighteenth century would locate such behaviour in human nature. Readers were, like him, aware of other literature and of the discussion of the properties of human nature. Human nature was engaged in a struggle between benevolence and self-interest but constrained by social possibilities such as 'contracts' and social divisions created by education and the division of labour.

He knew his sources and his social and cultural context well and so borrowed, imitated and adapted by responding to his reading. Still and Warton put the idea of all writing in the context of any writer's experience of reading: '[s/he] is a reader of texts (in the broadest sense) before s/he is a creator of texts, and therefore the work of art is inevitably shot through with references, quotations and influences of every kind' (Jasinski, 2001, 323; Still and Warton, 1990). He also knew how to transform a good workable example when he saw one, and this he could even have considered as an exercise of rhetorical imitation. He synthesised from a number of sources, though he did not swallow the arguments whole, and produced a text that was still his own. Hume's greyhound example is close to Smith's, but the use to which Smith puts the example goes beyond Hume. The fact that he can incorporate elements of Hutcheson (to whom Mandeville was anathema) – Smith does not deny benevolence, he just points out that in terms of commerce it is not relevant as a motivating passion – with Mandeville attesting to his writing skills, and the power of his synthesis. He is likely to have read other writers imaginatively, with his writing project in mind, and to have carefully identified passages – noting them either mentally or mechanically or simply by absorption – that he would draw upon for elaboration. In the passage on the evolution of the division of labour in a tribal society, for example, he has worked out the elements in Mandeville's brief example and translated those same elements into a convincing story of his own, even if modelled on the same moves as made by Mandeville. How he actually did this (i.e. by intuition or by careful plotting) remains unclear (what we know of his redrafting activities suggest plotting, by rewrite, though the differences between the passage in the early draft and in the published work are slight), though the textual outcome is carefully constructed. Either way, he turned a simple illustration into a more significant story in the context of a developing theoretical argument.

Another aspect of synthesis is his ability to paraphrase. Here, however, the notion of paraphrase is not precisely specified. It can be characterised as involving 'various types of transformations of expressions into the same language' (Yamamoto, 2003). The sentences identified in Smith and in others are not always doing the same kind of work, but there are elements in common: repetition of words and phrases being a significant element. We are dealing with more or less; sometimes there are common elements, and sometimes the relationship is more remote or elaborated. Sometimes the commonalities are distilled from more than one source. Paraphrasing was of considerable cultural significance in the sixteenth and seventeenth centuries and is likely to have found its way into non-theological writing in the eighteenth century. Its origins are to be found in biblical study but the practice was extended to secular writing. 'Paraphrases' were also part of Presbyterian services in Scottish churches. In modern discussion of 'paraphrasing', in the context of developing students' capacities to write, the issue of paraphrasing is linked to the avoidance of plagiarism. On the evidence supplied from book one, chapter two, there are no grounds for a charge of plagiarism. To understand Smith's writing, as writing, requires a cultural context that is more sophisticated than a simple search for origins.

A significant point about paraphrasing is that readers in the eighteenth century would have been expected to recognise the sources – texts were very long-lived. There would be an element of familiarity even though Smith, as a writer of a didactic text, would have aimed at transforming the target reader's experience. The familiar gives way to the new, and this is what happens in his contrasts between human and animal nature. The ideas are familiar, but the use that Smith finally puts them to is radical. His conclusions that invention is the product of the ordinary mind engaged in daily business or that street porters and philosophers differ only in situation and as the result of institutional arrangements and not essentially in nature must have been startling.

His second chapter demonstrates many of Smith's qualities as a writer, for not only does Smith use synthesis in his writing, but there is some evidence of different qualities (e.g. he writes as a moralist, a political economist, a logician, and, in this chapter above all, a storyteller). Evensky describes Smith's purpose, in book one, Chapter two, as that of telling 'a compelling story of mankind's evolution' (Evensky, 2003, 7). That story was told in ways that reflect the *Zeitgeist* and ways that help transform it. Smith also, then, achieves a synthesis amongst these different forms of writing. That he produces a whole with the reputation of gently leading the reader by the hand is a significant rhetorical achievement.

3 Nature's dupes

Irony and economic agency in Smith's writing

Irony was systematically analysed in the nineteenth century, and refinements in the analysis of irony have been an important part of the development of rhetoric in the late twentieth century, but it became a sustained part of literary acts in the eighteenth. And literary acts in the eighteenth century were undertaken by individuals capable of working in many different contexts and on many differing genres. The lines of distinction between disciplines, a commonplace in the modern world, were hardly drawn in the eighteenth century. The *philosophe* could turn his or her hand to a range of subjects and genres. Consider David Hume who wrote substantial works on moral philosophy, politics, economics, religion and history, and Smith himself who worked on rhetoric, on the history of astronomy, on jurisprudence, social philosophy and political economy. Hume read the output of the 'Augustan Age', and its 'ruling literary modes of satire and irony' (Price, 1965, 4), and so did Adam Smith. Eighteenth-century writing by Swift and Defoe and Hume and many others are noted for the need to be wary of the intended irony of the authors concerned, for their ironies can be subtle and treacherous, so treacherous that Defoe wrote a piece that was taken at face value by almost its entire readership. The social experience of being duped by intended irony is unpleasant and the victims can retaliate, as they did in their vigorous reactions to Defoe. The ironic intention escaped his grasp once the work was in the readers' hands. The literary distinction between deception (being duped) and self-deception does not necessarily sit so comfortably with readers' responses on discovering that they have been abused.

Irony is a strange, paradoxical trope, the preferred 'mode of intellectual detachment' and at the same time a device that can 'mock, attack, ridicule' (Hutcheon, 1994, 14–15). Like metaphor, itself a complex figure of speech, irony is not to be taken merely at face value, any more than an idiom or conceptual metaphor can. Irony is a trope that needs to be interpreted, but like some others, it can be slippery. It can be created deliberately in the text by the ironist/writer. It can be identified in the text by the irony-aware reader. It can be read into a text when read from the point of view of an experienced reader. It can be set up by an author but needs to be discovered and 'explicated' by a reader. Wherever it is detected, it is detected by a reader, the result of an act of reading and of interpretation, that is, by acts of discrimination, identification and interpretation. With 'irony' it is probably unwise to talk in terms of the monopolistic idea of 'the' reader. Irony only works as irony when a discerning reader or a set of readers treat it as such. (Hutcheon, 1994, 6). Different readers, operating under particular cultural or social conditions or expectations, may construct different meanings. Indeed, Hutcheon wonders who is held to 'make' the irony, the ironist as producer of the text or the experienced, irony-aware readers of the text (Hutcheon, 1994, 11 and 116–117). Just as the metaphorically unaware can be used by conceptual metaphors, the ironically unaware can fall 'victim' to the ironist whilst 'irony-aware' readers can create a surplus of meanings.

It is also difficult to place within a 'list' of figures that are covered by the theory of metaphor. 'Irony' to quote Price, '. . . is not only a concept, it is a way of dealing with concepts' (Price, 1965, 25). Irony, where it is unsubtle can readily fall from its bitter/sweet duality (different possible meanings being appreciated at the same time) into the more unpleasant form, sarcasm, and the associated notion of mockery, at the other end of the spectrum. It is also allied to another literary form, satire, and satire often brings in its train, paradox. So, as with other aspects of reading text in which what is said is not literally what is meant, any investigation of irony must either explicitly or implicitly consider what particular instances signify in interpretative terms. Smith himself draws attention in his work on rhetoric, of the problem of distinguishing hyperbole from metonymy or metaphor (*LRBL*, i.60). This is a specific example of a general problem found within the theory of metaphor. It may be difficult for some modern-day readers of the *Wealth of Nations*, preoccupied with Smith's writing as economics writing, to see an element of mild, and even not so mild, satire in his portrayal of merchants and landlords and of their economic fears and aspirations. His first readers, reading in the same cultural context as Smith was writing, would have, according to Butler, recognised the satirical elements (Butler, 1992, 28). Irony in Smith has recently been highlighted by Rothschild with reference in particular to Smith's use of the notion of an 'invisible hand' (Rothschild, 2001, 5 and 119). This chapter will contextualise irony and economic agency in Smith within the context of Smith's explication of a sustained contextual irony.

In open and democratic societies irony tends to have a bad name, for it suggests more than one meaning and a secret and undemocratic code of interpretation. When irony is successfully communicated it can set up a 'secret intimacy' between the writer or speaker and that part of the audience that grasps the meaning (Fowler, 1966, 306). 'Intimacy' here means nothing other than the shared capacity to correctly interpret a message that is in some sense coded (Cooper, 1986, 156). Such discrimination may not be the case of situational irony, for all human beings are subject to mortality but tend to live their lives on the unreasonable assumption of immortality, though there are those who will appreciate this irony and those who will not. In this case, as Smith himself argues, it is 'nature' that is sending the message rather than any human agent. Even here, some will be aware whilst others are unaware of the ironies. In societies that are (potentially) fragmented as a result of diversity and differing modes of interpretation, irony can be divisive. There are institutions in the Western world, and universities in the English-speaking world are numbered amongst them, in which irony is a privileged mode of discourse. There is a suspicion of elitism in the distinction between irony's intended victim, one who cannot arrive at the available meaning, and the master of irony who can handle its subtleties without being fooled. This is a point indirectly elaborated upon by Weinsheimer in his analysis of Swift's *Tale of a Tub* (a work that we know Smith read for it is specifically mentioned as a juvenile work in *Rhetoric and Belles Lettres*). Swift's work, according to Weinsheimer involves the false interpretive dichotomy between the fool, who sticks to external appearances, in interpretation, and the knave, who deals with levels and hidden meaning (Weinsheimer, 1993, 2–6). This discourse is seen as a discourse concerning hermeneutics and the position of the knave or of the fool, inadequate. But irony 'cuts both ways' and in this respect requires integration of the knave's and of the fool's perspectives. It can be used 'tactically, in the service of a wide range of political positions, legitimating or undercutting a wide variety of interests' (Hutcheon, 1994, 10). Furthermore, to condemn 'irony' because it is potentially hierarchical carries with it the possibility of also condemning allegory, another vehicle for more than one available meaning.

Hume, Smith's friend, is acknowledged as a great ironist, though Hume's motivation is not usually taken to be based upon simply the exploitation of a fashionable and culturally acceptable mode of writing. Price presents Hume's choice of irony in terms of his place within a society that equated 'religious scepticism with moral degradation' holding that it was his particular circumstances in combination with a cultural mode that lead to Hume's way of writing: 'I would like to suggest that this initial religious scepticism combined with the predominantly satiric–ironic mode in literature to lead Hume to seek irony as a method of expressing himself' (Price, 1965, 4). Price sees Hume's irony as a strategy to enable his works to be read by an audience that was potentially hostile. Where his irony is read, understood and interpreted, Hume is successfully working against a dominant point of view, one that would have attempted to prohibit the development of that point of view in the first place. Hume's ironies are raw and un-explicated; it is the readers who do most of the work.

Smith's views on religion and on God are less precise and more ambiguous than Hume's. Smith fairly readily talks of 'Providence', especially in the *Moral Sentiments* and even of 'that benevolent wisdom which governs the universe' (though this is in the context of reporting on and discussing ancient philosophy) (*MS*, VII.Ii.1.21). Smith is also prepared to talk about 'Nature', 'nature's intentions' and of 'the Author of nature', the 'Deity' and sometimes 'God', though my impression is that he tends to use attributes or associated ideas within the Deist repertoire (*MS*, II.ii.3.4; III.5.7; II.ii.3.5). He even refers, in one amendment, to 'the great judge of the world' who is obscured from 'the weak eye of human reason' (*MS*, III.2.3), a notion that transforms 'God' into an undeceived spectator and reduces the capacity of the 'eye of human reason', a notion extended later in the form of 'the all-seeing Judge of the world, whose eye can never be deceived' (*MS*, III.2.33). The 'all seeing eye of God' is a powerful eighteenth-century symbol that is also rooted in Freemasonry. The physical eye and the eye of human imagination are capable of being deceived.

Smith's notions of 'spectatorship' are complex. His concerns are those of the providentialist intent on seeking some form of order, in this case social order, by design, and sometimes, it would appear, by regulation. It must be kept in mind, however, that all of this is also a manner of speaking and writing. Smith's vocabulary in this respect is derived from stoicism. According to Viner, providentialism was a way of looking at the world favoured in the eighteenth century by 'Deists' many of whom were unhappy with Christian concepts or doctrine (Viner, 1966). 'Deism', although there is no 'consistent usage' and no 'complete consensus as to who the deists were' in eighteenth-century Britain, encompasses a number of propositions including the notion of a universal human nature, the use of reason to explore how to live a moral life in accordance with nature, an 'intelligent general providence' and hence the possibility of a well-ordered world (Brown, 1996, 8). Hume found deism to be intellectually weak and unconvincing, though he also admitted the possibility of an intelligent prime-mover but not the possibility of any certainty in that respect.

Smith disliked religious monopolies, just as he disliked other monopolies and exhibits a concern similar to that of Hume over the eradication of 'enthusiasm' (on balance the Protestant disease) and 'superstition' (on balance the Catholic one), but this approach is found more in the *Wealth of Nations* than in *Moral Sentiments*. 'On balance' for at the centre of Christianity, there is a miracle or mystery. Hume split discussions of human nature from the a priori discussion of divine nature, and this marks his work out from that of others before him. Human kind is not made in the image of God nor does it share 'reason' with God. Hume's starting point is human nature as it is revealed in history or contemporary society or by introspection and there is no 'transcendental investigation' or reasoning (Stroud, 1977, 11). A starting point for Hume is the properties and propensities of the mind. He is more interested in comparing human nature with animal nature than he is in any relationship, essentially not capable of exploration, in his eyes, between human nature and divine nature. His starting point is that which is observable about human nature and he is interested in the consequences that flow from human nature as it is.

Although Smith worked with notions of Providence, he may have followed Hume's lead, on human nature, in the *Wealth of Nations*. In that work, Smith is writing in the context of historical evolution and social development rather than in the potentially static world of providentialist thinking. In the *Moral Sentiments* he pursues a providentialist discourse as a means of integrating his ideas on morality. His construction of political economy is rooted, in book one, chapter two of the *Wealth of Nations*, in human nature and its propensities, in his case the 'propensity to truck, barter and exchange' and propensity to struggle towards self-betterment, not withstanding the reference to an 'invisible hand' (once) in the

Wealth of Nations. So if Smith is an ironist or if we read Smith and discover irony, the context may not be Hume's context even if the cultural orientation towards a combination of satire and irony, for Smith was also, from the evidence supplied in his work on rhetoric, well-read in modern, as well as in ancient literature. Smith, who has been described as a 'professional explainer', rarely seeks to hide his meaning (though he too as a skilled writer occasionally plays with his readers as in his passages on charging for the teaching of wisdom and abolishing slavery in Pennsylvania in the *Wealth of Nations* illustrate). In this respect we may assume that Smith and his readers may not have used the term irony but could, given its cultural significance, at least suspect that irony, and related concepts, were textual possibilities. Particularly in the context of the *Moral Sentiments*, Smith is drawing attention to the ironies inherent in human life (situational ironies) and, as will be shown, explicating them. Hume encodes irony and the skilled reader understands that Hume undercuts his own words and implies something different from what is superficially apparent. In his passages dealing with riches and ambition, Smith detects and explicates irony. Nature is the ironist and Smith the un-fooled, philosophical reader/writer, though even he, in life rather than in text, can only avoid being fooled some of the time. In this context, other ironies may be created.

In his studies on rhetoric Smith makes no specific reference to the term irony (the advance in the analysis of irony seems to be a nineteenth-century phenomenon) but he is well aware of the concepts of 'ridicule' and of 'parody' and associated ideas such as satire (*LRBL*, i.95 and i.v.116). 'Ridicule' implies 'mockery' and other forms of castigation though it is meant to cause laughter (Bryce, 1983, 20). The notion itself exhibits duality, in Smith's treatment of Swift's writing, for some will treat with 'admiration' (those who are themselves prone to such behaviours, for example) and some with 'contempt' those who engaged in human follies. The subject of ridicule Smith sees, in his discussion of Swift, are the 'follies and silliness of men' (*LRBL*, i.118). Smith accepts 'ridicule as more to the taste of the times' and accepts Shaftesbury's implicit judgement, which is that 'ridicule' works better than 'confutation' (*LRBL*, i.147). However Smith's analysis is not highly innovative, even if it has some critical insights such as the notion of appropriateness and 'suitability' of expression.

Irony and economic motivation in Smith

Smith, like Hume, is a student of human nature. This is the case both for *Moral Sentiments* and for the *Wealth of Nations*. Like Hume, who is very concerned with establishing a relationship between economic life and human nature, Smith locates economic behaviour in human nature itself. He does this in many places, for the drive to self-betterment is a drive found in 'every man' (his universal economic agent) but with very great deliberateness in chapter two, of book one of the *Wealth of Nations*. At the heart of Smith's construction of political economy, is an understanding of human nature as intrinsically social and intrinsically change oriented. Smith's opening words in chapter two:

> This division of labour, from which so many advantages are derived, is not originally the effect of any human wisdom, which foresees and intends the general opulence to which it gives occasion. It is the necessary, though very slow and gradual consequence of a certain propensity in human nature which has in view no such extensive utility; the propensity to truck, barter and exchange.
>
> *(WN*, I.ii.1)

The propensity to 'to truck, barter and exchange' is posited, in the paragraph that follows, as a universal aspect of human nature, 'common to all men, and to be found in no other race of animals'. It is the basis on which Smith constructs the drive in all men, in all social conditions, towards self-betterment, a basis in human nature for Smith's 'system of natural liberty'. The consequences of this propensity, the development of specialist labour and the growth of 'general opulence' is not the result of any grand plan. Rather it is the unintended consequence of human action in the world – action guided by a natural propensity, not quite located in passions and not quite located in speech and reason, rather than by human reason ('human wisdom'). The potential of the propensity to transform human economy experience is at its greatest in commercial society (an aspect of Smith's developmental thinking that Force analyses in the context of writing by Mandeville and Rousseau) (Force, 2003). Smith's universal economic agent is 'every man', but he is normally working with specific and located agents: landlords, merchants, shepherds, philosophers and so on.

There is a potential irony in this, developed later by the notion of the 'invisible hand', for the general good is not intended. Although agents are capable through benevolence of intending the well-being of others, and sometimes do, located agents are motivated by their 'interests'. The notion of self-interest suggests both a subjective and objective aspect to material and social circumstances. The objective 'interest' of rulers is their kingdoms, of shepherds, their sheep. 'Vanity', or how we appear in the eyes of others would seem to be the subjective counterpart. The consequences of conditions created by the propensities to economic action can be interpreted as (given what is written elsewhere in the *Wealth of Nations*) neither implied by God's will nor by any other agency capable of collectively expressing the purposes of human life. The development of human society, as a result of the propensities in action, along specialised lines, is the work of time, as suggested by Mandeville, and the result of accumulated experience (see Chapter 2). Whilst the 'invisible hand' metaphor is used only once in the *Wealth of Nations*, the notion of positive collective outcomes, stemming from human propensities to engage in economic activity and the notion of positive but unforeseen ends as the outcome of individual human effort, is fundamental to Smith's notion of the relationship between economy and human nature. The irony is that by engaging in economic activity, in pursuit of their own interests, unforeseen consequences are generated that promote the wider good. Self-interest is pursued in commercial society through individual calculations of advantage situated in given contexts of action, but as a result society is provisioned, entertained and supplied with professional services. A full analysis of the ironies associated with the notion of 'the invisible hand' will be postponed until later.

Another significant irony found in the *Wealth of Nations* (*WN*, I.ii.4) is that the division of labour itself leads to a division of social class. Smith, in contemplating the generation of the 'philosopher' and of the 'common street porter', may well have reflected upon his childhood companions and on his own development. The example feels too nice to be otherwise. He certainly considered the duality of the division of labour both as providing a means to general opulence and in restricting the opulence of particular individuals and classes. Irony consists in the fact that the means to that opulence is also a means to alienation. Smith's consideration of the need to educate for cultural and social purposes to off-set the disadvantages of the division of labour has its origins in insights encoded into his opening chapters.

The profoundest combination of situational irony and mild satire is set forth by Smith in his discussion of 'riches' in the *Moral Sentiments* and what is said about riches and motivation in the *Wealth of Nations* can be seen as but a reflection of the earlier work. This would seem to be Force's view, and there are many who would read the *Wealth of Nations* through the *Moral Sentiments*. It is as well to remember that chapter two of book one locates agency not in either self-interest or in moral approbation or disapprobation but in the 'propensity to truck, barter and exchange'. In *Jurisprudence* Smith is reported as having used in 1763, the term 'disposition' in an otherwise similar phrase (*LJ*, vi.64). Such a propensity must be located in both a drive to self-interest and to negotiate, and the act of negotiation requires 'sympathy'. It is not need in this formulation that drives economic life but psychological conditions inherent in what it is to be human. If economic actions are to be repeated, as they will be in any small-scale society, there needs to be a socially acceptable basis for exchange. Provided this is kept in mind, it is useful to look at the ironies involved in the consideration of agency in both works.

It would be hard to exaggerate the satirical elements in *Moral Sentiments*, especially in those many passages in which it contemplates aspects associated with the motivations for, and the status credited to, those who hold wealth. Although the satire in the *Wealth of Nations* may be less visible, there are textual links between Smith's earlier and later works both with respect to human nature and to human motivation. It has to be clear, in our reading of these two works, that in *Moral Sentiments*, Smith is reflecting upon individual 'riches', whereas in the *Wealth of Nations*, Smith is focusing more, though not exclusively, on national wealth and on formal analysis. The *Wealth of Nations* is composed of narrative passages and of 'lists'. I opine that the narrative passages often carry sentiments, important to Smith both in relation to ideas expressed in *Moral Sentiments* but also in the wider context of his belief about how to persuade. The lists, I suspect, often carry generalised analytical material presented as 'timeless'. Any divide between the two needs to be investigated, though not here.

Strictly speaking, Smith's first significant extensive passage on 'riches' and the social attitudes towards them is in *Moral Sentiments* and headed, 'On the origin of Ambition, and of the distinction of Ranks' though there are many comments on 'rank' and 'riches' elsewhere in the *Moral Sentiments*. Although there is an element in the writing at this point that is concerned with ambition, or as Smith puts 'that great purpose of human life which we call bettering our condition', ambition is to be taken to mean both the ambition of the rich to stay rich as well as of the poor to better their condition. Smith reverses the point of view: 'Do they [those in the 'higher ranks of life'] imagine that their stomach is better, or their sleep sounder in a palace than in a cottage?' (*MS*, I.iii.2.1). A man aspires to riches, 'because he feels that they naturally draw upon him the attention of the world'. A poor man, 'ashamed of his poverty' is placed, he feels, 'out of the sight of mankind' and so 'goes out and comes in unheeded, and when in the midst of a crowd is in the same obscurity as if shut up in his own hovel'. 'Vanity', the need to seen and admired, and 'shame' are prime motivators. Smith is careful to show, by his evaluations of these notions – such as the inverted point of view carried by 'Do they imagine...?' or his undercutting of the associations around obscurity, 'to be overlooked, and to be disapproved of, are things entirely different' – that he does not necessarily share the conventional judgements. However, being noticed is the motivator:

> It is this, which notwithstanding the restraint it imposes, notwithstanding the loss of liberty with which it is attended, renders greatness the object of envy, and compensates, in the opinion of mankind, all that toil, all that anxiety, all those mortifications which must be undergone in the pursuit of it; and what is of yet more consequence, all that leisure, all that easy, all that careless security, which are forfeited for ever by the acquisition.
>
> (*MS*, I.iii.2.1)

Smith sees, in the *Wealth of Nations*, that: 'With the greater part of rich people, the chief enjoyment of riches consists in the parade of riches' (*WN*, I.xi.c). The urge to be seen to be rich is presented as a strong motivator. Force sees this as 'vanity' and the equivalent of 'amour-proper' in Rousseau's thinking (Force, 2003).

Smith elaborates on the way in which 'we' tend to imaginatively paint 'in those delusive colours' the state of being rich. And therefore as we also aspire to the imaginative context of the rich, we also think:

> What a pity...that any thing should spoil and corrupt so agreeable a situation! We could even wish them immortal; and it seems hard to us, that death should at last put an end to such perfect enjoyment. It is cruel, we think, in Nature to compel them from their exalted stations to that humble, but hospitable home, which she has provided for all her children.
>
> (*MS*, I.iii.2.3)

So the mockery and sense of satire are not only constructed through Smith's writing, it is inherent in Nature, in the human condition. Smith regards this 'disposition to admire, and almost to worship, the rich and powerful' as 'the great and most universal cause of the corruption of our moral sentiments' (*MS*, I.iii.3.2) though it is also a source of social stability. Smith's mockery, in these and related passages, is reserved for the 'superior stations in life' and his sympathy (in the sense of concern) for the 'poor and humble' though even the poor are subject to satirical comments, as in the case of the 'poor man's son, whom heaven in its anger has visited with ambition' (*MS*, IV.1.8). The image is both a 'representative anecdote' (in common with, say, the 'lovers of trinkets') in Burkean terms and at the same time, 'the imagistic source out of which the story has flowed' (Burke, 1969, 339). The end of the story challenges the assumptions of the start. In the search for a means of depicting true values, Smith is driven towards narration, towards stories located in the social or lived experience of his readers. Logic, in this context, is not enough to understand and resolve human issues, particularly those of understanding, of sorting the real from the deluded and imaginary. The context is that of paradox and this had already been explored in the writing of Pascal who held that people search, inconsistenly, for both 'le divertissement et l'occupation' on the one hand and 'le repos' rather than 'le tumulte', on the other (Force, 2003, 119). This kind of paradox or con-tradiction is not rare in Smith's writing. On examining problems that have in 'the nature of things' a remedy and those that do not, Smith comes to the conclu-sion that it takes longer to accommodate the consequence of those that have a remedy: 'the prisoner, who is continually plotting to escape from his confine-ment, cannot enjoy that careless security which even a prison can afford him' (*MS*, III.3.33).

After a life devoted to self-improvement, such a one 'begins at last to find that wealth and greatness are mere trinkets of frivolous utility, no more adapted to procuring ease of body or tranquillity of mind than the tweezer-cases of the lover of toys' (*MS*, IV.1.8). The paradox here is that the tranquil world is always poten-tially available to the 'poor man's son'. If only he could see that in his journey the postponed end is always potentially available in the beginnings of the story. Smith himself is not fooled and comically constructs and ridicules those who seek after trinkets (a point of view sustained in the *Wealth of Nations*) including the para-doxical behaviour of the person who is 'curious in watches'. Such a one admires the 'machine' capable of keeping accurate time but neglects to be punctual (*MS*, IV.1.5). And consider the comic figures of the 'lovers of toys' who 'contrive new pockets, unknown in the clothes of other people, in order to carry a great number'. The usefulness of the toys is 'not worth the fatigue of bearing the burden' (*MS*, IV.1.6). Smith's lightly drawn, comic cameos, products of observation, in as much as Smith is pointing his readers to a social phenomenon that they too can observe, and imagination, are effective and show that he understood very well how a comic effect can be created and used for reformist ends, in line with his thinking on rhetoric. Smith reveals here and in the passage on the ambitions of the 'poor man's son', an almost Ciceronian understanding of 'social intercourse, precedent, tradition, and the manners and disposition of his fellow-countrymen', necessary for the construction of convincing narrative (Cicero, *De Oratore*

2.30.131). It would seem that Smith's 'lovers of toys', located in a specific historical context, are essentially still with us.

Smith is convinced that 'In the middling and inferior stations of life, the road to virtue and that to fortune, to such fortune, at least, as men in such stations can reasonably expect to acquire, are, happily in most cases, very nearly the same' and in these contexts 'real and solid professional abilities, joined to prudent, just, firm, and temperate conduct, can very seldom fail of success' (*MS*, I.iii.3.5). This is the social context of Smith's own life and outlines the path that he and David Hume took for the improvement of their position. A possible irony here is that Smith seems objectively to choose his own social class, a class that he felt comfortable with and whose values he also holds, as the one least likely to confuse the demands of virtue and the demands of wealth accumulation. Not only that but such people probably constituted the bulk of Smith's readership. He may be playing essentially to their self-regard.

Nonetheless, at the heart of human endeavour is a delusion, a delusion also recognised by Plato, that wealth, far from ushering in a life of ease, is also a burden, a notion from Plato that the nineteenth-century social critic John Ruskin used to illustrate problems with Mill's theory of value, interpreted, by Ruskin, as 'more means better' (Henderson, 2000). In this sense Ruskin inadvertently anticipated Jevon's innovation in the theory of value. For Smith, at this point in the exposition, the 'spectator' misunderstands the actual condition of the rich, as do the rich themselves when they first set out. Under threat from disease or from old age, the rich man 'curses ambition' though Smith is careful to write 'in his heart'. It is almost as if Smith holds that the rich do not wish to give the game away, that they too are engaged in an inauthentic conversation or display. In old age, the rich man comes to see power and wealth as

> ... enormous and operose machines contrived to produce a few trifling conveniences to the body, consisting of springs the most nice and delicate, which must be kept in order with the most anxious attention, and which of all our care are ready at any moment to burst to pieces, and to crush in their ruins their unfortunate possessor.
>
> (*MS*, IV.1.8)

At last the gaze of the rich penetrates below the surface of things and sees the instability and futility of the structures that have been relied upon. The re-interpretation is dramatic.

It is not economic necessity that drives individual acts of accumulation. This would require no interpretation as it would suggest itself as clear and unhidden. Necessity is quickly dismissed. It is not need but vanity and the desire to be admired: 'it is chiefly from this regard to the sentiments of mankind, that we pursue riches and avoid poverty' (*MS*, I.iii.2.1). Smith seems that what we would now call conspicuous consumption is motivated by pride and vanity. These motivations were ridiculed by the poet Robert Burns, who knew, also, of the 'impartial spectator' and constructed him or a power like him, in a famous verse in a way that almost parallels Smith's own words: 'If we saw ourselves in the light in which others see us, or in which they would see us if they knew all, a reformation would generally be unavoidable' (*MS*, III.4.6). Notice in this quote the phrase 'or in which they would see us if they knew all'. Actual spectators do not know all. Smith uses the notion of spectator in a number of different ways though here it is not intended to be the equivalent of conscience. There are, however, at least two psychologies at work, that of the observer and that of the observed, and these individuals must change roles with others in the different parts of their social lives. The actual spectator cannot be reliable, for we are predisposed to conceal any negative aspects of our situation. The sentiments concerned are that 'mankind are disposed to sympathize more entirely with our joy than with our sorrow', and for this reason 'we make parade of our riches and conceal our poverty'. Wealth and its conveniences seem 'something grand and beautiful and noble, of which the attainment is well worth all the toil and anxiety which we are so apt to bestow upon it' (*MS*, IV.1.9). The motivation is sentimental though this is not quite the same in the *Wealth of Nations*. It is not that there is no sentiment in the *Wealth of Nations*. Rothschild has made the role of sentiment abundantly clear and economic agents, in that work, remain deluded as to the ends, given the nature of unintended consequences, which they are promoting by acting in their interests. Economic actors in the *Wealth of Nations* continue to operate under conditions of risk and fear, but in the opening moves of the work, Smith calls upon the propensity to truck, barter and exchange as the urge to action. He also pays greater attention in the *Wealth of Nations* to the logic of economic life, and this reduces or rather repositions, for it does not remove, the role of narrative.

But in all of this we are also fooled by Nature: 'And it is as well that nature imposes upon us in this manner'. We are all duped and it is this deception which 'arouses and keeps in continual motion the industry of mankind' (*MS*, IV.1.10). But how precisely are we duped? When we are old we can see the problem but when we are young we cannot (see later). This would seem to be, by implication, a matter of experience. Later, in a passage that Force takes as a direct response to Rousseau, Rousseau being identified because of his criticisms of contemporary society as 'the splenetic philosopher' (Force, 2003, 159). Smith uses the term 'splenetic philosophers' in an early chapter and the editors suggest a reference mainly to Mandeville despite the use of the plural form (*MS*, III.2.27), and elsewhere he refers to 'whining and melancholy moralists' (*MS*, III.3.9).[1] Plural forms are rhetorically useful for the strengthening of a case made by opposition; however, Smith wrote against both Mandeville and Hume as Force has emphasised. The editors of the *Moral Sentiments* suggest that Smith may have had Mandeville and Rousseau in mind in the passage below, citing, as evidence, Smith's translation of a passage from Rousseau and its apparent repetition on the paragraph that immediately follows the reference to 'splenetic philosophy'. Smith writes

> But though this splenetic philosophy, which in time of sickness and low spirits is familiar to every man, thus entirely depreciates those great objects of

human desire, when in better health and better humour, we never fail to regard them under a more agreeable aspect.

(*MS*, IV.i.9)

Force takes this to be a direct reference to Rousseau's *Second Discourse*, a work 'which consists in denigrating the value of all human endeavours in civil society' (Force, 2003, 159). Smith, who appreciates the role of sentiments in all aspects of human life, is illustrating the ways in which nature conspires to fool us to keep us working at the accumulation of wealth and possessions. Smith needs a natural means of continuing the situational irony and hope (what political analysts now call 'the feel good factor') seems as good as any. This understanding of the reversal involved seems to be psychologically acceptable and consistent with his earlier passages rather than simply a counter-argument to Rousseau. One explanation does not preclude the other.

Nature, as constructed by Smith, is itself an ironist and it is the philosopher who works to interpret the irony, to distinguish what is real from what is merely imagined. The rich are 'led by an invisible hand' to work towards the provision of human kind and 'In ease of body and peace of mind, all the different ranks of life are nearly upon a level, and the beggar, who suns himself by the side of the highway, possesses that security which kings are fighting for' (*MS*, IV.1.11). This is one of Smith's social paradoxes that call upon readers to reflect on motivations and to re-evaluate their concept of what is to be valued or admired.

However Smith was not alone in this view. Plato has Socrates mention the alleged 'lack of happiness of a king or rich man', and Horace too proclaims that the poor have fewer cares than the rich (Viner, 1966, 99). Viner also points to a number of eighteenth-century discussions concerning what can and cannot be achieved in the way of happiness, and of course salvation, by the accumulation of wealth. Thus, in what is a complex sermon concerning 'mutual subjection' Swift argues that 'great riches are no blessing in themselves, because the poor man, with the common necessities of life, enjoys more health and has fewer cares without them' (Swift, 1744). However the next sentence, not quoted by Viner, asks the question of how riches become blessings. The answer is by 'feeding the hungry, clothing the naked, rewarding worthy men, and, in short, doing acts of charity and generosity'. Swift's context is that of Christian stewardship in line with the natural law thinking of Thomas Aquinas. Viner does not identify a source for the pronouncement of La Bruyère, who lived in the seventeenth century but whose sayings predicted the eighteenth, on the issue. La Bruyère thought that 'He who is powerful and rich, and to whom nothing is lacking, may well formulate the question; its answer, however, should be left to the poor man', a stance that would seem to be, on the face of it, more critical than that taken by Smith (Viner, 1966, 99). At issue is not essentially the equality or inequality of wealth but the equality of happiness.

Smith's view of the potential difficulties of wealth is followed through in the different context of the *Wealth of Nations*, though not, I think, with the same dramatic force. The rich man cannot sleep at peace in his bed at night:

> It is only under the shelter of the civil magistrate that the owner of that valuable property, which is acquired by the labour of many years, or perhaps of many successive generations, can sleep a single night in security. He is at all times surrounded by unknown enemies, whom, though he never provoked, he can never appease, and from whose injustice he can be protected only by the powerful arm of the civil magistrate continually held up to chastise it.
>
> (*WN*, V.i.b.2)

The satire on ambition and wealth and on the cupidity of human nature is one that is sustained. And the satire is also to be found in the pages of the *Wealth of Nations* where 'Princes' and 'Chief Magistrates' and landlords and merchants are subject to ironic and satirical comment, and contextual paradoxes, but not in such a concentrated and amusing form (see, for example, *WN*, V.ii.a.6). Smith was aware of the literature of his age and sees Swift as writing on the 'follies' of mankind. He is essentially doing the same in the passages in which he analyses riches and attitudes of admiration towards the rich. The ironies are complex and 'vanity' (taken by Force to have an equivalent role in Smith's thinking to '*amour propre*' in that of Rousseau) is an easy target. We are duped. It is in our nature to seek attention and rich people get more attention of a positive kind than the poor. This seems as true of today's world of 'celebrity' as it was in Smith's time. All the striving and energy that goes into making and conserving riches does not lead, according to Smith, to peace of mind, and since there is only so much food that the stomach can take, riches lead to the accumulation of trinkets and other things that need to be maintained, guarded against theft and worried about:

> It is to no purpose, that the proud and unfeeling landlord views his extensive fields, and without a thought for the wants of his brethren, in imagination consumes himself the whole harvest that grows upon them. The homely and vulgar proverb, that the eye is larger than the belly, never was more fully verified than with regard to him. The capacity of the stomach bears no proportion to the immensity of his desires, and will receive no more than that of the meanest peasant.
>
> (*MS*, IV.1.10)

There is only so much that we can physically consume and if we try and consume beyond this, then ill-health induced by immoderate consumption will be the result. The landlord does not intend to help poorer people, but this is the inevitable outcome of his labours.

And in the end, we are all brought low by death, and it is only when faced with ill-health, decline and the possibility of death that we are capable of making a correct interpretation of the drive to accumulate. In the end, according to Smith, the real banishes our imaginative delusions and paradoxical behaviours. No matter how hard we strive, we are exposed 'to anxiety, to fear, to sorrow; to diseases to danger, and to death' (*MS*, IV.1.8) – just as much a theme in the *Wealth of Nations* as it is in *Moral Sentiments*. This is situational irony, constructed by Smith as an essential human condition, and it is the context of this irony that leads to the need for the philosopher to interpret human aspirations, for it is only in extremes that individuals recognise in themselves, with respect to power and riches 'what they are', that is dangerous burdens (*MS*, IV.1.8). The 'poor man's son, whom heaven in its anger has visited with ambition' is fooled by the apparent condition of the rich. The narrative is emotionally charged and in the style of the better sentimental novels. He works and fatigues his body and is very much deluded: 'through the whole of his life he pursues the idea of a certain artificial and elegant repose which he may never arrive at, for which he sacrifices a real tranquillity that is at all times in his power' (*MS*, IV.1.7). There is no logic involved here, the situation just is. The modern day commonplace equivalent is the social understanding that few are likely to say on their death-bed that they wished they had 'spent more time in the office'. The economy, nature and human nature, according to Smith, need to be interpreted and understood, however difficult it may be to separate the 'real' from the apparent. If 'we' collaborate, Smith seems to say to his readers, you will be provided with, what Booth has called in a different context, the 'pleasure of deciphering', except it is the philosopher who deciphers overtly for us (Booth, 1961, 301).

But there are other ironies. The 'spectator' is fooled by the working of the imagination, especially 'in times of ease and prosperity' (*MS*, IV.1.9). At such times, the imagination deceives, though the power of the imaginings is likely to vary as individuals vary. The rich parade their wealth, the 'spectator' imagines that to be observed and admired is good but does not see the loss of freedom and the price that is paid for the gathering together and maintenance of wealth. Smith values liberty highly and elsewhere writes that:

[E]xcept for the frivolous pleasures of vanity and superiority, we may find, in the most humble station, where there is only personal liberty, every other which the most exalted can afford; and the pleasures of vanity and superiority are seldom consistent with perfect tranquillity, the principle and foundation of all real and satisfactory enjoyment.

(*MS*, III.3.31)

Contrasts are to be made between 'idle fancy' and 'real', between the 'apparent' and the 'actual'. The 'spectator' like the fool in the *Tale of a Tub*, stays on the surface of things: 'The great mob of mankind are the admirers and worshippers [of riches], and, what may seem more extraordinary, most frequently the disinterested admirers and worshippers, of wealth and greatness' (*MS*, I.iii.3.2). This admiration, however misplaced, has a significant part to play in the maintenance of the established social order.

This is another of Smith's delightful paradoxes. The spectator is not likely to gain anything materially from those that he so admires, though, we could reflect that a spectacle is only a spectacle by dint of those who take pleasure from watching it. So there is an exchange relationship and the spectator gets some sort of vicarious pleasure. In the context of this social theatre, it is worth pointing out that Rousseau uses 'theatricality' as a 'metaphor for dishonest discourse' and sees the unreformed role of the spectator as 'passive' and 'captive of the despotic prince' (Morgenstern, 1996, 44 and 45). In Smith, any active participant in seeking out wealth is fooled, but, in old age and in ill-health, when the burden of wealth overwhelms and the body cannot sustain the level of activity required to maintain wealth, he acknowledges the truth in his heart, though not necessarily openly, for that would destroy the surface appearance, an essential part of duping and of being duped. What is 'real' is decrepitude, old age and death. This rather than beauty is what is significant about human existence. All, it seems, in the spirit of the Hebrew scriptures, is vanity and vexation of spirit.

The 'spectator' is both fooled and capable of fooling for:

> If we examine, however, why the spectator distinguishes with such admiration the condition of the rich and the great, we shall find that it is not so much upon account of the superior ease or pleasure which they are supposed to enjoy, as of the numberless artificial and elegant contrivances for promoting this ease or pleasure. He does not even imagine that they are really happier than other people: but he imagines that they possess more means of happiness.
>
> (*MS*, IV.1.8)

Even the spectator's perceptions, as illustrated by the examination made by Smith, need to be evaluated and interpreted. Smith's 'spectator' is, in this context, a necessary but unreliable narrator rather than the perhaps more familiar God-like 'impartial spectator' and Smith the insightful philosopher. This makes Smith himself, in a sense, an impartial and hence reliable spectator.

Smith himself is not always duped, in his own eyes, for he shows us both the surface of things and what the actors, misread by the mass of human kind, actually experience:

> If we consider the real satisfaction which all these things are capable of affording, by itself and separated from the beauty of that arrangement which is fitted to promote it, it will always appear in the highest degree contemptible and trifling. But we rarely view it in this abstract and philosophical light.
>
> (*MS*, IV.1.9)

The philosopher, who claims to be able to interpret Nature's irony, sees the significance but at the same time the philosopher seems to be powerless to alter mankind's opinions as 'we' are not consistent in our point of view. The philosopher labours essentially in vain, 'And it is well that nature imposes upon us in this manner' (*MS*, IV.1.9). 'Nature' here plays a God-like role as the master ironist and

Smith resorts to a kind of misplaced deism for there can be no external evidence of his proposition. His story goes this way:

> Nature has wisely judged that the distinction of ranks, the peace and order of society, would rest more securely upon the plain and palpable difference of birth and fortune, than upon the invisible and often uncertain difference of wisdom and virtue. The undistinguishing eyes of the great mob of mankind can well enough perceive the former: it is with difficulty that the nice discernment of the wise and virtuous can sometimes distinguish the latter. In the order of all those recommendations, the benevolent wisdom of nature is equally evident.
>
> (*MS*, VI ii.1.20)

The world goes its own way and whilst it is not the 'fool' and the 'knave' that is contrasted, but the 'mob' and the 'wise and virtuous', Smith's construction of the interpretation is akin to the contrast between the surface and deep meaning of things that is explored by Weinscheimer's interpretation of Swift. Smith values 'wisdom and virtue' and disapproves of the fact that 'wealth and greatness' usually gets the honours due to 'wisdom and virtue' (*MS*, I.iii 3.1). In this he is refining and elaborating a view also put forward by Hume in the *Treatise of Human Nature* (*THN*, II.ii.5). In the passage quoted above, Smith concedes that even the philosophically inclined find it hard to discern 'wisdom and virtue'. The contrasts evidence Smith's hermeneutics as in line with a wider understanding of eighteenth-century hermeneutics as analysed by Weinschiemer. The 'mob' and its 'undistinguishing eyes' reads only what is immediately obvious. The 'virtuous' can (only sometimes) penetrate deeper though it would take a superhuman effort to directly detect 'the invisible'. 'Wisdom and virtue' cannot, according to Smith, sustain the 'peace and order of society'. The 'eye' or 'eyes' is used many times both on the *Moral Sentiments* and in the *Wealth of Nations* as a synechdoche for 'spectator' or 'spectators' though there are many possible eyes including 'the eye of the body' and 'the eye of the mind' (*MS*, III.3.2). 'Spectators' also come in a variety of forms, 'spectators', 'impartial', 'indulgent and partial', 'real and impartial', 'generous', 'discerning', 'indignant' (as in the phrase 'the sympathetic indignation of the spectator') and others. There are also synonyms including the notion of 'impartial judge' (*MS*, II.ii.2.4) and attentive and 'inattentive observers' (*MS*, I.iii.3.3).

What seems really interesting about Smith in this respect in that he writes, as Weinscheimer argues Swift does also, implicitly of the necessity of both superficial and deep interpretations of the human predicament. An understanding of the surface of things pushes humans forward but the possibility of critical reflection, under the gaze of the speculative and curious philosopher, allows deeper or hidden understandings to surface. For the understating to be complete, the two must work together. Smith is engaged in an act, in Weinscheimer's terms, of 'interpretive curiosity' taken to be the 'ferreting out of the real beyond the apparent', but at the same time reflecting upon that and integrating the revealed understanding with the superficial (Weinscheimer, 1993, 1). That the task of interpreting nature and human nature is difficult is suggested by the variety of ways in which Smith attempts to specify the activity of interpretation. The 'apparent' and the 'real', deception and self-deception, are returned to time and again in different ways in the *Moral Sentiments*. Fiori has recently drawn attention to Smith's notion of 'visible' (available to the 'eye') and 'invisible' (available to the 'mind's eye' and so to philosophy) (Fiori, 2001, 434). That the attempt is significant is supported by the fact that interpretation and judgement is a recurrent theme. But, in this example, the interpretation given by Smith is less powerful than the thing interpreted and so, for this reason, the world goes its own way. This is a situation that he acknowledges elsewhere in *Moral Sentiments*: 'The natural course of things cannot be entirely controlled by the impotent endeavours of man: the current is too rapid and strong for him to stop it . . . ' (*MS*, III.5.10). Smith is not, of course, merely nature's interpreter, for it is he who has imaginatively constructed nature's ironies, albeit within a wider and developing cultural understanding of hidden and 'superior' structures (Fiori, 2001, 430) and within a range of what I take to be established Stoic or perhaps Deist vocabulary. It is not nature but Smith who imaginatively constructs, narrates and explicates, within a providentialist tradition (with hints of Plato?), the irony of the human condition.

Because they are limited in what they can physically consume, the rich, 'in spite of their natural selfishness and rapacity', must perforce 'divide with the poor the produce of their improvements' and so are 'led by an invisible hand to make nearly the same distribution of the necessities of life, which would have been made, had the earth been divided into equal proportions among all its inhabitants, and thus without intending it, without knowing it, advance the interest of society, and afford means to the multiplication of the species' (*MS*, IV.1.10) This is a very convenient outcome, but it is restricted to the 'necessities' of life, as required by the natural law tradition with respect to the fruits of the earth, as is evidenced by the natural law comparison contained within the sentence, and not to anything beyond those. The context is that of a sustained, explicated situational irony and of an unintended link between 'interest' and 'justice' or 'virtue'. The link with 'natural justice' in this example is found within the same sentence as the metaphor is expressed. Although the reference to 'an invisible hand' (*WN*, IV.ii.9) in the *Wealth of Nations* is not so well sign-posted as part of a situational irony in the same sense, the elements are there. There, the next but one sentence states: 'By pursuing his own interests he frequently promotes that of society more effectually than when he really intends to promote it' (*WN*, IV.ii.9). This paradox has an ironical force and the agent is duped. Indeed, claiming virtue is not likely to lead to success: 'I have never known much good done by those who affected to trade for the publick good' (*WN*, IV.ii.9). The phrase is used once but the theme as analysed here is found in many different passages in the *Wealth of Nations* (*WN*, III.iv.17; IV.b.3). Intentions are selfish but the results can be virtuous.

The middle classes of society can bring the worlds of virtue and the world of riches together through economic aspirations that are translated into action by wisdom, application and prudence. The need for social and political discussions is an implication of this view. This seems to provide Smith with a way of integrating the problems of superficial and deeper interpretive understanding. As Force puts it, people work under the guidance of the universal desire to better their condition, but they also have the power of speech and the capacity to reason (Force, 2003). There is hermeneutics at work involving reading and interpreting Nature, which seems to be something purposeful and directed, in the *Moral Sentiments*, and human nature. This is illustrated in the phrase 'Nature has wisely judged...' (earlier). The relationship between human nature and nature is problematic. Sometimes the nature that Smith talks about is located in human nature, by which he means something akin to human psychology, and sometimes it is a force superior to human nature that intends or causes outcomes in the manner of a deity, though through the exercise of natural laws rather than miracles. Sometimes it is directed precisely towards certain causes such as the social fabric sustained by justice, a 'fabric' that seems 'to have been the peculiar and darling care of Nature' (*MS*, II.ii.3.4). The propensity 'to truck, barter and exchange' in the *Wealth of Nations* is located, in contrast, more in human nature and the outcomes of this human nature are unintended and the ends only realised through changed historical circumstances. It is possible in the context of the *Wealth of Nations* for the actual condition of society to be in contrast to the natural condition of society as a result of particular socio-economic and historical circumstances (see the Chapter 7). Either way, human agents are both individualised (i.e. seek their own 'interests') and socialised (i.e. contribute to social well-being in intended and unintended ways).

Irony and interpretation seem to rub off one another in Smith's text. This fact suggests a need to reflect upon Smith's approach to interpreting nature, and hence upon his notion of hermeneutics, on the interplay between surface and deep meanings, or between the 'visible' and 'invisible' as organising principles, between the 'intended' and 'unintended'. The distinction between the 'apparent and the real' is a philosophically ancient one, going back to Plato, as is the notion of a God-like view of the world. Smith could be seen as providing an old understanding with a modern context and twist. Smith as a hermeneuticist is involved in reading Nature's book. Smith textually constructed economic motivation around the notion of being duped, of acting in contexts in which the apparent actions or motives are not the real ones. Wealth cannot deliver what it seems to hold out in terms of 'happiness', a state to be envied, and 'happiness' itself can be achieved actually and potentially, under a variety of conditions and restrictions but action to obtain wealth can have significant unintended benefits for society in general. Providence, variously construed, fools us into action and only the most discerning and virtuous in society can sometimes struggle free of the duped state. In the resulting social competition, who is it that is likely to win out, Smith asks, the 'knave' of the person of 'virtue'? Using 'natural' in two different contexts, Smith holds that the 'natural course of things decides it in favour of the knave: the natural sentiments of mankind in favour of the man of virtue' (*MS*, III.5.9). Either way in the context of Smith's thought, we assist others either on a voluntary or involuntary basis. Of course, Swift's knave and Smith's knave are not the same, but the problem of obtaining a full interpretation is. This split corresponds to Weinsheimer's characterisation of 'the problem of eighteenth-century hermeneutics' that is, the distinction between 'credulity and curiosity' (Weinsheimer, 1993, 1). What Smith gives away he takes back and, in this context, links virtue and economic action with his own social class. Even then, the philosopher may be duped. As an act of rhetoric, Smith is upholding his readers' interests against the follies of the great, and the indiscrimination of the 'mob', showing himself to be working, Cicero-like, with and for, in this case, potentially 'good men', capable of self-awareness, self-command and compassion (Cicero, *De Oratore*, 2.51.206).

4 The political economy of *Castle Rackrent*

Maria Edgeworth and Adam Smith[1]

Maria Edgeworth's *Castle Rackrent: an Hibernian Tale*, a short novel written in the period 1793–1799 and published in 1800, is a conundrum. On the face of it, it is an innovative though straightforward tale of a family in decline – narrated by the comic figure of the faithful family retainer, Old Thady. It could be taken as a comedy of manners, written in an ironic tone and set in an Ireland that either has disappeared or is in the process of disappearing. Here, it will be used to illustrate the consequence of a reading of Smith's *Wealth of Nations* as social satire as a vehicle whereby notions developed by Smith, the Scottish Historical School and by David Hume were insinuated into society. Smith's concern with economic growth, the consequences of land monopolisation, primogeniture and 'institutions', 'customs and manners' (illustrated in Chapter 7) are in *Castle Rackrent*, given a sustained social context in a comic novel on Irish social conditions. Maria Edgeworth had read the *Wealth of Nations* and later produced educational tales, such as *The Cherry Orchard* and *Lazy Lawrence*, with overt economic themes for parents to read to children (Henderson, 1995). *The Cherry Orchard* transforms Smith's account of the division of labour in a pin factory into a rural idle of plaiting straw and of social discipline and harmony. *The Bracelet of Memory* ridicules, in the context of a child's story, the love of trinkets, a subject for ridicule in both *Moral Sentiments* and the *Wealth of Nations* (Henderson, 1995). By such means, Edgeworth extended the influence of Smith's (and Hume's) economic writings and underscored the cultural significance of political economy. *Castle Rackrent* in this view, first developed by Butler, is a response to the satirical aspects of Smith's writing, as well as to his concerns with the 'institutions', 'customs and manners'. It influenced Walter Scott's writing, thus adding an indirect influence from Smith on Scott's approach to his novels of 'customs and manners' to a more direct influence through Dugald Stewart, and, in combination with Edgeworth's other economic stories, the development of socio-economic themes in later writers (Butler, 1992; Henderson, 1995). Together with her economic stories for children, it prompted further work on socio-economic themes by writers such as Jane Marcet and Harriet Martineau who in turn stimulated later socio-economic writing of a more evaluative and critical nature (Henderson, 1995).

Numerous analysts of *Castle Rackrent* find it to be something other than a simple text. Mortimer (1984) sees the layered historical contexts of the novel as problematic. Why, for example, Mortimer asks, is the religion of the Rackrents left undefined when Protestantism was the religion of the landlord class and a defining feature of the Ascendancy (Mortimer, 1984, 13)? And why is there a displacement in time as highlighted by the author in the preface? The temporal displacement raises interesting questions about the novel though it was assumed by English readers that the novel had current cultural significance. Mortimer explores the ideology of the work in terms of presences and absences in Edgeworth's narrative, including the absence of any discussion of the violence of 1798, the events of which had had direct implications for Edgeworth's father arising out of his anti-sectarian stand (Mortimer, 1984, 112; Murray, 1971, 20–21). As will be argued below, Smith suggests the possibility of sustained change over 'half a century or a century more' as a time period within which 'the old system' (taken to be one of feudalism and of lack of land improvement) will wear out and a new one, based on 'frugality' and accumulation, will be initiated (*WN*, I.ii.97). Mortimer challenges, amongst other things, the notion, held by Flanagan and Mercier, that Thady delights in the fall of the Protestant Ascendancy (the family name of the Rackrents was originally O'Shauglin and hence of Celtic and therefore, Catholic origin) (Flanagan, 1966, 77; Mercier, 1962, 186; Mortimer, 1984, 112). Thady, also, is an ambiguous character, perhaps both 'victim and cause of the present state of Rackrent failed affairs' (Schneller, 1989, 130). He has a more complex role than is sometimes superficially read. He appears, for example, to disapprove of the manipulative actions of his son Jason but, nevertheless, furthers Jason's land-grabbing cause (not once but twice). Thady also remains passive with respect to the interests of the Rackrents at key points in the narrative. Butler sees the unreliability of Thady and his ambiguous role within the household as a central to the development of the novel (Butler, 1992, 9–12).

The introduction ('Author's Preface') is itself fictionalised. Edgeworth writes as the male transcriber of Old Thady's tale and intermediary between the native Irish and the 'ignorant' English (i.e. 'ignorant' of Irish customs and manners). This much analysed 'Author's Preface' is part of the deceptions and possible confusions of the novel itself – Saguaro suggests that Edgeworth, Thady and 'The Editor' are engaged in a 'mime' (Saguaro, 1998, 151). That Edgeworth chose to fictionalise the preface means that it must be considered part of the novel. As part of the novel, it acts to put 'constraints on our freedom to interpret her work' (Butler, 1992, 9). The editor's comments frame the work as one concerned with the expectation of social and economic change as a result of the impending Act of Union. (For various analyses of the Preface see Belanger, 1998; Butler, 1972, 1992; Corbett, 1994; Saguaro, 1998.)

Schneller (1989) sees parallels between *Castle Rackrent*, Crabbe's *The Village* (1783) and Goldsmith's *The Deserted Village* (1770). The themes in common are the destruction and ruin, as a result of 'waste', 'individual responsibility' and of 'greed and selfishness', of a given agricultural economy (Schneller, 1989, 130). Indeed, Crabbe's work is normally seen as a 'critical response' to Goldsmith. This is to misplace, to some extent, *Castle Rackrent* for the depicted decline is the result of misunderstanding and mismanagement rather than necessarily underlying economic conditions. The introduction of such themes illustrates, however, a point made by those who pursue the 'new economic criticism'. Economic concerns (such as rural depopulation) become incorporated into fictional works in ways which lead to congruency between prevailing economic circumstances, and any economic theories formulated to account for them, and fictional writing. Two developing discourses – that of political economy and that of the novel – were, in the course of the eighteenth- and nineteenth centuries, according to this new economic criticism, engaged in conditioning each other, even if they finally diverged over concepts of value (Woodmansee and Osteen, 1999, 11). The novel itself is a consumable object, produced by given authors working in specific historical contexts. Edgeworth's was that of the 'Big House', albeit a progressive one, and all that that implied. In exploring the political economy of *Castle Rackrent*, there are other linkages to be made, stronger, as will be shown, than those made by Schneller.

Saguaro (1998) is intrigued by the novel's 'narrative complexity and its attention to the politics of language in a colonial context' (Saguaro, 1998, 147). Saguaro places Edgeworth as 'Anglo-Irish, liberal, Protestant, middle-class and female' and the novel in the context of the Act of Union of Ireland with Britain, 'an overt issue in the text' (Saguaro, 1998, 147). Saguaro also highlights Edgeworth's belief in the 'developmental power of commerce' (Saguaro, 1998, 158).

Adam Smith and the Scottish Historical School

It is the purpose of this essay to develop, further, using notions of social and economic progress derived from Adam Smith, the discussion of *Castle Rackrent* as a fictional work heavily influenced by theoretical proposition found in political economy. The notion of a direct Smithian influence on *Castle Rackrent* is not new. Butler, in her extensive introduction to *Castle Rackrent and Ennui*, devotes almost six pages to considering possible influences from Smith. She notes that, for Maria Edgeworth, the *Wealth of Nations*, was 'the first major book that R. L. Edgeworth gave her to read when he took her from her English boarding-school in 1782' (Butler, 1992, 28). Butler, in her pioneering analysis, locates the key influences in Smith's satirical style when dealing with 'unproductive people', in his 'evolutionary model of history' and in his 'labour theory of value' (Butler, 1992, 28). As has been shown in the chapter 'Irony and Economic Agency', the satirical elements are even stronger in *Moral Sentiments* and this is a work that Edgeworth, as an intellectual, is also likely to have read.

Butler does not explicitly justify her view that 'Smith's contemporaries were more aware than are many of his modern admirers' of his satirisation of landlords and other 'non-productive people' (Butler, 1992, 28). It can, however, be justified. The *Wealth of Nations* no more favours merchants and manufacturers than it does the lifestyles and values of the landed rich (Brown, 1994, 7; *WN*, II.iii.7). The situational ironies found in the text, which include the notion that wealth is unlikely to lead to fulfillment, are multiple and have already been rehearsed in

'Irony and Economic Agency'. The fact that wealth holds out a promise of happiness that it cannot fulfil is irony because, in a sense, it cannot be helped. Irony, a privileged manner of writing in the eighteenth century, is closely related to mocking which can be, itself, a form of satire (Muecke, 1969, 27). Mocking can be about behaviour and behaviour can be challenged and corrected, for example, by taxation or by ridicule. Given eighteenth-century literature's tendency to ridicule, it is hard to see Smith's readers not detecting a satire on 'manners and customs' whatever Smith may have intended. Smith's writing mocks landlords. For example, he states, after a long list of specific examples of the negative impact of courts and great magnates, drawn from historical circumstances, that 'the inhabitants of a large village, it has sometimes been observed, after having made considerable progress in manufactures, have become idle and poor in consequence of a great lord having taken up residence in their neighbourhood'. (*WN*, II.iii.12). His first readers, given the significance of irony and ridicule in the existing literature available to them, are likely to have been able to identify instances in the text.

This is a conceptual example that reflects his theory of growth based upon the unproductive bias in landlord expenditures. The phrase 'it has sometimes been observed' is vague and may point either to a specific reference in other work or to a general presupposition or prejudice, shared with his readers. Its lack of specificity precludes, perhaps, its ready acceptance as an authentic example. Smith may have his tongue firmly in his cheek. By 'great lord' Smith seems to have intended *grands seigneurs* though the juxtaposition of 'great' and 'lord' could, it self, also have ironic potential, given the other juxtapositions in context.[2] Not all landlords were 'great lords' and Smith certainly does not imagine a landlord class that is uniquely composed of such. His disapproving view that landlords make money 'in their sleep', a view that some would consider fortunate, is one example of his attitude towards the behaviour of the propertied class. Another is that they charge rent for 'what is altogether incapable of human improvement'. His comments on the purchases of 'trinkets' (both in the *Wealth of Nations* and in *Moral Sentiments*), and the images of the 'folly' and 'vanity' that he creates are further examples. The 'tone', is established early: 'As soon as the land of any country has all become private property, the landlords, *like all other men, love to reap where they never sowed*, and demand a rent *even* for its natural produce' (*WN*, I.vi.8, my emphasis). The italics highlights the authorial comment that serves to set an evaluative tone. Notice, however, that Smith both attacks landlords, who were also part of his set of actual readers, as men who 'love to reap where they never sowed' and undercuts his attack by the comment that this is a feature that they share with 'all other men'. The sentence could have been written descriptively without the elements underlined above. It is a matter of what and how it is written.

Given their social position and experience, many of Smith's readers are likely, as Butler argues, to have spotted the quality of his mocking. A critical view of landlords and landlordism became a feature of the Classical School as a whole.[3] Edgeworth, in developing a satire on the negative aspects of traditional landlordism, is following an approach already hinted at in Smith.[4] The novel is then a 'literary extension' of Smith's views on landlords in a fictional and alternative setting, though it may be not in any very simple sense (Henderson, 1995). *Castle Rackrent* has, in this sense, and in the historical evolutionary sense outlined below, a conceptual significance that goes beyond its 'Irishness'.

Butler sees Smith's critical approach to class and landlordism as supplying 'a general gloss to Edgeworth's writing about the estate in all her Irish tales' (Butler, 1992, 31). Butler does not however develop these ideas much beyond the notion of a general gloss, largely ignoring, probably because of her encyclopaedic approach to Edgeworth's Irish novels, her own insight with respect to Smith's 'evolutionary model of history'. By way of supplementing Butler's work, this chapter will argue that notions derived from Smith have a more pervasive contribution to make to the details of the structure and content of the novel.

The method, derived from critical themes explored by 'critical economics' and 'the new economic criticism', will be to match strategies and narrative of the novel to ideas from and passages in Smith's *Wealth of Nations*. Smith's work was published in 1776, and is generally regarded as the first analysis of a dynamic economic system considered as a whole. It made a profound impact on late Hanoverian economic and social thinking and was a subject of discussion in social as well as political contexts. Smith, a social philosopher, also wrote *The Theory of Moral Sentiments* (1759) in which he develops the concept of an internal 'impartial spectator' responsible for aiding an individual to reflect upon the morality of any actions that that he or she may take. Although the argument will not be developed in this essay, Edgeworth's 'Old Thady' could be construed as an externalised 'spectator', though given his role in shaping as well as reflecting upon conditions with the novel, he also can be seen as an 'unreliable spectator' (not unknown, as we have seen, in *Moral Sentiments*) as well as an 'unreliable narrator' used within literary criticism (Butler, 1992, 9). However, Smith has 'the spectator' as a social category in *Moral Sentiments* and this spectator, as has already been illustrated in 'Irony and Economic Agency', often misinterprets the condition of the rich. 'Old Thady' serves as narrator, spectator and protagonist for the maintenance of feudal values, and reflects such values back to the other protagonists, but does so in ways that are not incompatible with wider and ill-informed acts of spectatorship depicted in *Moral Sentiments*.

Smith worked out his political economy in many contexts, including the observation of longer-run development of lowland Scotland as a result of the Act of Union (1707) and against a background of extensive reading in classical thinking and of widespread discussion and reading of contemporary Enlightenment social thought.[5] His approach to historical analysis was based upon elements common to the Scottish Historical School as a whole. These were, according to Ross, the idea of stages in the development of civil society; 'impartiality in the writing of history'; and a concern for 'philosophical history' (usually referred to as conjectural history). Conjectural history suggested 'the causes and consequences of events to be traced and where no firm evidence for cause is available a commitment to explore natural causes' (Ross, 1995, 90–91). The transformation from one stage to another is social but given classical political economy's preoccupation with the social classes (i.e. holders of types of income), – landlord (rent), labourer (wages) and mercantile capitalist (profit on stock) – it must be fundamentally economic. Smith's four stages of society, based upon contemporary experience, are 'hunting, pasturage, farming and commerce' (Skinner, 1980, 31). The fullest expression of modernity, and of the challenges that it brings to 'virtue', is to be found in the commercial stage. Changes in the economic base of society would call forth changes in behaviours. Institutional arrangements such as primogeniture fixed by law and custom and its associated legal notion of entailment, could, in Smith's approach, hinder the development of agricultural change by reinforcing monopolies in land ownership.

Others pursuing a stadial and conjectural approach to history included Adam Ferguson, Francis Hutcheson and Lord Kames (Henry Home). In addition, Smith was a close friend of the philosopher and historian David Hume who was also interested in the 'change in the manners and customs of the people' (Spiegel, 1971, 214) and who developed links between trade and social practices in his political essays. Hume is not usually considered a member of the School, although he held some ideas in common with these writers.

Even if we were to treat Edgeworth's novel merely as a comedy of 'manners and customs', its development would still be linked to stadial thinking. Smith, as we will see in Chapter 8, constructs 'customs and manners' in historical terms. Hume also shared with Smith the notion that the improvement of domestic conditions can follow increased foreign trade, under certain historical, rather than theoretically ideal circumstances (Skinner, 1993, 30–31). Smith and Hume were concerned with the conceptual analysis of change. The *Wealth of Nations* is, then, a mixture of systematic economic analysis of, and comment on, policy and historical reflection upon, economic conditions and economic change. The proposition is that Edgeworth's imagination was stimulated by her reading. Edgeworth picked on the sense of historical change over time (from 'rude' to civilised; from feudal to commercial) and on the potential confusion of 'customs and manners' in a transition from a pre-modern to modern eighteenth-century commercial society.

Smith sees economic growth as a consequence of competition and the division of labour (itself sustained by increases in the size of the potential market by, for example, increased export trade) and the accumulation of capital. Investment capital can be accumulated in Smith's argument by deferred gratification ('frugality'), a notion almost totally absent from the social psychology of the Rackrents. Drawing upon, but at the same time altering, physiocratic analysis, Smith takes, according to Skinner, manufacturing to be the sector in which the division of labour can find its highest expression, depending upon the extent of capital accumulation and the size of the market. Manufacturing and agriculture interact, through the development of towns, and so improvements in manufacturing increase the demand for agricultural output and hence stimulate agricultural improvement (see Chapter 7). At the same time, Smith makes an analysis of wealth on the basis of categories of income and income holders and so rent, in all its forms, is subjected to close analysis.

The Wealth of Nations is far from parochial, but the fact that Smith could observe socio-economic conditions in Scotland meant that he had access to examples of different social and economic stages drawn from the same country at the same time. Although the theoretical books of the *Wealth of Nations* mentions Ireland, a partial or incomplete Union, and the consequences of Union, he treats the topic more directly in the policy analysis made in book five. Educated and politically aware readers such as the Edgeworths would have been capable of drawing out implications for their own situation. What is striking about Smith's approach, and that of the Scottish Historical School more widely, is that changing economic stages implied 'radically changing patterns of political authority and power' (Skinner, 1993, 31). Ireland was faced with both the need for change (as the rebellion of 1798 had illustrated) and the possibility of change through complete Union and the abolition of the Irish Parliament. Smith mentions Union, and the changed power relationships that it could be taken to imply, in a passage that is bound to have struck a cord with the Edgeworth family. The passage both promotes radical change whilst at the same time setting it within 'natural' limits, that is in a manner that could be thought typical of Smith it both promotes and textually under cuts radicalism. Given his general views upon religion and on the oppression of the poor, he is sharp and to the point though also hopeful:

> By an union with Great Britain the greater part of the people of all ranks in Ireland would gain an equally compleat deliverance from a much more oppressive aristocracy; an aristocracy not founded, like that of Scotland, in the natural and respectable distinctions of birth and fortune; but in the most; odious of all distinctions, those of religious and political prejudices; distinctions which, more than any other, animate both the insolence of the oppressors and the hatred and indignation of the oppressed...
>
> (*WN*, V.iii.89)

Wealth of Nations **and** *Castle Rackrent*

What then is the political economy inscribed in the novel? What is the significance of the Rackrent economy or lack of it? How are we to interpret the actions and events and their narrator? What ideas or ideology does Edgeworth incorporate into the text and how does all of this relate to Smith's political economy?

Maria Edgeworth chose to write on aspects of the political economy of landlordism. The elements of landlordism present in the novel include the religious basis of the land tenure system, absenteeism and the associated transfer of income, and of any benefits gained from its expenditure, from Ireland to England and the associated phenomenon of land agents and middlemen. Mortgages and debt, common features of late eighteenth-century land ownership, jointures, entailments, abatements and rent, also feature. Edgeworth constructs a satire around Smith's notion of the unproductive and inefficient nature of the landlord class and its 'predilection' for expenditures that encourage 'generally more idle than industrious people' (*WN*, II.ii.7; Butler, 1992, 29). Even if she sets the events of the story in the fifty years or so before 1782, itself a significant date in the legislative history of Ireland, Edgeworth is dealing with potentially controversial subject matter. This subject places the topic of the novel at the centre of a historical problem of considerable magnitude. Mortimer treats the novel within the context of known historical conditions. Here, by way of complementarity rather than contrast, they will be treated within the context of theoretical propositions.

Consider the name Rackrent. The name implies, according to Mortimer the Protestant Ascendancy, though the Rackrents are portrayed as minor gentry who combine land ownership with (ineffectual, for the most part) professional activities rather than as *grands seigneurs*. The O'Shaughlins took this name as a result of the political conditions under which they inherited the estate. Although the issue is not made explicit in the text, the fact that they took the name by Act of Parliament suggests that they renounced Catholicism in order to obtain the estate as a whole. Neither Sir Kit nor Sir Condy could have pursued their respective careers in the army and in Parliament had they been Catholic, though the religious situation is muddled by the ambiguous description of religious practices of Sir Murtagh's wife. Mortimer interprets this thus: 'The Rackrents, therefore, are not alien usurpers, but native gentry who can only maintain their position by conforming to the colonial system' (Mortimer, 1984, 113). That the novel can be viewed in colonial terms (though this is in itself a contested concept with respect to Ireland) is a theme common to other critics, such as Saguaro. The subtitle of Edgeworth's novel is 'an Hibernian Tale', though this is usually taken to signal its satirical tone.

Another way of looking at the ambiguity of the Rackrents' religion and hence social position might be to consider them as representatives of an economically 'unimproved' society. Such a society can then be considered within the context of a sequence of historical development as suggested by the Scottish Enlightenment. The term 'unimproved' is also used by Young to describe the practices associated with the land tenure system in Ireland (Mortimer, 1984, 115). If this view is taken then it would not have served the wider comic purposes of the writing had the family been unconditionally Anglo-Irish. The role is already occupied by 'The Editor'. Edgeworth, given the underlying radicalism of the text, may have chosen to hedge her position in ambiguity. The ambiguity (and the questioning which goes with it) serves to point indirectly to, in Smith's terms, 'the most odious of all distinctions', i.e. religion as the basis for land ownership (*WN*, V.iii.89). Besides, Anglo-Irishness, a nineteenth-century term and hence being used here out of historical context, could not have been taken as a defining characteristic of Irishness, characteristics essential to realisation of the parochial comic aspects of the novel.

Watson defines 'rackrent' as 'extortionate rent', rent that is being stretched. Butler, however, in the Introduction to the Penguin edition, suggests that the direct source is Smith's *Wealth of Nations* (Saguaro, 1998, 149; see also Butler, 1992, 348–349). Smith does not appear to use the expression rackrent but has an associated and analysed concept, that of 'racked rent' (*WN*, IV.ix.7). The concept of 'racked rent' is contrasted with that of 'reasonable rent' and implies a rent that eats into a farmer's legitimate returns necessary to keep him in business upon the given land. Smith puts the point nicely. If the landlord demands 'racked rent' this not only destroys the farmer's capacity to produce but the landlord 'necessarily reduces the produce of his own land, and in a few years only disables the farmer from producing this racked rent, but from paying the reasonable rent which he might otherwise have got from his land' (*WN*, IV.ix.7). That this term is found in Smith is significant, though according to the *OED*, it is one that had been in use from the late sixteenth century. By using it at all Edgeworth is identifying the concept of the 'Big House' with a system of exploitation that itself can give rise to rural depression. The title of the comic novel hints of radicalism on the part of the daughter of a progressive 'Big House'. If the novel can be viewed as the passing away of a particular set of social, economic and political behaviours and the anticipation of economic progress as a result of political Union, as Saguaro suggests, then Edgeworth is setting up in literary terms a discussion of rural demoralisation. This is a subject on which Smith had something to say. The anticipation of progressive change is contained not directly within the novel itself, save at the very end, but in the preface:

> When Ireland loses her identity by an union with Great Britain, she will look back with a smile of good-humoured complacency, on the Sir Kits and Sir Condys of her former existence.
>
> (Edgeworth, 1895 [1800], xlx)

According to Smith, mercantile capitalists who turned to investment in land brought with them a different attitude towards agricultural improvement. Traditional landlords only invest for improvement out of income whereas merchants are 'more spirited' in the way of improvements 'than those of mere country gentlemen' (*WN*, III.iv.2). The Rackrents could not improve their estate because their income was constrained and their priorities, as a class, were influenced by pre-capitalist values. The Rackrents are so hopeless in their household economies that they are diametrically opposed to the ideal management methods, esteemed in the Middle Ages, set out by the classical writer Xenophon in his *Oeconomicus*. Smith also acknowledges Xenophon's ideas on estate management. But it is Smith's advice on the balance of expenditures on productive and unproductive purposes, set out in book two, chapter four, of the *Wealth of Nations*, which the Rackrents consistently offend against.

Mortimer, who places *Castle Rackrent* in the context of the need for an Agrarian Revolution and modernisation of the land tenure system, comments:

> Serious agricultural improvement in Ireland meant, above all, reclamation of bogland, and this required greater capital investment and slower returns than most Irish landlords...were prepared to envisage.
>
> (Mortimer, 1984, 114)

The fact of improved commerce, in Smith's system two-sector analysis, also improved, indirectly, agricultural productivity. At the very end of the novel and using 'The Editor' as a device, Edgeworth adds a note of uncertainty concerning the consequences of Union for some of the

> few gentlemen of education who now reside in this country will resort to England. They are few, but they are nothing inferior to men of the same rank in Great Britain. The best that can happen will be the introduction of British manufacturers in their places.
>
> (Edgeworth, 1895 [1800], 73)

Is this a modified version of Smith's radical understanding of the social consequences of Union that is, the destruction by trade and by the concomitant changes in political power of the Ascendancy landlords?

The Rackrents are not men of education in Edgeworth's sense. Might they not stand also to illustrate 'the rude state of society' as considered by Smith? Here is Smith on the relationship between stock and land improvement:

> Without some increase of stock, there can be scarce any improvement of land, but there can be no considerable increase of stock but in consequence of a considerable improvement of land; because otherwise the land could not maintain it. These natural obstructions to the establishment of a better system, cannot be removed but by a long course of frugality and industry; and half a century or a century more, perhaps, must pass away before the old system, which is wearing out gradually, can be completely abolished through all the different parts of the country.
>
> (*WN*, I.xi.l)

Agriculture had prime importance for Smith as a source of revenue and as a significant location for the application of factors of production in a productive way. Indeed in his theoretical system, that is his notion of natural liberty, as in his stadial theory, it had prime place (Brown, 1994, 175–176). In *Castle Rackrent*, agriculture is the economy and the Rackrents are depicted as a class that stands in the way of progress within agriculture itself. The Rackrents are given neither to 'frugality' nor to 'industry'. Smith's 'half a century or a century more', is a reasonable close fit to the novel's time-scale and puts a different spin upon our understanding of *Castle Rackrent*'s temporal displacement.

Edgeworth seems to believe, as Smith did, that it is 'commerce and manufactures' which introduce 'order and good government, and with them, the liberty and security of individuals'. This is a consideration which may have been on Edgeworth's mind given the disturbances of 1798 (*WN*, III.iii.12; Mortimer, 1984, 110). In Edgeworth's text, Jason Quirk may represent the possibility of a new, more rational Irish middle class, that is, when seen from the point of view of progressive, ordered, economic life, and hence the possibility of amelioration through domestic change. 'Jason' is a surprising name in the context of Thady's social status. Is it a reference to the Argonauts and, hence, to the theft of the Golden Fleece? Or can Jason also be read as a satire on mercantile economic motivation? Ambiguities abound. Indeed, if Edgeworth is inscribing a Smithian historical understanding, rather than an ideal theoretical one, (see Chapter 7) then strong domestic change has to be preceded by changed patterns of external trade as analysed by Skinner. The possibility of such changed patterns, that is, the removal of English controls on imports from Ireland were potentially available as Edgeworth indirectly acknowledges at the end of the novel. In the meantime, domestic change as represented by Jason would only be capable of sustained and radical change under natural circumstances. Edgeworth was constrained, perhaps, by the possibilities as she experienced them.

Smith holds that stability of large estates is a sign of lack of wider economic change. Monopoly, such as local monopoly of land ownership perhaps, 'is a great enemy to good management, which can never be universally established but in consequence of that free and universal competition which forces everybody to have recourse to it for the sake of self-defence' (*WN*, I.xi.5).). From his actions (rarely directly observed) in the novel it is clear that Jason is unlikely to confuse gross and net rent or sentimentality and self-interest. Although doubt has been thrown on the nature of the relationship between Thady and his son, the fact that Jason 'never minds what poor Thady says' suggests that Jason rejects the sentimental feudal values that Thady represents (Edgeworth, 1895 [1800], 2). Though Jason may well represent a spirit of competition and self-interest, and although he is the means whereby an intact estate is transferred to someone with potentially a different set of attitudes, he does not come from a mercantile background. He is a lawyer, that is, part of the unproductive class that Edgeworth is satirising, though it must be added that he earns his income through work. Towards the end of the novel Jason becomes ensnared in a lawsuit with Sir Condy's widow. This lawsuit is of a type that would have mired Sir Murtagh. The circular pattern of landlordism in a static society looks as if it could re-establish itself. Jason has perhaps the potential to become a 'rich independent farmer' as identified by Smith (*WN*, II.iii.9), but, given the circumstances in the novel, more likely to become what came to be known later as a 'gombeen man', essentially a manipulative and exploitative money lender. The only way out of the circularity may be a re-colonisation by 'British manufacturers', as 'The Editor' suggests, in keeping with the (non-ideal) analysis found in the *Wealth of Nations* and with Hume's notions of 'progress in the arts'.

The economy depicted by Edgeworth is one of rural stagnation and decay. Indebtedness is a problem not only for the Rackrents but also for their tenants. The Rackrents need to renegotiate rent is based upon the fecklessness of their nature, their tenants on the fickleness of nature, a fickleness which is no doubt exacerbated by the unimproved quality of the land. Commerce and manufacturing are absent from the body of the novel as is, for the most part, towns. They are only introduced as a means of progress at its end. The Rackrents consume but rarely produce. True there is evidence that they attempted to farm in their own right and to make improvements – at some stage prior to Sir Kit's return from England some miserable 'trees' had been planted – but the activities are half-hearted (Edgeworth, 1895 [1800], 170). Even the neglect of the fences of the estate is seen as a means of parasitic consumption: fines imposed on stray cattle are added to the family income.

In addition, their notion of what constitutes wealth is firmly embedded in the unimproved agricultural system and in landlordism, bound up as it is in leases, rent negotiations, duty rent, abatements, jointures and law suits. Sir Murtagh sees going to law as a source of wealth, a costly folly, on which Thady comments with biting irony. He also rejoices in the ownership of land under any condition, for example the unproductive bog of 'Allyballycarricko'shaughlin' which, according to Thady, cost 'Sir Murtagh two hundred good pounds to defend his title to it' (Edgeworth, 1895 [1800], 17). Mortimer sees this action as feudal 'sentimentalism' (Mortimer, 1984, 117). This money would have been better spent on improvements elsewhere on the estate – an idea implied by the text. Smith lists 'improvements of land' as 'clearing, draining, enclosing, manuring and reducing it into the conditions most proper for tillage, and culture' (*WN*, II.i.16). Improvements are scarcely the concern of the Rackrents.

Lady Rackrent, nee Skinflint, is alleged to be of 'Scotch' ancestry. Her reputation for meanness is commented upon by Thady. Her character could also be a satire on Smith's notion of 'frugality' or 'parsimony' or rather on what happens when they go beyond what is judged socially, by prudence, to be a proper limit. Smith himself was well aware that 'prudence' to which 'frugality' is allied would be subject to a 'certain cold esteem' (*MS*, VI.i.14). Lady Rackrent knows 'to a tub of butter everything the tenants had' and exploits to the full the obnoxious and harmful system of duty rent whereby tenants supply produce or labour to the landlord (Edgeworth, 1895 [1800], 6). It is at this stage in the novel that a clear description of rural economy is provided. Apart from a mention of bleaching linen, industry is absent from the rural scene. It is also here that 'frugality', a central virtue in Smith's notion of the accumulation of stock and a notion that both Smith and Hume followed within their own domestic spheres in the early and middle years of their own careers, appears, even if it is satirised as meanness. Smith's notion of 'frugality' is, of course, developed, in *Moral Sentiments*, at least, within the context of a set of related virtues such as 'prudence', 'industry', 'moderation', 'patience' and 'self-control' (Griswold, 1999, 185). What matters to Smith the social philosopher is the whole set. Sir Murtagh and his wife may have pulled the estate together by such parasitic means, provided the tendency to 'racked rent' could have been avoided, had a quarrel over her vociferous intervention in an abatement not resulted in Sir Murtagh's death as a result of breaking 'a blood-vessel'. His death is a consequence of an immoderate response, lacking in self-control, to his wife's intervention (Edgeworth, 1895 [1800], 8). The proper expressions of the 'selfish passions' including self-control, were not available to him.

Sir Kit sees marriage and a diamond cross as a source of wealth (Adam Smith would have thought of this as a 'trinket'). He achieves the marriage although he fails to obtain the diamond cross. Sir Kit's wife – described, perhaps mistakenly by Thady as 'a Jewish' – manages to cling to her diamond cross. Here is another example of the religious ambiguities of the text – why a cross if she is Jewish? Although she secures the cross, she suffers being incarcerated by her husband for a period of seven years as a result of her refusal to yield it. The lusting after 'trinkets' – ridiculed by Smith in both *Moral Sentiments* and the *Wealth of Nations* – misdirects Sir Kit's efforts even if his lust is based on the desire to turn the jewel into cash. His labours could have been invested in more productive activity.

For Sir Condy, political office seems to be a way forward though this also proves to be a false path. Honest work is rarely considered an option by members of the Rackrent family, given as they are to gambling, drinking and, in Sir Kit's case, duelling. The aspiring Jason, Thady's son, starts out, in contrast, in honest, even if 'unproductive' work (according to Smith's political economy), until he learns to manipulate, by means fair and foul, the economic environment in which he finds himself. Edgeworth, as Butler has hinted, is engaged in a satirical development and extension of Smithian notions of unproductive labour, of misplaced 'customs and manners' and the dangers associated with a lifestyle based on consumption un-sustained by direct production. The ambiguity of Jason's actions undermine any simple 'solution' to the problems posed by literary analysis as it also undermines any simple 'solution' to the condition of the Irish economy.

Edgeworth's depiction of the landlord system, its possible social relations and legal contexts is fiction, which may be aligned to fact. As the preferred daughter of a 'Big House', Edgeworth would have a capacity to draw upon her own experience, though the Edgeworths were enlightened landlords. For the social aspects of the novel and the cultural values she no doubt drew upon the stories of John Langan, her father's steward. Observation is also significant, or as 'The Editor' puts it – though care has to be taken in interpreting what 'The Editor' claims – 'from the life' (Edgeworth, 1895 [1800], 73; Watson, 1964, xi).

However the structure of the novel and its ideological tenor can be interpreted otherwise. Edgeworth was also an avid reader who enjoyed the world of ideas, a world that her father encouraged her to explore. Mortimer points to Arthur Young's work *A Tour of Ireland* (1780) as a source of ideas, echoing what 'The Editor' says at the end of the narrative: 'Mr. Young's picture of Ireland, in his tour through that country, was the first faithful portrait of its inhabitants' (Edgeworth, 1895 [1800], 73). Young's documentation of his Irish tour is itself written in language which shows the influence of the *Wealth of Nations*, a point also noted by Butler (Butler, 1992, 31). Mortimer has already shown how Young's unfavourable account of key features of Irish landlordism – duty rent, the lack of compensation for improvement and the use of middlemen – feature strongly in Edgeworth's narrative (Mortimer, 1984, 115). Either directly through the *Wealth of Nations* or indirectly, through Young, Smith's writing seems to be a major source.

In the *Wealth of Nations* (1776) Smith considers many other topics which would have been relevant to Edgeworth. His analysis of rent is set forth in books one and two of the *Wealth of Nations*. Smith views landlords, as a class, as predatory, demanding rent for the improvements which tenants have themselves made and even, in some instances, demanding rent 'for what is altogether incapable of human improvement' (*WN*, I.xi.3). Landlords concentrate, in their relations with tenants, not on what 'the landlord can afford to take; but to what the farmer can afford to give', necessitating hard bargaining (*WN*, 249). This insight in itself throws further light upon the fatal dispute, concerning an 'abatement' between Sir Murtagh and his wife (whose desire for money sometimes put her on the side of any abatement-seeking tenant who offered it 'properly' in order to gain her intervention) (Edgeworth, 1885 [1800], 8). Given the 'unimproved' nature of the economic system, production can be expected to be uncertain and hence easily lead to a conflict between landlord and tenant concerning the possibility of 'racked rent' (in Smith's terms).

Smith also, in various places, outlines the social relations of feudalism. Whilst the political economy of *Castle Rackrent* is not feudal, it has been described as one of 'pseudo-feudalism' because 'it is revealed as a feudalism of forms from which the substance has departed' (Mortimer, 1984, 116). Mortimer located this feudalism of forms in the character of 'Old Thady' who lives, and whose family has lived, 'rent-free time out of mind' upon the Rackrent estate. This is another example of parasitic behaviour. Unproductive labour in Smith's terms is always 'maintained by revenue' (*WN*, II.iii.7). The Rackrents' ruin would be Thady's ruin too if it were not for Jason's rise. Thady carries the 'feudal' values of Sir Patrick's time forward through time and plants them in Condy's mind from a young age.

Consider what Smith says both of feudal social behaviour and of the feudal lord: 'Before the extension of commerce and manufacture in Europe, the hospitality of the rich and great, from the sovereign down to the smallest baron, exceeded everything which in the present time we can easily form a notion of.' (*WN*, III.iv.5). Smith also talks of the 'waste which attends rustic hospitality'. This is the pattern of the first Rackrent, Sir Patrick O'Shauglin, who, 'On coming into the estate...gave the finest entertainment ever was heard of in the country; not a man could stand after supper but Sir Patrick himself, who could sit out the best man in Ireland, let alone the three kingdoms itself' (Edgeworth, 1895 [1800], 3). Sir Patrick even had the chicken-house 'fitted up for the purpose of accommodating friends and the public in general, who honoured him with their company unexpectedly at Castle Rackrent' (Edgeworth, 1895 [1800], 3). This was in the time of Thady's 'great-grandfather' and the behaviour is the start of the Rackrents' problems (Edgeworth, 1895 [1800], 4). But aspirations towards this behaviour are never quite absent: the great funeral of Sir Patrick O'Shaughlin is recalled by Thady during the decline of Sir Condy and drinking, for a bet, from 'the great horn' which had belonged to Sir Patrick, is the cause of Sir Condy's death just as it probably had been for Sir Patrick himself (Edgeworth, 1895 [1800], 70).

Furthermore, if Maria Edgeworth did believe in the possibility of progress through commerce, given her intellectual pre-dispositions, this idea must stem from some theoretical understanding of the possibility of economic transformation through trade. Smith's *Wealth of Nations* has at least some of its origins in the recognition of the transformation in lowland Scotland which followed upon the commercial conditions created by the Act of Union with England in 1707 (*WN*, I.xi.l.3). Smith shared the optimistic view of the impact of 'commerce and manufactures' with Hume (Spiegel, 1971, 237). The case for Union with Ireland was put and won by Pitt the Younger, a 'scholar of Smith's', of whom, 'there is reason to believe that he had read *WN* with some care' (Ross, 1995, 295). Smith's writings were part of the lengthy political debate, and Richard Lovell Edgeworth, Maria's father, was closely involved in arguing the case for and against Union. At the time of the Union with Scotland, some depicted Ireland as the 'jilted party'. The emphasis on marriage in *Castle Rackrent* is in this context another discomforting feature of the novel for Rackrent marriages are not portrayed as either happy or economically successful (Hack, 1996, 161).

Edgeworth may have hoped that Union would produce economic progress, but elements in the novel may suggest that this was not a hope to which she was firmly attached. The economic landscape of *Castle Rackrent* is that of what Smith would have called, just as Young did, an 'unimproved' country. If Ireland were to experience economic benefits from Union, then Smith's text is one to which Edgeworth is likely to have turned when shaping her novel. A consequence of increased trade in both Smith and Hume's account of economic development is the changes in production (and consumption) arising from, in Hume's words, 'our imitation of foreigners' (Skinner, 1993, 31). The novel ends with what has been seen as an enigmatic question, involving the imitation of foreigners, which in the context of Hume's ideas point to the mutual benefits and exchanges which freer trade may bring: 'Did the Warwickshire militia, who were chiefly artisans, teach the Irish to drink beer? Or did they learn from the Irish to drink whisky?' (Edgeworth, 1895 [1800], 73). The hints suggest a critique, inspired by Hume and by Smith, of trade relations between Britain and Ireland.

Conclusion

Maria Edgeworth was ever someone to whom ideas mattered. In *Castle Rackrent*, she creates a satirical version of a fictionalised political economy of landlordism within the context of an unimproved country, drawing from her experience and her reading. It is more than just an eighteenth-century temptation to read *Castle Rackrent* as a social document. Her overall vision fits the kind of historical pattern of the evolution of social structure and social order, so strong a theme both of the Scottish Enlightenment as a whole and also depicted by Smith in the *Wealth of Nations*. The rational processes and development of appropriate patterns of land ownership and of mercantile capitalism and foreign trade are, in theoretical terms, both the causes and consequences of order. The passing away of rude states of society, of inappropriate values and outmoded forms of tenure, and agricultural production, are all to be expected as a historical fact.

Edgeworth depicts this theoretical understanding, in a satirical account of the decline and elimination of the Rackrents, essentially, and in this account necessarily, an Irish family. The discontinuity in time allows the historical process, as understood by the stages of development approach of Smith and of the Scottish Historical School, to work, whilst also allowing Edgeworth to distance herself from representing the Rackrents as a portrayal of contemporary Irishness. A new domestic order is potentially available on which to build further change. The Irish are not then in 1800 being presented as 'drunken, litigious and generally irresponsible' for 'new habits and a new consciousness' have been acquired (Belanger, 1998, 243; Edgeworth, 1895 [1800], xlx). Edgeworth is more certain of the negative aspects of feudal values than she is about the positive attributes of individualistic capitalist values, for these are largely absent or at best merely implied by implicit contrast with behaviours illustrated, save in the limited form of Jason's actions, from the tale as told by Thady.

This understanding of the political economy of the novel, helps place Mortimer's and Saguaro's analyses in a context of contemporary theories of historical process and economic growth. It extends Butler's notions of the relationship between Edgeworth's writing and Smith's economics. It offers an alternative explanation of the time-span of the novel. It also helps with the conceptualisation of Edgeworth's creative process, moving the novel's fictionalised structure and content further away from a simple transcription of tales told within the Edgeworth family and so, helps reconfigure our understanding of some of *Castle Rackrent*'s problematic features.

Edgeworth's writing, in this account, reflects her interpretation of Smithian notions of social progress though the details of this expected interplay are not all present in the main body of the story. In linking questions of culture, power and economic well-being in a context of social change and linking future change to future patterns of trade, Edgeworth is clearly setting out a fiction which is highly influenced by Scottish and specifically Smithian economic and historical themes. Whilst Edgeworth remains uncertain of the precise outcome of Union, her hope seems to be that it would accomplish in Ireland what it had clearly accomplished, according to Smith, in the lowlands of Scotland. What is remarkable is that she can take such grand ideas and still produce a comic novel of strictly domestic proportions.

The conclusion that Edgeworth is incorporating theories of political economy into her writing is in keeping with a central proposition of the new economic criticism, that not only do economic conditions become inscribed in literature but also the economic theories used either to evaluate or to justify those conditions. The conclusion that *Castle Rackrent* deals with economic themes is not new. That it specifically incorporates, in a highly innovative way, Smithian theory of the development of civil society and Smith's theory of economic growth into the novel's structure and content, is. This strengthens the claim that *Castle Rackrent* anticipates, by a generation, the development of the socio-economic novel of the nineteenth century. It also extends our understanding of ways in which Smith's thought was read and interpreted by his first readers, including helping to nuance the contemporary sense of radicalism and satire in Smith's writing. It also points to Smith as a major influence in the development of the socio-economic novel, a feature of the 1830s and onwards, but originated, in this account by Maria Edgeworth.

5 Exemplification strategy in Adam Smith's *Wealth of Nations*[1]

Adam Smith's *Wealth of Nations* (1776) is, in the annals of the history of economic thought, a work of major significance. It has been analysed and reanalysed over many decades with particular attention paid to the consistency of Smith's theoretical constructs, the origins and impact of his writing and the methodological and other links between Smith, his predecessors, his followers and so on. Hardly a month goes by without some new perspectives on this work appearing in learned journals or in collected volumes. In all of this, Smith's rhetoric has been analysed, though it would be true to say that the attention given to Smith's rhetoric (how Smith argues) has been significantly less than to more specifically content issues (what Smith argues). And within the concerns about Smith's rhetoric, the search has been either to match Smith's writing to eighteenth-century notions of persuasive argument, including Smith's own, or to explore the system and invisible-hand metaphors. Such 'canons of correct taste' include notions of 'order, symmetry, balance ... harmony and love of system' as well as an eighteenth-century preoccupation with irony (Brown, 1997, 291; Harrison, 1995, 99).[2] More recently, Brown has looked at Smith's writings in terms of 'dialogical' ('novelistic') and 'monological' rhetoric. The *Wealth of Nations* is, in contrast to *The Theory of Moral Sentiments*, seen, in Brown's analysis, as 'monological' (Brown, 1994, 31).

Smith's writing, especially in the *Wealth of Nations*, exhibits a number of interesting features not the least of which is, I find, a sense of reading something that has been already spoken and the recurrent use of examples. It is this recurrent use of examples which creates a balance between theoretical propositions and social possibilities.[3] In approaching Smith's work, it should not be forgotten (the 'death of the author' not withstanding) that he had earned his living for a substantial part of his working life as a successful university teacher and personal tutor. Smith is also known to have dictated parts of his manuscript: he often experienced difficulties with the physical aspects of writing and resorted to clerical help (Ross, 1995). Smith was both a teacher and rhetorician and, as pedagogy grew out of rhetoric, it seems likely that Smith would know how to convince his readers. It would be surprising if there were no traces, in the structure of Smith's discourse, of a systematic and 'teacherly' approach, based on an understanding of what a lecture is and what is required pedagogically to convince others of the effectiveness of an argument.

In all the sophisticated literature that has grown up around Smith's seminal text, there is little concerning what might be called the mechanical aspects of Smith's writing. Some studies, particularly by Endres, have taken specific chapters and attempted a textual analysis though such works have often been motivated by study of Smith's *Lectures on Rhetoric and Belles Lettres* (*LRBL*) (Endres, 1991, 1992, 1995) rather than simply making a direct response to the text, as recommended by Brown (Brown, 1994, 18). Smith, though evaluating, synthesising and developing the work of other theoreticians, was not writing a theoretical text for the sole attention of other theoreticians (the work as a whole is a complex of theory, historical analysis, narrative episodes and reflections on policy and practices). For most of his readers, apart from a few *philosophes*, the *Wealth of Nations* was, in effect, an introductory text, a novel reading experience. In this context, can a descriptive examination of Smith's writing help us take a different view of what Smith wrote?

This paper will examine samples of Smith's writing drawn from the opening chapters of the *Wealth of Nations* in order to establish how Smith develops and uses examples. Smith goes to great lengths to illustrate his ideas with examples drawn from contemporary events and situations or from historical circumstances (Endres, 1992). Perhaps his most well-known example is that of the pin factory which he uses to illustrate a key concept in his theoretical system, that of the division of labour. But his whole work is packed with exemplifications and these are often presented within a wider pedagogical strategy that we could think of, initially at any rate, as 'planned repetition' or even 'extensive familiarisation techniques'. Smith re-states and repeats key ideas throughout the text, for example his treatment, some would say satire, of landlords and their expectations, behaviours and 'predelictions' for the support of unproductive rather than productive workers is one such recurrent theme treated at various points in the work.

Modern-day, first-year economics textbooks spend much of their time in defining, exemplifying and familiarising (by repetition and variation) technical terms required for the analysis of more complex economic problems. The use of definitions and examples in modern-day economics textbooks was analysed by Henderson and Hewings several years ago, testing a model developed by Bramki and Williams (Henderson and Hewings, 1987). The research itself grew out of co-operation between Willie Henderson, a development economist by training of the then Department of Extramural Studies and colleagues, Tim Johns and Tony Dudley-Evans in particular, of the Department of English, University of Birmingham.

Since that time of close cooperation, I have been making application of a variety of discourse techniques to nineteenth-century writers marginalised by the mainstream economics canon. In making a further extension of discourse analysis to a canonical text in the history of economic thought, this time from the eighteenth century, it is fitting that work undertaken during a period of close subject – language cooperation should form a basis (perhaps in the extensive familiarisation techniques identified by Henderson and Hewings) for the chapter published here (Henderson and Hewings, 1987, 125). At that time, and under the influence of Tony Dudley-Evans, the degree of subject–language cooperation at Birmingham was certainly innovative and probably unique. The hope is that by undertaking an analysis of the way in which Smith textually develops examples, a systematic pedagogical strategy will be found that may or may not be similar to that found in modern-day, introductory economics writing. The corpus is an eighteenth-century text and the analysis of examples, and the methodology used, will have to adjust to the text itself. Since exemplifications are intended to assist readers understand and extend an argument, the relationship between the proposition and example and the role of exemplification in the wider discourse is also of significance.

Some general notions of Smith's writing in the *Wealth of Nations*

There is a literature on Smith's 'rhetoric', though the literature within the field of study known as the history of economic thought does not tend to approach the analysis of Smith's discourse through either details of language or the establishment of textual moves or patterns. Brown has surveyed a variety of critical approaches to the study of Smith's writing (Brown, 1997).

Some of this literature tends to approach the *Wealth of Nations* through the principles that Smith himself outlined in his *LRBL*. This is a method of approaching the *Wealth of Nations* that Brown is sceptical about, though no one would wish to deny that Smith understood what was required to secure the attention of different kinds of lectors and readers (Brown, 1997, 285). He had explored the issue in both theoretical and practical terms (if what we know about his teaching is allowed). The literature has also established that Smith understood what was required, rhetorically, for the development of a scientific argument (Campbell, 1971, 29). Brown's scepticism is based on a desire to read text as text, and respond to it as text rather than as authorial product. Although the methods of analysis in general are not the type that will be pursued here, for the method used is closer to, though different from, Brown's, nonetheless, the existing literature has drawn attention to a number of features of Smith's text.

At the 'macro' level of textual organisation, it is generally held that the first three books of the *Wealth of Nations* are concerned with 'generalised description' (i.e. 'the analysis of the market economy and its vicissitudes through history'). The last two books are concerned, then, with 'generalised prescription' (i.e. 'alternative systems of policy and the functions of the State') (Robbins, 1981, 7, quoted in Endres, 1991, 76). Thus, different sections of the *Wealth of Nations* are doing differing kinds of work, building a different kind of relationship with the reader or perhaps identifying different kinds of (implied) readers. Within each of these broad sections, differences in the style of writing have been recorded. Chapter five in the first book is widely regarded as a rhetorical failure and the whole of book four has been described as 'propagandist'. Endres has tested out such insights in relation to chapter five, book four by investigating what he calls the 'compositional rules'. His conclusion is that Smith's chapter on bounties conforms to Smith's 'compositional rules' and is therefore best seen as 'a disciplined exercise in advocacy rather than as a crude polemic' (Endres, 1991, 94).

It is also clear that Smith's *Wealth of Nations* is didactic in the sense that it is a teacherly text but also in the sense that it attempts to evaluate propositions by balanced argument (though this has been subjected to qualifications). It is also clear that it is based, like some of his other writing, on the development of 'a system comprised of a few core principles capable of accounting for manifold observed appearances' (Endres, 1991, 82; Skinner, 1972, 311–314). This is a central feature of Smith's writing and it may be a consequence of his understanding of the demands of Newtonian science, as he and other figures of the Enlightenment understood that science. But the textual implication is, of course, that there will be many textual repetitions of principles and their application as well as many different instances (examples) leading to the same result. Any 'planned repetition' in Smith cannot be, therefore, a simple consequence of an educational strategy as it is also implied by the preference for working with a few simple predictive or explanatory concepts. The rhetorical underpinnings suggest 'extensive familiarisation'.

The work undertaken here, initially at any rate, will not examine *LRBL* as a means of examining passages from the *Wealth of Nations*. It will as far as possible look at the first three chapters of the work simply as text, though given the subject-knowledge of the researcher there will be some constraints on this. The text will be analysed in terms of structure and language in order to establish generalisations about the use and purpose of exemplifications in Smith's discourse. Its primary aim is to describe the text, account for its coherence and so illustrate how examples are used, in the hope that such a description will allow for the development of an informed critical appreciation, capable of revealing something new about Smith's method of argument.

Initial classification of examples

There are probably three broad categories of examples to be found in Smith's text: current examples drawn from contemporary economic experience and written about in the present tense, historical examples, and, for the want of a clearer expression, 'hypothetical examples'. Current examples are likely to consist of two kinds. First, those which are directly observable and within the experience of the target reader, for example everyday examples of economic behaviour. Examples are found in references to 'carpenters', 'smiths' and 'tanners'. Second, those that are contemporary but which would be more difficult to directly verify. This is either because they are drawn from a different geographical environment ('France', 'Poland') from that of the target reader but which are in principle verifiable by observation or because they are drawn from some 'macro' economic experience. The use of current examples, written in the present tense, in the section on the division of labour must have given the text an 'up to-the-minute' quality for its first readers.

Another set of examples is historical, such as the economic conditions in the classical world or in medieval England. These are drawn from Smith's reading and understanding of historical texts. It is to be expected that Smith will make a special effort to select and shape the historical examples to assist the reader in understanding the concept, analysis or 'policy' that is being investigated, proposed or evaluated. As it happens, historical examples in the sense of located historical events, circumstances or policies are relatively unimportant in the three chapters under detailed consideration. From what is known about the 'macro' structure of the work (see later), historical examples can be expected to be significant in books four and five.

There is yet another set that can be called 'hypothetical examples'.[4] These may or may not have an authentic existence in the world beyond Smith's text and they are often 'stylised' in ways that are not always easy to describe. For example, the text may refer to a location such as the Scottish Highlands and make statements about conditions in 'a' remote village. The context is not specific – no definite village is being referred to though the example is within the bounds of social possibilities, but, nonetheless, the example is not 'outside' the text. Such examples are therefore 'imaginary' or 'hypothetical' (and have an equivalence in the modern-day first-year economics textbook). When faced with such examples, the question of textual location and function perhaps needs to be explored in detail. In modern-day textbooks such examples are frequently located within a small-scale text pattern of situation–problem–solution–evaluation, signalled by imperatives such as 'assume', 'suppose' or 'take'. The 'hypothetical examples' provide a setting for a small-scale application of a concept (Henderson and Hewings, 1986, *passim*). In Smith (see later) they tend to be located within a dynamic narrative. Such examples tend to illustrate a theoretical principle or extend a principle to a dimension of economic life that would be difficult or impossible to 'observe' (e.g. the process of change) or where specific detail is irrelevant (e.g. 'a' highland village).[5] They also tend to appeal to the shared cultural experience between the text and the reader such as with commonplace examples ('farmer' or 'merchant' in some given context) drawn from 'common sense' or 'everyday experience', though the common sense that is appealed to is one that is heavily influenced by other Enlightenment writers. Such examples can give rise to problems of interpretation concerning their status and significance.

However, these are for the time being at any rate to be thought of as broad categories only as, given eighteenth-century referencing conventions, some examples will appear to the modern reader as vague whereas others will be more precisely located. The example of the pin factory is a general example that is not precisely located as a given pin factory. Nor is it uniquely located in that sense either for it has been 'often observed'. Smith, however, supplies us with evidence that he has seen just such a factory. Such a pin factory did exist but whether it existed or not it remains an example. The classification of examples cannot be expected to be clear cut; judgements will depend on how they are presented to, or interpreted by, the reader. So the schema set out here can only be taken as provisional. It may be, say, that the notion of 'vague examples' is a better way of approaching a whole set of exemplifications, but this remains to be seen. As 'evidence', Smith's 'examples' are both 'qualitative' and 'quantitative', and the 'qualitative' (sometimes based upon third-party observation) evidence can also be 'vague'.

Contextualisation of examples: overview of opening moves and development in the first three chapters of the *Wealth of Nations*

Smith is concerned with illustrating the 'causes of…improvement in the productive powers of labour' (*WN*, I.5). He concentrates on the concept of the division of labour in the first three chapters of book one of the *Wealth of Nations*. The discourse structures of the three chapters are themselves interesting. Each chapter begins with an assertion of analytical or practical significance. Even without detailed knowledge of economic thinking prior to Smith's work, it is clear from the language that the assertions are bold. Chapter one, paragraph one:

> The greatest improvement in the productive powers of labour, and the greater part of the skill, dexterity, and judgement with which it is everywhere directed, or applied, seem to have been the effects of the division of labour.

Chapter two, paragraph one:

> This division of labour, from which so many advantages are derived, is not originally the effect of any human wisdom, which foresees and intends that general opulence to which it gives occasion. It is the necessary, though very slow and gradual consequence of a certain propensity in human nature which has in view no such extensive utility; the propensity to truck, barter and exchange one thing for another.

Chapter three, paragraph one:

> As it is the power of exchanging that gives occasion to the division of labour, so the extent of this division of labour must always be limited by the extent of that power, or, in other words, by the extent of the market. When the market is very small, no person can have any encouragement to dedicate himself entirely to one employment, for want of the power to exchange all that surplus part of the produce of his own labour, which is over and above his own consumption, for such parts of the produce of other men's labour as he has occasion for.

Each one of these opening paragraphs conveys a striking proposition to the reader, though the detailed linguistic construction of each differs in detail. In a way, Smith has already signalled the boldness of his plan: the first sentence of the *Wealth of Nations* has already been provided in the 'Introduction And Plan of the Work'. It reads:

> The annual labour of every nation is the fund which originally supplies it with all the necessaries and conveniences of life which it annually consumes, and which consist always either in the immediate produce of that labour, or in what is purchased with that produce from other nations.

This striking sentence has, given knowledge of economic thinking prior to Smith, the force of a cannon shot. According to early economic doctrines, the 'fund' was a monetary fund consisting of gold and silver, either as money or as plate. But even without such insider knowledge, the paragraph's textual location underlines its importance. The linguistic construction of the sentence itself also signals its importance as a significant, formal proposition. It is in fact two definitions, one concerning the nature of the 'fund' ('annual labour') and another of the 'annual' consumption defined as the produce of the 'fund' of labour. The relationship between the rest of the 'Introduction' corresponds to the structures revealed by the analysis of the first three chapters (later).

The opening sentences in each of the three chapters considered here follow the same formal pattern and suggest an origin in Smith's lecturing style or in other formal, scientific texts. The propositions (topics?) are all, in effect, key analytical statements, central to the development of Smith's economic analysis and must be, in a sense, conclusions that Smith has already reached. Indeed the structure is found in various places in the *Wealth of Nations*, to a greater or lesser degree. The lead sentences are presented as assertions and what follows in each chapter is a justification for, and extension of, the key ideas. Extra-textual evidence, from chapter two, part two of *The Theory of Moral Sentiments*, and comments by John Millar (one of Smith's students) suggest that Smith's method of lecturing in Moral Philosophy consisted in presenting distinct 'propositions' and then proving and illustrating them (*TMS*, Raphael and Macfie (eds), Introduction, 4).

Chapter one, paragraph one relates increases in the productive powers of labour (whose annual application gives rise to the means of consumption) to 'the effects of the division of labour'. The pin factory is such a well-known example that it is difficult at first sight to be certain that there is anything new to be said about it. However, when looked at from the point of view of the development of Smith's argument in writing, several interesting things emerge. Smith does not offer, for example, a definition of the division of labour but merely highlights the link between the division of labour and increases in productivity. Instead he opts for an example: 'the effects of the division of labour, in the general business of society, will be more easily understood by considering in what manner it operates in *some particular manufactures*' (my emphasis) (*WN*, I.i.2). Smith then reverses the order of treatment: the text deals *first* with the question of *illustrating* what is meant by the division of labour before it explores the analytical link between the division of labour and increases in labour productivity.

In paragraph three, Smith introduces his famous (though not innovative) example of 'the trade of the pin-maker'.[6] But before working through his example, Smith considers some methodological issues. He first challenges the erroneous notion that the division of labour is carried further in 'trifling' occupations than in bigger undertakings. This notion arises from the capacity to observe small-scale operations, under 'the view of the spectator'. Smith lays great stress on the capacity to observe economic processes: 'the view of the spectator'; 'seldom see more'; 'not near so obvious'; 'I have seen a small manufactory of this kind...'; 'I have seen several...';

or have them confirmed by other people's observations, 'I am assured...'; '...must frequently have been shown...'. Such instances, right at the start of the work, attest to the Baconian influence on Smith and to the active nature of his researches. Smith is envisaging something more systematic than mere idle curiosity. He is very much concerned that evidence should support his argument, and it is clear from samples of his writing that he both practised direct observation and encouraged others to do so (see Skinner, 1972, 309). He uses similar phrases elsewhere in the *Wealth of Nations*, for example in chapter five, book four (Endres, 1991, 88).[7] But some 'great manufactures' cannot be readily observed (*WN*, I.i.2).

Smith, then, is careful to justify his example and stress that it is suggestive of a greater process found in other types of enterprises and economic activities of even greater significance. This is important for Smith never defines the division of labour itself. His approach, here, is inductive. He merely illustrates it in the pin factory by spelling out the processes involved and extends it, by informal analogy or by metaphorical extension, to a whole series of other simple examples that call upon the implied readers' existing but unorganised knowledge of economic life or on their capacity to observe it. Smith works to reorganise their experience of observing such life. These examples are: 'farmer'; 'manufacturer'; 'linen and woolen manufacturers'; 'growers of flax'; 'bleachers and smoothers of linen'; 'dyers and dressers of cloth'; 'carpenter'; 'smith' – also, later, in the context of 'a common smith' who 'has never been used to make nails', and so on. In this sense, the pin trade is taken as a case study from which the organisational and productive features of the division of labour can be extended to other economic contexts, subject, as in the general case of agriculture, to certain provisos. In short, Smith is saying that the principles that operate in example 'X' also operate in example 'Y', and by this process unlike things can be reduced to one common process: the division of labour. It is up to the readers, for most of the examples, to spell out the process for each type of work. McCloskey has drawn economists' attention to a similar process of metaphorical extension found in modern-day economic argument; for example, a 'child' is just like a 'durable good' and so in explaining 'family size', notions of investment can be applied (McCloskey, 1994, 327–328). An aim of Smith's rhetoric of repetition is to fix the underlying principles in the reader's mind and relate them to diverse social practices and historical contexts.

In the sixth paragraph, Smith initiates discussion of the circumstances that give rise to the increases in productivity. The textual structure repeats the pattern, generalisation–exemplification. In each paragraph a generalisation is supported by evidence. In two out of the three paragraphs the evidence is supplied from contrasting situations. One passage is adequate by way of illustration:

> First, the improvement of the dexterity of the workman necessarily increases the quantity of the work he can perform, and the division of labour, by reducing every man's business to some one simple operation, and by making this operation the sole employment of his life, necessarily increases very much the dexterity of the workman [*theoretically backed empirical generalisation*]. A common smith, who, though accustomed to handle the hammer, has never

been used to making nails, if upon some particular occasion he is obliged to attempt it, will scarce, I am assured, be able to make above two or three hundred nails in a day, and those too very bad ones [*authentic empirical example without benefit of dexterity*]. A smith who has been accustomed to make nails, but whose sole or principal business has not been that of a nailer, can seldom with his utmost diligence make more than eight hundred or a thousand nails in a day [*authentic empirical evidence with some benefit of dexterity*]. I have seen several boys under twenty years of age who had never exercised any other trade but that of making nails, and who, when they exerted themselves, could make, each of them, upwards of two thousand three hundred nails in a day [*authentic empirical evidence with high levels of dexterity*].
(*WN*, I.i.6)

As nail making was a significant activity in Smith's home town, extra-textual evidence suggests Smith had engaged, once again, in direct observation. The comparative method (i.e. 'compare and contrast' or even, in formal economics terms, some sort of 'comparative statics') is taken to a high degree in this extended example or mini-case study. Several examples, in the sample of text considered, exhibit this pattern. Elsewhere in the *Wealth of Nations* other contrasting examples are to be found, for example 'rude' and 'civilised', 'improved' and 'unimproved', 'servant' and 'slave'. The opening paragraph of part one of book one chapter ten contains five paired examples of contrasting conditions that systematically, in Smith's estimate, influence the structure of wages.[8]

The long final paragraph of chapter one consists of a narrated series of intellectual speculations and examples in which readers are invited to work with Smith ('let us consider', 'we shall be sensible that . . .' and the use of the exclamation mark to signify a sense of intellectual excitement), to enter, as it were, his world of economic wonder and explore the remarkable social and economic consequences of the division of labour.[9] The specific example, this time of a compound product rather than of a simple manufacturing process relying on individual dexterity, that gives rise to a sustained narrative, is that of 'that very simple machine, the shears with which the shepherd clips the wool' (*WN*, I.i.II). The consideration of the inputs and other specialisations gives rise to a long list of occupations and activities, tied together in a mutual dependence of interlocking exchanges. The examples are set within the framework of a great economic drama that starts with a consideration of the number of people involved in preparation of the accommodation of 'the most common artificer or day-labourer' and ends with:

Compared, indeed, with the more extravagant luxury of the great, his accommodation must no doubt appear extremely simple and easy; and yet it may be true, perhaps, that the accommodation of a European prince does not always so much exceed that of an industrious and frugal peasant, as the accommodation of the latter exceeds that of many an African king, the absolute master of the lives and liberties of ten thousand naked savages.
(*WN*, I.i.23–24)

In between comes the long list of examples with the associated danger of incoherence. Smith's closure must be judged little short of masterly, for it guarantees the coherence of the paragraph. Smith has a capacity for generating memorable images and the creative or imaginative aspects of his writing should not be underestimated. The *Wealth of Nations* is a blend of fact and fiction. And to think that Ruskin was accused of a romantic approach to economic life! The long list of economic specialisations united round consideration of one product became a staple of Victorian economic story telling, Smith's 'shears' being dropped in favour of the 'Christmas pudding'. A modern-day literary manifestation of a list of economic activities contributing to a final product is satirised in David Lodge's *Nice Work*, an 1980s reworking of themes from the Victorian socio-economic novel (Lodge, 1988).[10] The evidence from 'outside' the text is that Smith's wondrous nature of economic life had a huge impact on his readership and those influenced by it.

The opening paragraph of chapter two signals an insight that is of fundamental importance to Smith's approach to the whole of economic life: the principle of natural propensities in human nature which give rise to unintended consequences. The organisational and productive implications of propensities 'to truck, barter and exchange' emerge slowly over historical time, the unintended consequences of individual human beings trying to better their position through trade. Here it is, clear and plain and located at the core of his fundamental principle of productivity, central to his theory of economic growth.[11]

Smith then develops the theme of human nature by a series of exemplifications, developed within the context of 'truck, barter and exchange', which contrast (in the manner of David Hume in his *Treatise of Human Nature*) human nature with animal nature. Smith's examples are also formed within the general framework of wider enlightenment thinking. Fawning is presented as an attribute of both human and animal nature. However, humans stand 'in need of the co-operation and assistance of great multitudes' (*WN*, I.ii.2) and need to gain that co-operation (instinctive in animals, through the 'accidental concurrence of their passions') by other means. The exemplifications lead up to the following observation:

> It is not from the benevolence of the butcher, the brewer or the baker that we expect our dinner, but from their regard to their own interest. We address ourselves, not to their humanity but to their self-love, and never talk to them of our own necessities but of their advantages.
>
> (*WN*, I.ii.2)

'[A]ddress' and 'talk' serve to remind the reader that Smith has opened the discussion with a speculation that the human propensity 'to truck, barter and exchange' may be located in 'the faculties of reason and speech'.[12]

The lead sentence in the third paragraph in chapter two is:

> *As it is by* treaty, by barter, and by purchase, that we obtain from one another the greater part of those mutual good offices which we stand in need of, *so it is this same* trucking disposition which *originally* gives occasion to the division of labour. (my emphasis)
>
> (*WN*, I.ii.3)

This is, as far as I can see, the first use in the text of the construct 'as it is . . . so it is', a construct Smith uses in the following chapter to present implications to the reader. I have italicised 'originally' because Smith's thought was developed within the context of vision of the historical evolution of society and accounting for origins is a significant aspect of his social thought. The rest of the paragraph consists of examples designed to illustrate 'origins' within the conceptual framework of the division of labour. Thus 'In a tribe . . .' introduces a set of stylised, that is 'hypothetical', examples of growing specialisation that allow an individual 'to cultivate and bring to perfection whatever talent or genius he may posses for that particular species of business'. The individual examples have, in context, a kind of plausibility with 'realistic' narrative touches helping to paint an idealised picture of the developmental process. The division of labour is arrived at on a voluntary or natural basis. The specialisations are in making arrows, frame building and cover making for 'their little huts or moveable houses', smithing, skin dressing, dressed skins being presented as 'the principal part of the clothing of savages'. In this narrative passage Smith uses the present tense: this gives immediacy to the examples, in keeping with the 'of the moment' approach found elsewhere in the sample. Furthermore the details of the narrative appeal to a shared body of knowledge concerning the nature of the 'rude' or 'savage'. Although a story of 'origins', the specialist members of the tribe learn the lesson in one generation. The paragraph that follows corrects the impression that these differences are entirely innate: they are themselves 'the effect of the division of labour'.

The final paragraph opens with '*As it is this disposition* which forms that difference of talents, so remarkable among men of different professions, *so it is this same* disposition which renders that difference useful' (my emphasis) (*WN*, I.ii.5). The exemplifications, most of which are stylised, again a series of contrasts, tracing out distinctions between animals and men, are designed to illustrate the utility of the 'general disposition to truck, barter, and exchange'.

The opening paragraph of the third chapter is more complex but just as bold as those of the preceding chapters. It is an analytical proposition presented as an *implication* of what has gone before: 'As it is the power of exchanging . . . so the extent of this division'. This in itself signals that Smith's argument has already progressed, the principle of exchange having already been explored in the preceding chapter. The reader has something to build upon. And this is reflected within the organisation of the paragraph. The second sentence is an exemplification of the 'hypothetical' type, designed to illustrate the analytical statement. It is an exemplification but it is not located in any given concrete situation and the reader is supplied, given what has gone before, with just enough information to make sense of the proposition. The two sentences together follow the 'rule–example' pattern found in modern-day introductory economics writing.

What follows in the rest of the third chapter is at first sight (and especially for the modern reader) rather dreary, considering the dramatic opening. Closer reading shows it to be otherwise. It is in fact a series of carefully contrived more or less concrete examples illustrating the analytical relationship in a series of linked sets of contrasting examples, rising from the village up through cities and so to the whole world. Overall for the rest of the third chapter taken as a whole the pattern is 'specific-general' but there are variations within this. Smith, however, continues to use the same basic pattern of subsets of analytical propositions with implications. He does this, strikingly, in paragraphs three and four.

In paragraph two the contrast is between town and country and the paragraph develops from the 'hypothetical' example of a general nature, becoming progressively more detailed in terms of specific trades. In other words a 'general-specific' text structure within the paragraph. It terminates with the example of the impossibility of a 'nailer' finding the means of specialised employment in a remote part of the Scottish Highlands. Again the example is hypothetical but it serves the purpose of re-applying a key concept by exercising the imagination. The 'nailer', a parallel example to that of the pin maker and already treated as such, and in some detail, by Smith in chapter one, requires only a thumbnail case study as the process is close to that already examined in the first chapter. This textual variation must also count as a kind of deliberate repetition that at the same time extends, without too much intellectual effort, the reader's experience.

Paragraph three opens 'As by means of water-carriage ... so it is upon the sea coast and along the banks of navigable rivers'. In fact it is useful to set out the whole of the complex lead sentence in this paragraph:

> *As by means of water-carriage* a more extensive market is opened to every sort of industry than what land-carriage alone can afford it, *so it is upon the sea coast, and along the banks of navigable rivers*, that industry of every kind *naturally begins to subdivide and improve itself*, and it is frequently not till a long time after that those *improvements extend themselves to the inland parts of the country* (my emphasis).
>
> (*WN*, I.iii.3)

The first part of the sentence illustrates an application of the idea through a means of extending the market and the implication relates the general principle to the world beyond Smith's text 'sea coast and banks of navigable rivers'. The bold type picks out language that is consistent with Smith's concept of 'natural' behaviour and unintended consequences, 'improvements' 'extend themselves'. The pattern of development is not planned. Rather it evolves, under the influence of competition, as each individual pursues his interests in trucking and bartering. Smith's ideological position is here found within the details of the language choices that he has exercised while writing. His overall system is founded upon a notion of 'natural liberty', operating in this example at the 'macro' level. The rest of the paragraph consists, again, of a series of teacherly contrasts between the movements of goods on land and sea. It is in such 'compare and contrast' exercises that the didactic nature of the text is manifest. The comparisons start with the detailed domestic example of London and Edinburgh but extending to the international arena by the addition of a question: 'What goods could bear the expense of land-carriage between London and Calcutta?' (*WN*, I.iii.3). Smith explicitly justifies his choice by pointing out that London and Calcutta in fact carry out 'a very considerable commerce with each other'. The comparisons cannot be extended to London–Calcutta because the land alternative is impractical: its absence is used to effect.

Paragraph four maintains the general form of the argument and opens with:

> *Since such, therefore, are* the advantages of water-carriage, *it is **natural** that* the first improvements of art and industry should be made where this conveniency *opens the whole world for a market* to the produce of every sort of labour, and that they should always be much later in extending themselves into the inland parts of the country (my emphasis).
>
> (*WN*, I.iii.4)

Smith continues to demonstrate reasoning by moving from, in this case, an empirical generalisation based upon comparative costs, to a 'natural' implication. In the previous paragraph, the pairing, Edinburgh–London and London–Calcutta has given way to 'the whole world for a market'. But the position of the 'sea coasts' and 'navigable rivers' is contrasted with that of inland parts whose development is limited by local conditions. Once again the paired contrasts, this time 'inland–coastal', is maintained. The text repeats a basic pattern but the variation maintains the interest.

The final series of paragraphs, in a sense, focus on more or less concrete examples that treat 'the whole world' in terms of what has gone before. Again the textual pattern is 'general–specific'; the general concept 'the whole world' is then divided into its component parts: China, India, Central Asia and Africa. Considerable emphasis is placed on exemplifying, further, the consequences of the division of labour for economic well-being, in the contemporary and historical world as known by Smith, and in relation to access to coastal or riparian navigation. This principle, based upon comparative costs, is used to explain the lack of development in interior locations or on continents, such as Africa, with few navigable waterways. Thus, through a careful pattern of exemplifications, Smith effectively illustrates that his theoretical insight is valid, over time, and in local, regional, national and international contexts.

Conclusions

The primary purpose of this paper was to explore Smith's use of examples and to relate his use of examples to the wider discourse. A number of interesting aspects of Smith's writing have been revealed. First, the general scheme for considering examples has proved to be useful in context. In the passages under consideration, the 'hypothetical' example, essentially an appeal to the active reasoning power of the implied reader predominates though there are several instances of the more-or-less authentic case study. 'Hypothetical' examples are sometimes set within plausible if somewhat idealistic narratives. Second, the macro structure of each chapter considered seems to follow a pattern. This consists in a single-paragraph introduction that sets out the topic or proposition that is to be explored in the chapter. The rest of the, chapter consists of the justification of the proposition, by exemplification, some of which corresponds to styles of exemplification found in modern-day economics textbooks, and its extension, again usually by exemplification, to other contexts. Third, it has also been revealed that the use of examples is not accidental or incidental but, for at least two of the chapters concerned, fundamental to the development and justification of the proposition that is being presented. Considerable effort has gone into the specification and selection of examples (used inductively and deductively) and into their textual organisation and presentation. It is by weaving a simple principle or set of principles in and out of largely contemporary examples (in the case of the sample considered here) that a few simple propositions are demonstrated to have a powerful explanatory and predictive role. Even in this small sample of writing, Smith's hierarchy of examples aims for universal appeal. Fourth, it would seem that the implied reader has, sometimes, to activate the knowledge of certain working environments and apply the principle to the understated examples, real or imaginary. Fifth, the cohesion of the chapters is secured by recurrent patterns in the structure and handling of examples within the framework of simple text patterns such as 'general–specific' and 'compare and contrast' and by details of the language used. This textual organisation, which a quick check shows to be found elsewhere in the text, would seem to correspond to a pattern most likely found in scientific discourse (either written or spoken) of the time. Sixth, the analysis has also revealed a linguistic pattern 'As it is . . . so it is' for the presentation of any theoretical or empirical implications of key propositions. A quick look in the introduction to book two shows that there it is reduced to 'as . . . so', a construct suggestive of the 'if/then' formula found in elementary modern-day positive economics (Mead and Henderson 1983). The construction is in evidence also in *The Theory of Moral Sentiments*. Further work is required to see if this pattern is found elsewhere in Smith's writing.

It would seem, however, that a primary interest in textual description gives rise to interesting possibilities for textual exploration by other (extra-textual) means. It provides detailed evidence for existing propositions about Smith's text and suggests additional ways of understanding Smith's economics writing.

6   A very cautious, or a very polite, Dr Smith?

Hedging in the *Wealth of Nations*

Adam Smith opens book one, chapter one, of the *Wealth of Nations* (*WN*) with the following statement:

> The greatest improvement in the productive powers of labour, and the greater part of the skill, dexterity, and judgment with which it is any where directed, or applied, seem to have been the effects of the division of labour.
>
> (Smith, 1976, *WN*, I.i.1)

This is a striking opening sentence for it goes straight to the heart of Smith's treatise on the nature of economic growth. But it is a hedged statement. Smith does not claim in this sentence that all the improvement in productive powers of labour arise from the division of labour; and a similar modification is made with respect to the application of 'skill, dexterity and judgment'. Nor does Smith claim that the increases in the productive powers of labour are the consequences of the division of labour, only that they 'seem' to be.

Smith's sentence avoids the use of the unmodified verb 'to be'. The 'seem' is easily missed, and indeed there are, no doubt, some experienced readers who have missed it. Thus for example, although Groenewegen quotes the phrase in his investigation of Smith's notion of the division of labour, he makes no reference to the hedged nature of Smith's claim (Groenewegen, 2002, 389).[1] Smith repeats the use of 'seems' later in the chapter: 'The separation of different trades and employments from one another, seems to have taken place, in consequence of this advantage' (*WN*, I.i.4). Repetition of the verb suggests that this use of 'to seem' is not an accidental feature of the writing, but the result of authorial choice.

Another hedging word – 'perhaps' – also appears early in the opening chapter, in the context of the famous example of the pin factory, as well as (later) in a discussion of the price and quality of corn. It may be the case that 'everyone knows' that Smith is a highly hedged writer (though such an unhedged generalisation could easily be shown to be rash). Even if it were to be the case, and that this is an obvious aspect of Smith's style, such a view cannot be used to suggest that the problem of investigating Smith's hedging is trivial. Far from it: if the phenomenon is so striking this in itself suggests a need for analysis. That some have noticed is not in doubt. Rothschild, without presenting much by way of evidence or of context with respect to making a judgement, contrasts Smith with Condorcet, a writer of considerable robustness, and says: 'Smith was, by contrast, extraordinary cautious and circumspect. The writings he published during his lifetime are replete with qualifications ("it seems", "frequently", "no doubt"); Dugald Stewart speaks of "those qualified conclusions that we admire in his writings" ' (Rothschild, 2001, 221).[2]

Smith goes on to demonstrate, in detail, the significance, through a number of examples, of his opening knowledge claim. He is also prepared, in other contexts, to use the unmodified verb 'to be' in making claims. Why then does he hedge this opening claim? There could be many reasons – including modesty. With respect to this particular proposition, it is clear that Smith sets out to support the proposition in the rest of the chapter. Is Smith suggesting that the proposition is yet to be proved? Smith is starting a book-length project, does not wish to claim certainty (in line with, say, David Hume's notion concerning the weakness of systems in which significant ideas are 'taken upon trust') for a proposition *a priori*, but nevertheless has to start somewhere (Hume, 2002; *THN*, Intro.xiii).[3] The pattern of a proposition (set out in each of the opening paragraphs of the first three chapters) followed by supporting evidence, is in keeping with Smith's view of an appropriate structure for didactic writing – didactic writing being 'best in all matters of science' – as set out in the *Lectures on Rhetoric and Belles Lettres* (*LRBL* i.83; ii.126, 133).[4] A hedged statement avoids the implication of certainty before the matter has been supported by evidence.[5] Or it could be that Smith is aware of the exceptional weight he is putting on his claim as part of his theory of economic growth. Other influences on the growth of output, such as better nutrition, are possible, but such influences are covered by 'the greatest improvement'. We are not likely to have direct access to Smith's motives, in this respect, other than what is inscribed in the text.

Answering this question would contribute but a footnote in the study of Smith's work. Though, if Schumpeter is correct in his judgement that 'nobody, either before or after A. Smith, ever thought of putting such a burden upon division of labour', it may well be that Smith had every reason to be cautious (Schumpeter, 1954, 187). Schumpeter also makes the point, without exploring the details of the writing whereby the features are realised, that Smith 'led them [his readers] on gently' (Schumpeter, 1954, 185). This notion is common in studies of Smith. Brown refers to Smith's 'elegant eighteenth-century prose' that 'carries his reader along' (Brown, 1994, 10).

It is not too difficult to show that Smith hedges propositions elsewhere, even in the opening chapter.[6] Groenewegen refers to the first three chapters as 'the oldest part of the building', echoing Schumpeter, and, again, as, 'by far the most polished part of the whole' (Groenewegen, 2002, 389; Schumpeter, 1954: 187). However, in the unpublished Early Draft (ED) of a part of the *WN*, a key reference to the division of labour is unhedged: 'The division of labour, by which each individual confines himself to a particular branch of business, can alone account for that superior opulence which takes place in civilized societies . . .'. (Smith, 1978, ED 6). This suggests that Smith, when it came to the prospect of publication, paid attention to the hedging of propositions.

How does Smith establish knowledge claims in writing and if he hedges them, how and why does he do so? What part, if any, does hedging play in 'gently' leading on the (target) reader? Insight on hedging in modern academic texts will be used to initiate an examination of knowledge claims in a sample of Smith's writing. The paper defines and categorises 'hedging' with respect to Smith's writing, and attempts to identify Smith's approach to his target reader through an examination of hedged passages. Motivations for hedging, based upon 'politeness' and eighteenth-century views about scientific reporting, will be suggested. Since the notion that Smith is a writer who uses hedging in a distinctive way is essentially a comparative one, reference will be made to hedging in the philosophical and economics writing of David Hume.

What is 'hedging'?

By 'hedge' is intended 'any linguistic device by which a speaker avoids being compromised by a statement' that turns out not to be valid. This is at least the essence of the definition in the *Concise Oxford Dictionary of Linguistics*. The term seems to have been first introduced into applied linguistics by Lakoff, who intended it to describe 'words whose job it is to make things more or less fuzzy' (Lakoff, 1972, 183). Lakoff's notion is that of vagueness, and degrees of vagueness, with a purpose. There have since been many studies of hedging in academic writing (Bloor and Bloor, 1993; Hyland, 1998; Markkanen and Schröder, 1997; Myers, 1985, 1989). These have been focused on modern academic discourses. The term itself has been criticised for it suggests, at least in general English, 'pejorative connotations of deviousness and self-interest'; and this is not, according to Bloor and Bloor, what the use of modifiers is usually about (Bloor and Bloor, 1993, 155). The substantive issue is that of an author legitimately moderating a commitment to a textual proposition or claim.

Myers suggests that hedging is a strategy that may be used not only because of any lack of certainty with respect to the knowledge claim that is being made, though this is one use, but, in addition, in order to show a degree of respect to others in the discourse community (Myers, 1985, 1989). 'Hedging' in this context becomes another authorial device for creating a community of interest between an author and the target or imagined reader. Making knowledge claims is, in Myers' approach, potentially threatening, as it threatens the knowledge contribution of others and imposes restrictions on what the research community can subsequently do.

Smith was not, strictly speaking, writing for an established research community. This does not mean that Smith was exempted from social interactions with peers or with actual readers through his writing. As an act of communication, writing is socially situated and subject to authorial assumptions and expectations about the imagined or target reader (Coulthard, 1994, 4). The notion of a target reader helps the analyst understand the assumptions that an author makes concerning, for example, what is taken as given (already known and understood) and what is new. In this approach, according to Coulthard, actual readers are understood to be working towards becoming the target reader. It could be argued that interpretations of the *WN* helped, over time, to create just such a specialist research community. Smith has to start somewhere and so assumptions about (target) readership and reader behaviour are therefore built into his writing. According to modern views, when hedging strategies are adopted this is so because writers are following 'rational strategies for dealing with the social interactions' involved in publishing (Myers, 1989, 3). How this works out for actual readers cannot be determined by a textual study.

The point about rational strategies in writing is one that can be explored. Rommel, for example, has shown with respect to metastylistic comments, that Smith's narrative strategies are 'deliberately adapted to the form, content and implied reader' (Rommel, 1997). According to Rommel, by drawing attention to aspects of his style, Smith is demonstrating his trustworthiness as narrator.[7] It is likely that Smith's hedging is also socially adapted to purpose.

In addition, although the term 'hedging' is a recent one, awareness of the phenomenon as an aspect of scientific writing is not. The nature of scientific writing is one that was extensively discussed from the late seventeenth century onwards within the developing institutional context of the Royal Society. Robert Boyle is credited with creating 'a rhetoric which laid the foundations for scientific communication' (Hyland, 1998, 19). Boyle and other members of the Royal Society were clear that some thought had to be given to the reporting of scientific evidence. The issue of 'veracity' and 'verification' were issues current in the late seventeenth century (Cope, 1990, 5). Even if participants in the discussion misunderstood, as Brown suggests, the role of metaphor in thought and language, a significant concern was the accurate communication of scientific results through written language, rather than directly through participant observation and demonstration (Brown, 1994). Boyle was well aware of his resort, when writing, to words and phrases such as 'it seems', 'perhaps' and 'it is not improbable', and he argued for the need to distinguish between facts and interpretations (Shapin, 1984, 495). A context for the development of scientific writing in which talk of certainty was restricted only to 'matters of fact' already existed (Shapin, 1984, 496). The language, conventions and attitudes required for the reliable communication of science were not self-evident. Even now, it takes undergraduates time to learn the conventions. Boyle, according to Shapin, tried to become a 'reliable purveyor of experimental testimony and to offer conventions by means of which others could do likewise' (Shapin, 1984, 493).[8] Being a 'reliable narrator' is relevant to thinking about Smith's writing strategy in the *WN*.

Smith may have absorbed the literary aspects of the developing scientific culture.[9] His stress on the significance of rhetoric may have also influenced his understanding of theory as a process of 'successive approximation' (Endres, 1992, 231). Although Smith was not writing an experimental report, he is likely to have been aware that he himself was writing a didactic text. It is useful to keep in mind Endres' understanding that 'it is not immediately obvious to the reader what predominant discursive mode Smith had in mind' (Endres, 1992, 223). The text is not wholly or merely a didactic text – Smith uses historical narrative as well as other forms of story. However, given what Smith says about such a text in the *LRBL* – that a didactic writer had a responsibility not to push interpretative claims further than the evidence would allow – then this and the consistency of use suggest a self-conscious strategy (*LRBL*, i.150). In this context Rommel's notion that Smith sought to be a 'trustworthy narrator' takes on added significance, as it aligns Smith to the scientific rhetoric of the Royal Society.

The notion of being a 'trustworthy narrator' also links Smith's writing in the *WN* back to issues that he explores in *LRBL*, where issues of 'character', 'civility' and politeness are recurrent themes. The issues of 'civility' and 'politeness' are not simply concerns for Smith alone, they are part of eighteenth-century notions of sociability and manners. These notions informed an array of activities, including that of 'polite knowledge' (Klein, 1994, 3–8). Politeness assumes sociability and the possibility of reconciling differences. According to Klein, it assumes intersubjectivity and exchange of 'opinions and feelings'. It also, as a technique, sets rules – such as the avoidance of 'excesses of assertiveness' in 'conversation' – 'governing the "how" of social relations' (Klein, 1994, 4). An originating champion for 'civility' and 'politeness' was Shaftesbury, though the essays of Addison and Steel were also of significance.[10] Shaftesbury's aims were, according to Klein, political, concerned with securing the Revolutionary settlement and the 'dominance of gentlemen over English society and politics' (Klein, 1994, 1).[11] Hume's contribution was that of making the systematic and objective discussion of political and economic life a subject fit for polite conversation (Phillipson, 1988, 54). Smith, who may also have been concerned with making political economy fit for polite conversation, comments on English politeness and its integration into the political discourse of the House of Lords, where what is admitted (from outside) is expected to be 'a plain, just and exact account', in keeping with its own sense of political decorum (*LRBL*, ii.251). There is direct textual evidence, in the *Wealth of Nations*, of the significance of polite sentiments. Here is Smith on 'plans' for education: 'The good temper and moderation of contending factions seems to be the most essential circumstance in the publick morals of a free people' (*WN*, Vi.f.40).

There is also reason for caution that comes from the nature of the evidence available to Smith. There are two key aspects to hedging, as established in today's literature, that may be relevant to Smith's work: politeness in discourse and the degree to which the writer is committed to a claim. The phenomenon of politeness in today's academic world is shorn of many of the social and cultural aspects of politeness in Smith's world. The word is the same but the social connotations and implications are different. Modern notions of politeness are reduced both in content and substance. The degree of commitment to a claim can be further divided, following Prince *et al.*, into 'approximators' (where claims made are approximate) and 'shields' (where the idea may be to deflect criticisms concerning over-generalisation, for example, 'perhaps') (Prince *et al.*, 1982). Established interpretations of Smith's theory of growth take Smith's commitment to it to be total, but such interpretations delete Smith's hedging.

English makes possible a range of 'hedging devices'. Myers establishes, for modern academic writing, a list of possibilities that include the use of modal verbs ('may', 'might'), the use of modifiers ('perhaps', 'probably'), the avoidance of the verb 'to be' (at least in an unmodified form) and the avoidance of factive verbs ('show', 'prove') (Myers, 1989, 13; Dudley-Evans, 1993, 136). Recent work by Hyland reviews how 'hedging' has been extended by further empirical studies to include the use of a number of other devices such as personal statements using modals, the use of a general rule, impersonal agency and direct apology (Hyland, 1998, 45).

It has already been shown that Smith avoids the use of the unmodified verb 'to be' in the opening sentence. This is how he tells the reader that a common assumption about the division of labour is mistaken:

> It is commonly supposed to be carried furthest in some very trifling ones; not perhaps that it really is carried further in them than in others of more importance...
>
> *(WN,* I.i.2)

The 'commonly supposed' suggests some other discourse, though it is not necessarily implied that a given reader shares this view. The phrase distances Smith from the proposition and anticipates a possible challenge. The episode, even if on a small-scale, is constructed dialogically within a 'response–counter-response pattern' as identified as a textual possibility by Brown (1995, 277) drawing upon Bakhtin: 'It is commonly supposed'/'not perhaps that it really is...' *(WN,* I.i.2).[12] The challenge to this general view is modified by 'perhaps'. The full passage (including the skilful use of 'we' in the penultimate sentence) illustrates a carefully hedged strategy, based upon politeness or perhaps upon the, not unrelated, classical rhetorical notion of 'decorum' and even 'ethos'.[13] If contemporary readers shared this supposition (why write it if they did not?), then the text does not confront such readers directly. Smith, by using hedging, avoids challenging sensibilities unnecessarily. The dialogism is, in this case, gentle and is only formally revealed by close reading. As with many aspects of hedging, in this example another discourse is implied, either as an authentic discourse, presumed in this case, or as an imagined one.

Eighteenth-century conventions are different, with respect to outcomes, from modern conventions, but not radically so. The authorial contexts are, however, substantially different. It could be possible, nonetheless, to take all of the categories now used in hedging in academic writing and attempt to apply them to the *WN*. Here, a limited set of examples of hedged statements in Smith will be used to raise awareness of the issues involved in making such an analysis. The examples are drawn from the use of modals, the use of modifiers, the avoidance of the unmodified verb 'to be' and the avoidance of, or moderation of, factive verbs.[14]

Hedging and the use of modifiers in the *Wealth of Nations*, book one, chapter one

In this section only three modifiers are examined: the use of 'perhaps', the use of 'certainly' and the use of 'probably'. However, Smith uses a combination of elements in his approach to knowledge claims, and some of those combinations will be illustrated in the next section. Justification for the use of these terms is drawn from the *WN*, book one, chapter one, where Smith uses 'perhaps' and 'certainly' in the context of the operation of the pin factory. Here are three examples:

> [A] workman not educated to this business (which the division of labour has rendered a distinct trade), nor acquainted with the use of the machinery employed in it (to the invention of which the same division of labour has probably given occasion), could scarce, perhaps, with his utmost industry, make one pin in a day, and certainly could not make twenty.
>
> (*WN*, I.i.3)

And again:

> But if they had all wrought separately and independently, and without any of them having been educated to this peculiar business, they certainly could not each of them have made twenty, perhaps not one pin in a day.
>
> (*WN*, I.i.3)

And at the end of the chapter:

> Compared, indeed, with the more extravagant luxury of the great, his accommodation must no doubt appear extremely simple and easy; and yet it may be true, perhaps, that the accommodation of an European prince does not always so much exceed that of an industrious and frugal peasant, as the accommodation of the latter exceeds that of many an African king, the absolute master of the lives and liberties often thousand naked savages.
>
> (*WN*, I.i.11)

There are a number of interesting features in evidence in the first example. Take the claim that pin making is a distinct trade and that it has been made so by the division of labour. This is un-hedged, even though the role of the division of labour in creating new trades is hedged elsewhere in chapter one: 'The separation of the different trades and employments from one another, seems to have taken place, in consequence of this advantage' (*WN*, I.i.4). These are similar claims but presented textually in different ways. Specialisation of machinery is hedged: 'the invention of which the same division of labour has probably given occasion' (*WN*, I.i.3).

The hedge here is 'probably'.[15] The main idea, which is that of an ineffective worker's performance, is nicely hedged: 'could scarce, perhaps, make one pin in a day, and certainly could not make twenty'. The hedging is double in that it involves both 'scarce' and 'perhaps'. 'Could' in this instance is probably not a hedge as it is the 'ability' meaning rather than the 'degree of certainty' meaning that is stressed. The whole seems to be, therefore a mixture of approximators and shield.

In the second example, the order of 'certainly' and 'perhaps' is reversed. Smith's knowledge is imprecise at this point, whereas with respect to other aspects of the case study he is backed by two sets of observations, those of others (evidenced by 'has been very often taken notice of . . .' I.i.3) and those of himself

('I have seen a small manufactory of this kind...' I.i.3). It may not be the imprecision that suggests the hedging but the degree of Smith's commitment to the knowledge. What has not been observed is the operation of the workforce 'separately and independently'. If observation is a source of knowledge, then that which cannot be directly observed may have to be carefully hedged. Conjectural propositions are, therefore, likely to be hedged.[16]

Does this hypothesis help with aspects of the other examples? There has been no observation of a pin maker making pins by himself. No authentic example is reported upon directly by Smith in his text (even if his targeted readers may be assumed to know about the *Encyclopédie* article and illustrative plate on pin manufacture, already, perhaps, indirectly referred to with 'very often taken notice of' (1.i.3; Editors' note p. 15, n. 3)). It is not unreasonable to present the trade textually as a separate trade, and to provide the division of labour as the source of the specialist activity. What about machinery? No argument has been presented about machinery and hence at this stage the knowledge claim is hedged. Smith, however, follows through with the hedging. Later in the chapter he states: 'that the invention of all those machines by which labour is so much facilitated and abridged, seems to have been originally owing to the division of labour' (*WN* I.i.8). He puts forward a reasoned case for the proposition but, again, it is a process over time that cannot be observed except in the present. However, hedging can imply the existence of a counter-argument, acknowledged indirectly by the hedge but not necessarily explicitly stated. The implied counter-argument here is likely to be that of specialist machinery as the product of individual genius (see the next section).

The same would seem to be true for the passage on the accommodation of princes and peasants. It would be difficult in practice to observe all the elements required for the comparison and specify the basis for a correct judgement. It is an imaginative idea, the comparative elements are vague, and it is one that cannot be easily observed. Hedging assists with its plausibility.

Application to hedging elsewhere in the *Wealth of Nations*

The suggestion, from the analysis of book one, chapter one, is that 'to seem' is used when a process cannot be directly observed or a fact cannot be directly verified or where some nod is required in the direction of other sources of knowledge.

It is also the case that hedging is often double and hedged phrases are often combined with 'perhaps'. Are these insights confirmed by other examples in book one? Here are some further examples from book one.

'Seems' and 'perhaps':[17]

> The difference between the most dissimilar characters, between a philosopher and a common street porter, for example, seems to arise not so much from nature, as from habit, custom and education. When they came into the world, and for the first six or eight years of their existence, they were,

perhaps, very much alike, and neither their parents nor play-fellows could perceive any remarkable difference.

(*WN*, I.ii.4)

The first hedge is 'seems to arise' rather than 'arises' and is combined with another modifying phrase, 'not so much from'. The sentence could be rewritten so that the unmodified verb 'to be' is used rather than a modified 'arise'. The second hedge, modifying the verb 'to be', is 'perhaps'. But why is the idea hedged? Well, there is no possibility of any real observation (at this stage) and Smith is, in this respect, not in agreement with contemporary views on the nature of genius. This use of hedging would be in line with earlier uses. Even if the proposition, and its supporting argument (supplied in the second half of the paragraph), is plausible, some caution is likely to have been socially necessary to get the point accepted. This much can, by implication, be textually derived, for hedging often implies another discourse. Smith was writing against the prevailing notion of 'genius' and is therefore challenging views that 'took as the bases of social order the distribution of mental faculties and the accumulation of works of genius' (Tenger and Trolander, 1994, 171). Such an insight helps explain the pattern of hedging with respect to knowledge claims made in discussing aspects of the division of labour. Smith next, however, throws caution to the wind (though there is a hedge in the use of 'scarce') and attacks the vanity of philosophers: 'till at last the vanity of the philosopher is willing to acknowledge scarce any resemblance' (*WN*, I.ii.4).

A good contrast can be made, also in chapter two, with a related and un-hedged statement: 'By nature a philosopher is not in genius and disposition half so different from a street porter, as a mastiff is from a greyhound, or a greyhound from a spaniel, or this last from a shepherd's dog' (*WN*, I.ii.5). The differences, once the initial and potentially challenging hedged proposition has been presented to the reader, can be quickly and directly observed and reflected upon, and Smith's conclusion reached.

'Seems' and 'perhaps' (again):

The policy of Europe considers the labour of all mechanicks, artificers and manufacturers, as skilled labour; and that of all country labourers as common labour. It seems to suppose that of the former to be of a more nice and delicate nature than that of the latter. It is so perhaps in some cases; but in the greater part it is quite otherwise, as I shall endeavour to shew by and by.

(*WN*, I.x.b.8)

Two of the three sentences contain hedges. The hedges are 'seems', 'perhaps' and 'endeavour to shew'. In context, it would be hard for Smith to supply hard evidence, at this stage, of the 'policy of Europe'. 'Seems' is appropriate but Smith, next, wishes to challenge the supposition. The whole episode is one of small-scale dialogism with the putative interlocutor being personified as 'the policy of Europe'. 'Seem' and 'perhaps' belong to what is conceded to the interlocutor and the 'endeavour to shew' gently points to the challenge that Smith will mount. These small-scale examples of dialogism (see earlier paragraphs) may be more common in the *WN* than has been elsewhere supposed.

'Show' is an example of a 'factive' verb and modern analysis of hedging suggests that this will be hedged. Smith frequently uses 'show' in the main text of the *WN* but in the majority of instances, where he is making claims in the first-person singular for the impact of his own writing, he normally hedges by combination with 'endeavour'.[18] Smith is hedging in order not to claim, in advance, that his writing is effective and that therefore his argument is conclusive; the success of his argument, when it is made, is for others to judge. If this interpretation is correct, then motives for hedging would come from ideas, in formal discussions of rhetoric, such as 'ethos' or 'decorum' and, at a pinch, Boyle's related notion of 'modesty'.[19]

'Seems' and 'probably':

> Of all the countries on the coast of the Mediterranean sea, Egypt seems to have been the first in which either agriculture or manufactures were cultivated and improved to any considerable degree. Upper Egypt extends itself nowhere above a few miles from the Nile, and in Lower Egypt that great river breaks itself into many different canals, which, with the assistance of a little art, seem to have afforded a communication by water-carriage, not only between all the great towns, but between all the considerable villages, and even to many farm-houses in the country; nearly in the same manner as the Rhine and the Maese do in Holland at present. The extent and easiness of this inland navigation was probably one of the principal causes of the early improvement of Egypt.
>
> (*WN*, I.iii.6)

In this example, the hedging ('seems', 'seem', 'probably') implies the possibility of another discourse: the 'best authenticated history' mentioned in Smith's preceding paragraph (*WN*, I.iii.5). The evidence could in principle be disputed and evaluated elsewhere. The knowledge also relates to a process of historical development over time. It cannot be directly observed since it refers to an age long past. But, it is something that Smith and his readers could observe in the world of his time – for this is one of the purposes of the inclusion of references, by (hedged) analogy, to the Rhine and Maese. Notice how nicely the analogy is presented: 'nearly in the same manner as ...'. Smith's precision is remarkable: 'nearly' also because these rivers gave rise to communities that engaged extensively in foreign trade. It can be assumed that he agrees with the proposition for he explores it in a related paragraph and reaches a related conclusion, also hedged: 'It is remarkable that neither the ancient Egyptians, nor the Indians, nor the Chinese encouraged foreign commerce, but seem all to have derived their great opulence from this inland navigation' (*WN*, I.iii.7). He uses the verb 'to be' in the unhedged first part of the sentence but modifies it with 'probably' and so, to some extent, maintains his position whilst not encouraging any significant opposition. He is, modestly, not claiming expert knowledge in any direct sense – he is not an author of the 'best authenticated history' – but merely making a plausible argument. The tone is one of suggesting possibilities rather than of partisan advocacy. The passage follows his advice concerning exclamation in historical writing: the argument is entirely logical and unemotional (*LRBL*, ii.38). The target reader's sensibilities are not disturbed. Dugald Stewart, an actual reader, wrote of

Smith's 'judicious' synthesis and of his 'disinterested zeal for truth', features exemplified here (Stewart, 1980, 320, 323). Few actual readers could then disagree with such a reasonable proposition, especially when made in support of a fact that can be observed in the modern world: the commercial advantages derived from location on 'the banks of navigable rivers'.

'Seems' when the knowledge is uncertain:

> The denominations of those coins seem originally to have expressed the weight or quantity of metal contained in them. In the time of Servius Tullius, who first coined money at Rome, the Roman As or Pondo contained a Roman pound of good copper... The Tower pound seems to have been something more than the Roman pound, and something less than the Troyes pound.
>
> (*WN*, I.iv.10)

The examples are from the past. This may lead us to expect some hedging but, in addition, the knowledge is imprecise, even vague. Another discourse is implied – in this case, sources on knowledge of the values of ancient coinage. In the rest of the passage 'appears' is used as a hedge. So, unlike modern-day knowledge claims in some scientific contexts where the operating principle is 'social constructionist' – where the hedging originates in a relationship between the writer and the professional discourse community (Hyland, 1998, 82) – Smith is acknowledging his target readers who share his own sensibilities and understanding (Servius Tullius is a given; that he 'first coined money' is new). Smith is also recognising the uncertain and imprecise nature of the existing historical knowledge. Here 'seems' is working as an approximator (Bloor and Bloor, 1993, 153).

'Perhaps' is complex. There are at least three different uses of 'perhaps' that can be identified in the *WN* – derived from an analysis of sixty passages (a non-random sample of the whole). These are

(a) 'perhaps' as a hedge for a potentially verifiable proposition;
(b) 'perhaps' as a hedge in a hypothetical or conjectural situation;
(c) 'perhaps' as a hedge to signal usuality or successive approximation.

Potentially verifiable propositions are normally about situations that are current but which have not yet been observed, by the author, for some reason. The conjectural context of hedging in Smith has been noticed in the early literature with respect to the contested concept of conjectural history (Stewart, 1980, 293). What the present analysis has established for 'perhaps' is that hedging is associated both with counter-factual statements and other motives for hedging. The first two uses of 'perhaps', from the list provided, are illustrated in the passage that follows. Notice that there are other hedges such as 'seems', 'probably' and the use of hedged phrases including verbs. This pattern of multiple hedging in an argument is not untypical of Smith's writing in the *WN* and is certainly not confined to Book one. The category of 'usuality' or 'approximation' is used in contexts that do not require accurate reporting. In the following passage there is only one sentence that does not contain a hedge – 'It had not got to this height in any part of Scotland before the union'. No evidence is supplied here for the claim that is being made. It is simply reported as a matter of fact:

> There are, perhaps [hedge/verifiable], some parts of Europe in which the price of cattle has not yet got to this height. It had not got to this height in any part of Scotland before the union. Had the Scotch cattle been always confined to the market of Scotland, in a country in which the quantity of land, which can be applied to no other purpose but the feeding of cattle, is so great in proportion to what can be applied to other purposes, it is scarce possible, perhaps [hedge/conjectural], that their price could ever have risen so high as to render it profitable to cultivate land for the sake of feeding them. In England, the price of cattle, it has already been observed, seems, in the neighbourhood of London, to have got to this height about the beginning of the last century; but it was much later probably before it got to it through the greater part of the remoter counties; in some of which, perhaps [hedge/verifiable], it may scarce yet have got to it. Of all the different substances, however, which compose this second sort of rude produce, cattle is, perhaps [hedge/verifiable], that of which the price, in the progress of improvement, first rises to this height.
>
> (*WN*, I.xi.1.2)

The first hedge is used for a proposition that could in principle be verified but which has not been observed by the author for whatever reason. The second conjectural proposition is a complex one and is not capable of verification by observation. It is a theoretical notion and has the status of a counterfactual. Notice that, in the second example, the full hedged phrase is: 'scarce possible, perhaps…could…'. This is a very elaborate set of hedges. Both are examples of hedging as 'shield'. There are many other hedges in the passage, including other complex patterns.

This next example contains both 'perhaps' as 'usuality' and 'perhaps' as 'conjecture':

> Taking the whole kingdom at an average, nineteen houses in twenty, or rather perhaps [hedge: usuality/approximation] ninety-nine in a hundred, are not insured from fire. Sea risk is more alarming to the greater part of people, and the proportion of ships insured to those not insured is much greater. Many sail, however, at all seasons, and even in time of war, without any insurance. This may sometimes perhaps [hedge/conjectural] be done without any imprudence.
>
> (*WN*, I.x.b.28)

The approximation is not likely to be challenged since it would be reinforced by readers' experience of the insurance of houses. The second sentence also contains the verb 'to be' and asserts an unhedged matter of fact.[20] The whole passage is about risk and estimations of risk (the 'presumptuous contempt of the risk') and not about details of the insurance market (assumed to be known to target readers) and hence the approximation is acceptable. Notice, in the first example, 'perhaps' is placed before additional information in a series of approximations. This upward progression of hedge exemplifications is encountered elsewhere: 'It [public admiration] makes a considerable part of that reward in the profession of physick; a still greater perhaps in that of law; in poetry and philosophy it makes almost the whole' (*WN*, I.x.b.24).

This wider survey confirms the use of 'perhaps' in the earlier examples. The general pattern is also confirmed. Simple, directly observable statements tend not be hedged. Knowledge that could be observed in principle, but has not been so in fact, tends to be hedged. Conjectural statements, including predictions, tend to be hedged.[21] Indeed, Smith's characteristic method of linking many stages in a chain of argument (the 'Newtonian method', according to *LRBL*) itself suggests the need for multiple hedges (*LRBL*, ii.133). Hedging is also implied by the realisation of the didactic method in writing. Propositions are hedged before they are analysed and supported by evidence. Details of Smith's argumentation are suggested by characteristic arguments. Personal claims for what the writing has accomplished or will accomplish are, with few exceptions, also normally hedged.

Hedging in Hume's writing

It may be useful, for comparative purposes, briefly to consider hedging in David Hume's writing. Smith and Hume were friends and the opening chapters of the *WN*, chapter two in particular, attest to Hume's influence on Smith. Hume's relationship with the target reader is complex. In his philosophical writing, Hume is setting out difficult and socially unacceptable propositions about what can be known. His philosophical writing is shot through with irony, or rather multiple ironies, to which an unwary reader can easily fall victim (Price, 1992/1965, 370). Smith's situational irony is gentle when compared to the variety of Humean ironic strategies, though it would be a mistake to underestimate the role of irony in Smith's writing. If we can extrapolate from what Smith said about style in his *LRBL*, he would have accounted for some of the differences between his writing and Hume's writing in terms of 'character' (itself a reflection of the notion of 'ethos').

In the analysis of the *WN* mentioned earlier, emphasis was placed on verbs and modifiers, and little attention was paid to personal statements (except with respect to Smith's claims about the success of his own writing), impersonal agency and personal apology – all of which can also be used as hedges. Given the different relationship with the target reader, when Hume hedges, the patterns and intensity of hedging are not likely to be the same as in Smith's writing.

A survey of Hume's essays classified by Rotwein as economics writing, suggests that 'perhaps' is used hardly at all. This does not mean that Hume does not hedge, for phrases such as 'no doubt' or even 'in my opinion' (strictly speaking this is direct 'authorial comment') are used, in context, as modifiers. Where 'perhaps' is used, the context is simple and no different from simple uses in Smith:

> But we may observe, that, at a time when they [arts and sciences] rose to greatest perfection among one people, they were perhaps totally unknown to all the neighbouring nations; and though they universally decayed in one age,

yet in a succeeding generation they again revived, and diffused themselves over the world.

> (Hume, 'On the Populousness of Ancient Nations';
> Rotwein, 1955, 109)

A similar simplicity is found in 'Of the Balance of Trade': 'Our tax on plate is, perhaps, in this view, somewhat impolitic' (Hume; Rotwein, 1955, 69).

The overall function of 'perhaps' is similar, at the level of the sentence, to those found in Smith. 'Perhaps' as a hedge for a potentially verifiable proposition, as a hedge for a conjectural proposition and even as a signal of successive approximation can all be evidenced from the essays, as can the use of 'perhaps' as a form of politeness. But Hume is a different writer from Smith. Here is Hume's evaluation of '*abstruse* thinkers':

> They suggest hints, at least, and start difficulties, which they want, perhaps, skill to pursue; but which may produce fine discoveries, when handled by men who have a more just way of thinking.
>
> (Hume, 'Of Commerce'; Rotwein, 1955, 3)

The proposition, that such thinkers are not capable of pursuing a topic systematically, is modified by the use of the hedge 'perhaps'; politeness is in play. However, later on in the opening moves in the same essay, Hume says of his own writing:

> I thought this introduction necessary before the following discourses on *commerce, money, interest, balance of trade*, &c. where, perhaps, there will occur some principles which are uncommon, and which may seem too refined and subtile for such vulgar subjects.
>
> (Hume, 'Of Commerce'; Rotwein, 1955, 5)

Hume is writing in anticipation of the fact that just such principles, in his own mind, will be presented. He is hedging (the 'perhaps' is supported by the 'may seem') in order to keep the reader reading on in a sympathetic way. But in the next sentence, there is a robust challenge: 'If false, let them be rejected'. There is, when read in the wider context of the developing text, just a hint that he will be both abstruse and just. This potentially undercuts the initial 'perhaps' as Hume hedges his own potentially 'abstruse' contribution whilst maintaining his reputation as a 'just' reasoner.

In the *Enquiry Concerning Human Understanding* (*ECHU*), the use of 'perhaps' is spread evenly throughout the work with only one instance recorded of 'perhaps' being used more than once in a paragraph. The uses are not implied as part of a chain of reasoning (Hume, 1975, *ECHU*, Vi.43). There are no uses that match the serial and complex use of 'perhaps' and other forms of hedging that were illustrated for Smith's writing. Of the cases investigated from *ECHU*, a significant minority were accompanied by 'may' (in thirteen of the thirty-four examples). Although there were no examples of 'perhaps' being repeated in a series of hedged statements used in the construction of an argument, Hume's simple use of 'perhaps' does not mean that the relationship with the intended reader is straightforward. Consider the following two examples, found in close proximity in the *ECHU*:

> Can I do better than propose the difficulty to the public, even though, perhaps, I have small hopes of obtaining a solution?
>
> (*ECHU*, IV.ii.32)

> I must also confess that, though all the learned, for several ages, should have employed themselves in a fruitless search upon any subject, it may still, perhaps, be rash to conclude positively that the subject must, therefore, pass all human comprehension.
>
> (*ECHU*, IV.ii.33)

Both uses of 'perhaps' are conjectural and modify the relationship with the reader. In the first example, the question is itself a kind of hedge, an apology for inconveniencing the reader. It is also ironic, for this inconveniencing the reader is exactly what Hume intends to do. And does it not also carry a hint that Hume will, in fact, propose a solution? In the second example, Hume is on the face of it, avoiding the charge of arrogance but, once again, Hume's 'shot-gun irony' is in play (Price, 1992/1965, 39). Both are examples of 'perhaps' being used in the context of a question or a personal statement (direct authorial comment) being used as a hedge. Such uses are likely to be found frequently in Hume's writing.

This survey of Hume's *ECHU* does not reveal 'perhaps' and other modifiers being used as hedges in the same serial way as in the *WN*. There is no evidence either in the *Enquiry* or in the economics essays of whole paragraphs being made up of a variety of (mainly) hedged sentences, with the repeated use of 'perhaps' in a chain of reasoning, as exemplified in selected passages from the *WN*. Hume, in distinguishing between 'particular' and 'general' subjects, makes it clear that a chain of reasoning supported by principles is significant for 'general' subjects (Hume, 'Of Commerce'; Rotwein, 1955, 3). Both Smith and Hume are interested in making such connections but differ in the ways that such arguments are realised in argumentation as exemplified by the use of 'perhaps'. However, Hume also hedges, although the predominant use is likely to be based on personal statements, apologies and questions, all potentially negated by irony. Hume's politeness may be no politeness at all.

Discussion

Hedging of knowledge claims is a significant phenomenon in the *WN*, as it is likely to be for any serious discourse but, even so, there is a sense in which Smith may be a distinctively hedged writer. The comparison made with Hume's writing is merely indicative, with respect to modifiers, rather than definitive. In the textual relationship between author and reader, hedges serve a purpose. What is that purpose in the *WN*? The answer is complex. Smith is writing a 'didactick discourse' and, ideally, such a discourse would 'persuade us only so far as the strength of the arguments is convincing...' (*LRBL*, i.149). Of course, the *WN* exhibits a variety of traits, including story telling, but the primary aims are to explain and instruct. Cope categorises Smith as 'a professional explainer' (Cope, 1990, 168). The notion of a didactic text could imply, following through Smith's own terms, caution in stating the initial proposition and some form of authorial evaluation concerning the merits of an argument. Hedging – rather than formally and overtly stating possible weaknesses in the chain of reasoning, as direct authorial comment – is one way that this can be achieved since hedging often implies other possibilities, other arguments.

Because the observation of the details of hedging, and how it works, relies on close reading, the quantity, quality and nature of Smith's hedging can be over-looked, or read as 'obvious' and not worthy of reflection. This may well be a result of Smith's rhetorical strategy; if the (actual) reader is 'led on gently' then Smith has created a text that serves its didactic purpose without drawing attention to itself as writing, at least in this respect. It is polite discourse, in the sense identified by Klein, and culturally informed by notions of agreeable conversation (Klein, 1994, 3–8). If readers do not notice the hedged nature of significant claims, a community of interest and an agreement to read on quietly has been maintained. Awareness of hedging changes the experience of reading Smith, however, as a sense of robustness gives way to some caution or at the very least some curiosity.

Given all this hedging, is Smith's 'controlling voice' still in control (Brown, 1994, 191)? The instance of double and even triple hedging that have been presented here, including the phenomenon of 'negated hedging', carried by 'perhaps' . . . 'certainly not', suggests that any analytical reading concerned with evaluating Smith's ways of arguing ought to take hedging, and its varying intensity, into account. Are we justified in 'reading out' Smith's hedges? Smith's writing in the *WN* may work on two levels, rather than one. Too much awareness of Smith's hedging can serve to undercut the argument or at the very least to promote further reflection upon it. How actual readers negotiated hedged statements cannot be derived from a textual study.

It is important to locate the interest in hedging in the relationships revealed through text, with Smith's target readers and even with Smith's sense of self. Smith chooses to hedge some knowledge statements and not others. He is able to use the unmodified verb 'to be' in making knowledge claims about aspects of the world that can be simply and directly observed, and capable of independent verification by the target reader, though even here there may well be other forms of hedging that have not been explored in this chapter.[22] Smith is more likely to hedge claims that cannot be directly observed (statements about the past, or about processes in the present, or about process that are still being worked out), either because they rely on theoretical knowledge or because the facts are not likely to be readily ascertained or because he is dealing essentially with counterfactuals. If he is concerned with making the experience of observation of the economic world available to his readers, as Brown suggests, then, hedging where such observa-tions cannot be made is a rational strategy, closely related to the objectives of the writing overall. A didactic text aims to alter the target reader's understanding. Smith's hedges, by not alienating the reader, increase his chances of rhetorical success. In this respect, Smith is exhibiting through hedging, as suggested by Rommel for metasylistic statements, evidence of his reliability as a scientific nar-rator with respect to knowledge claims (Rommel, 1997). On these counts, Smith's use of hedging is compatible with Boyle's views on the reporting of scientific observations (reliability and 'verifiability') and the distinction between 'fact' and 'interpretation'.

Some of Smith's hedging is about lack of precise knowledge. His arguments, as in the case of the output of an unskilled worker trying to undertake every aspect of pin making by himself, or in the measurement of the value of former monetary units, can only be imprecise. Sometimes hedging is about modifying claims for which he would not be seen, and would not necessarily wish to be seen, as an authority. We may suppose, from evidence elsewhere in the text, that claims about river navigation in ancient Egypt are claims that Smith believes; but they are nonetheless hedged either because he is not an authority and does not wish to be seen as one, or because the process can no longer be observed even if it can be linked to a modern one. Hedging also implies the existence of other texts and discourses, and hence hedges can be associated with an implicit dialogism.

The case for observation of some of the conventions suggested by classical rhetoric, decorum and ethos, added to by eighteenth-century notions of civility and politeness, perhaps mixed with Boyle's notion of modesty and Smith's sense of character in *LRBL*, also suggest that motivations are more complex than a simple comparison with today's writing may imply. Smith usually hedges when, using the first-person singular and fictive verbs such as 'show', he makes claims about the standing and impact of his own work as author. Decorum and ethos may be the operating influence as far as such claims are concerned. Of course, caution and politeness can work in the same direction in the sense that both maintain a sense of reasonableness.

There is more, therefore, to hedging – and to leading readers along gently – than simple questions of style. There are cultural as well as logical and evidential aspects, some found explicitly or implicitly in Smith's *LRBL*. The textual realisation of hedging and the associated motives in Smith and other samples of eighteenth-century economic and philosophical writing are not likely to be identical to those established by Myers, Hyland, Bloor and Bloor, and others, for modern academic writing. Cultural practice and personal preferences are relevant as well as the nature of the evidence available in the eighteenth century to back knowledge claims. However, as with other aspects of Smith's economics writing, the motives and purposes are likely to share some family resemblance with hedging in (say) modern-day introductory economics textbooks. The distinction between 'actual' readers and 'target' readers is also a useful distinction to make, and further work is required if we are to develop a fuller understanding of Smith's economic and philosophical writing, as writing.

7 Natural and human institutions

Reading for argumentation in book three of the *Wealth of Nations*

Introduction

The theme of book three of the *Wealth of Nations* is 'Of the different progress of opulence in different nations'. Smith carefully announces the purpose of his 'Third Book' in the 'Introduction and plan of the work' as a whole: 'Nations tolerably well advanced as to skill, dexterity, and judgment, in the application of labour, have followed very different plans in the general conduct and direction of it' (*WN* [1].7). His focus will be 'the policy of Europe', in this respect, and somewhat ambitiously, 'since the downfall of the Roman Empire'. Smith's 'Third Book' is composed of a series of chapters in which history (sometimes stylized) and narrative predominate. The content largely follows the theme of the sectoral pattern of investment and therefore follows on naturally from the last chapter in book two. This is concerned with the 'Different employment of capitals'. Smith makes the link specific in the long final sentence of the last chapter in book two. The last chapter of book two becomes a foundation upon which books three and four are constructed. The section also deals with 'natural' conditions and with the potentially contrasting 'human institutions' and the results of the analytical reading in this chapter need to be put with the results of the analysis of Smith's writing on 'primogeniture' (the subject for textual analysis of Chapter 8).

As the chapters in book three generally consist of narrative, stories of historical evolution and change, the details of the writing differ from details found in books one and two. It is only in chapter four, for example, ('How the commerce of the towns contributed to the improvement of the country') that the overtly signalled list, such a feature of the earlier books, forms part of the way in which the argument develops and the chapter is structured.[1] The list is a method of exposition that is associated with logical argument rather than with narrative. Even in this case, the list is used but once and organises not more than four paragraphs of a chapter that consists of a total of twenty-two. Book three, the shortest of the five books, is constructed by different means, including the author's need to accommodate the issue of what is already 'given' by the fact of reading the earlier books and what is now 'new'. However the book does not deal only with historical description (an unlikely proposition anyway) for it sets out an ideal model of economic development, and it follows through themes established in the first two books, including the significance of the division of labour and of the returns to stock employed in different sectors.

This chapter has two main purposes. One is to demonstrate close reading techniques and the benefits in reading that such techniques bring. In this respect the paper is part of the continued exploration of economic rhetoric though the concern is not with the application of literary criticism and/or principles of rhetoric. Rather it is an extension of the language-based approach that I have used in earlier published work.[2] The method of analysis, that is ways of reading in detail, is deliberately left exposed in what comes, in order to demonstrate the nature of the process itself. The reading is focused on understanding Smith's writing first as writing and only subsequently as economic argument. However, it is a 'neutral' reading, in the sense that the first task is to try and understand how the text is constructed. Any useful reading ought to result in increased understanding. Any understanding achieved in this chapter will be based on what is, essentially, a re-description of Smith's writing. The idea is to lay aside presuppositions and try and look directly at what could be called the 'mechanics' of the text. This is, of course, not easy and can only be achieved 'more or less' for reading is an individualised and mentally located experience. What follows is not free of interpretation for there are always both overt and covert contexts in operation in any reading.

The initial aim is therefore a modest one, which is to be able to describe Smith's writing. But there is also the aim of creating the conditions for a reflection upon the reading experience that the method brings. An attempt has been made, also, to make the paper freestanding in the sense that it can be read without Smith's text. This puts a limit on the detail that can be achieved in the writing of the paper. What follows is not all of the evidence supplied by a close reading, but an edited version or a writing-mediated version of it. Even though the aim is to be as open as possible, audience awareness and the available rhetorical skills limit what can be written. There is no attempt to create something as detailed as Richards account of the close reading process. We are not sharing directly an experience of reading: what is here is a body of writing that relates in some way to that reading. Although the reading is purposeful rather than primarily aesthetic, it still seems reasonable to reflect upon the significance of the process and of the outcomes.

Another purpose, to which the first is inextricably linked, is to further the exploration of Smith's writing as economics writing, that is his methods of achieving in writing the economic argument that he is presenting. As book three is both conjectural (chapter one) and historical (the remaining chapters), narrative is of key significance. Specifying Smith's methods is likely to prove more difficult than with respect to arguments constructed along more overtly systematic lines. Smith's writing, from my experience of working on the *Wealth of Nations*, is usually constructed with great care. I hope to be able to show that book three is no exception in this respect. However, this chapter will do this by exploring in detail the opening chapter only of book three. In this chapter Smith sets up the significant proposition that there is a natural order in the sequence of economic development that goes from agriculture to manufacturing to the development of foreign trade.

The notion of a natural order, or something akin to it, is to be found behind those mid-twentieth-century theories of economic development that suggest, either, an ideal sectoral sequence of development, or the notion of balanced growth. In the 'Introduction', Smith specifically says that 'Scarce any nation has dealt equally and impartially with every sort of industry' (*WN*, [1].7). It could be supposed that Smith is an extreme proponent of the balanced growth argument.

The paper is divided into a section on close reading as a method of analysis plus three sections (a structure that follows the conventions of an analysis of beginning, middle and end of Smith's chapter) reflecting upon Smith's writing and a reflective conclusion.

Reading and close reading: purposes and limitations

Studying the economics writing of the past necessarily involves reading. It is clear that reading is something that we normally do but not necessarily something that we normally openly and self-consciously reflect upon. An aim of the collection is to encourage reflection on how Smith's economics writing can be read, that is, a focus on the act of reading Smith. In other words encouraging detailed contact with Smith's words. At a practical level, there are differences between a reading that it meant to give a quick overview of what the text is saying (say a strategy based on skimming) and a more analytical or richer reading. Equally there are differences between analytical readings. Umberto Eco posits the notion of the naïve reader. This is a reader who is intent on understanding a text and who engages in a process of understanding that is furthered by summarisation. This could be someone new to reading the *Wealth of Nations*. Textual summarisation (notes; any reduced form of writing out what is found in the text) and the reading and writing that takes place in order to produce a reduced version helps the reader gain insight and develop understanding. Summarisation is a significant way of producing understanding and a method that is used in the preparation of introductory histories of economic thought supplemented, of course, by critical reading. Czarniawska suggests, drawing upon Frye, that such readers, intent on understanding, are 'standing under the text'. Other approaches are engaged with (say) some form of textual deconstruction and 'stand over the text' (Czarniawska, 2004, 60–61). Drawing on the work of Hernadi, Czarniawska makes no distinction between the significance of the alternative approaches that are theoretically available: they are all at the same level in terms of significance though they use different means. Whilst any particular act of reading for academic purposes will be complex, involving inter-relating many different strategies – my own approach to text analysis, whilst informed by various methods is normally eclectic – this chapter applies a language-based close reading method to passages from the *Wealth of Nations*. This means that in passages other than the discussion section at the end, the method constrains the reporting and analysis.

Close reading is one approach to the promotion of richer reading that is concerned with establishing how the text achieves its ends through language.

Its origins are to be found both in literary criticism and in rhetoric, an area of inquiry that is better-developed in the United States than it is in Britain. The initial context for the development of close reading seems to be in the study of political speeches and works of fiction. Here, it is being used to study a work that is developing a theory of sectoral growth, so at first sight this seems far from the original locations in which close reading developed.

Close reading puts the text first. What does this mean? It means treating the given text, in the case of the work presented here, passages from the *Wealth of Nations*, first. The text, and not either the author's intentions or the writings and interpretations of other scholars, comes first. So if you are saying something about the text in a close reading, the evidence for what is being said is drawn directly from the text. Close reading in this sense is not about reading (say) the *Wealth of Nations* through the *Theory of Moral Sentiments*. If we wished to make comparisons using close reading then two close readings would be required in passages dealing with similar topics. Each reading would be undertaken separately and the results would then be available for comparison. The object of study is the text and this is conceptualised as potentially powerful and its construction lacking in transparency. This power derives from the fact that the text is organised through language, images and moves. It is coherent, engaged in (say) building an argument or shaping understanding of a topic and achieves this coherence by an internal process of links and implications. If we are dealing with a persuasive text, the ways in which the text persuades is hidden or at least not immediately apparent. Adam Smith's *Wealth of Nations* in particular, has long been taken as a text that leads its readers 'on gently' (Brown, 1994, 10; Schumpeter, 1954, 185). This is often repeated as a judgement on his work but the writing strategy that makes this judgment possible is rarely specified in any detail, being based on impressions rather than on close analysis. A close reading could help reveal how this capacity is achieved through language, image and (say) reader awareness on the part of the author.

Close reading subjects the selected text to detailed or micro-analysis. The idea is that if we understand the inner workings of a small part of the longer work, we can, as close readers gain insight into the work as a whole. To adapt a phrase from Ricoeur when discussing the 'reconstruction of reality' through oil painting, 'This strategy of contraction and miniaturization yields more by handling less' (Ricoeur, 1976, 40). Whilst there could be some point in undertaking a detailed analysis of a difficult passage as an end in itself, the idea of looking at significant but small samples of text is also to gain insight into the larger span of the work. Fish talks in terms of slowing the reading process in order to capture details of textual events (Fish, 1972). The aim is to pay attention to detail, to understand how a text persuades through language and image, style or what ever is found to contribute to its inner workings. Smith's way of dealing with historical time, for example, could emerge as a significant issue. A subsequent chapter will show that Smith speeds the passing of historical time. The method of 'slow down' used below is to subject the writing to a sentence by sentence analysis based upon discrete blocks that make up the developing argument. In other words the reading is 'microscopic' (Jasinski, 2001, 92). The reading is exacting and involves studying words, word order, sentences, verb tenses, repetitions and so up to bigger passages. It involves identifying forward and backward references, the identification of textual patterns (such as those outlined in the chapter on exemplifications) and other aspects exemplified later in this chapter.

Close reading aims to specify how a particular text works to further a persuasive argument or create an alternative world, but it will increase understanding whilst also problematising it. Seeing how it works may weaken and cast doubt on it or raise other questions in relation to it. In Smith's case the subject is an argument about the 'natural order' of economic development by sector but this fits into a wider argument beyond the passages analysed. Something that could emerge from the close analysis of the passage analysed here, and of other passages in which Smith is making claims about the 'natural' is the problematic aspects of the set of ideas claimed to be, or constructed as, 'natural'. The chapter prepares readers for Smith's attack on mercantilist policies. This placing of the passages for analysis has already been done in the introduction section (earlier). Any insights derived at this level should help suggest insights and problems in a wider span of text, so part of the method is to locate the passages being discussed with respect to the longer work (see the introduction section of this chapter). The rhetorical problem is that of changing readers' understanding of the economic development processes.

As a method, close reading does not make use of paraphrasing or summarisation. Summarisation is a way of understanding what the text is 'saying'. This is a common method in writings on the histories of economic thought and skills in summarisation have to be developed. But summarisation is not taken here as part of what is required in a close reading. Its concern is the way in which, for example, language is used to convince readers that it is worthwhile entering into the world that Smith is creating. Close reading is more about what a text is 'doing'. At a simple level this prompts us to look at categories of textual organisation (e.g. definitions and defining, exemplifying, questioning, answering questions already made explicit, classifying). However, close reading goes beyond such descriptive categories to answer evaluative questions such as: 'How does this text say what it says?' and 'Why does it say what it does?' (Silverman and Torode, 1980).

'Of the natural progress of opulence': the introduction to the argument

The chapter opens with a very long paragraph and a detailed reading of the paragraph will help further understand Smith's writing. It is a paragraph that is structured in a manner not untypical of Smith. It is united by the theme set out in the first sentence and by the overall conclusion. It contains, however, within it, clusters of sentences that a modern writer would split, perhaps, into separate paragraphs, though the linkages of the resultant paragraphs would not be from lead sentence to lead sentence as Smith has constructed them. In my reading it consists of four coherent units and these are used as a matter of convenience to further an analysis. What follows here is, then, a close analysis of the whole of the paragraph based on four units that have coherence of theme.

Here are the opening five sentences that form the first of those units:

> The great commerce of every civilised society, is that carried on between the inhabitants of the town and those of the country. [sentence 1] It consists in the exchange of rude for manufactured produce, either immediately, or by the intervention of money, or of some sort of paper which represents money. [sentence 2] The country supplies the town with the means of subsistence and the materials of manufacture. [sentence 3] The town repays this supply by sending back a part of the manufactured produce to the inhabitants of the country. [sentence 4] The town, in which there neither is nor can be any reproduction of substances, may very properly be said to gain its whole wealth and subsistence from the country. [sentence 5]
>
> (*WN*, III.i)

Sentence 1 presents the topic that is sustained in the whole chapter, that of the relationship between the development of the town and of the country. The notion of civilised society is not explicated, it is simply taken that readers know, given what has gone before or from their social experience, what this means. Sentence 2 spells out the context of the trade: the exchange of 'rude for manufactured product'. It also provides a set of conventions, barter, commodity money and paper money, whereby exchange is facilitated. Mentioning a hierarchy of different means suggest a general argument. In the rest of the sentences the relationship between the town and the country is presented in balanced ways, sentences 3 and 4 in particular. The notion of 'balanced writing' would seem to be at first sight an intuitive notion rather than one that can be easily identified in linguistic terms. Here it has some to do with the structure of the sentences, for example starting with the town and finishing with the country (1 and 5). There is also the pattern of word use in sentences 2 and 3: 'rude'/'manufactured' (2), 'country'/'town' (3). Even sentence 5, which appears to challenge the balance, maintains the same overall order of the previous sentence. This also starts with 'the town' and ends with 'the country'. The final sentence in the section is one that carries with it a strong sense of physiocracy in the notion that there can be in the town no 'reproduction of substances'. The town, it implies, deals solely with transformations of rude inputs.

The opening moves, by virtue of the writing, create a sense of balance in exchange (i.e. well matched with the content). This balance in the details of the writing sustains the analytical notion that Smith is working towards. The sentence structure throughout the opening section is simple thus helping the reader into the chapter. The paragraph builds up towards more complex ideas. Lest the reader get the wrong impression from sentence 5, the next sentence makes the relationship clear, 'We must not, however, on this account, imagine that the gain of the town is the loss of the country'. This overall pattern and its conclusion in sentence 5 is significant for sentence 5 assists the development of the later stages of the argument in the chapter overall. It establishes the primacy of 'rude' over 'manufactured' produce in terms of the 'reproduction of substances'. It is the first hint of a, as yet unstated, natural order of relationships.

The next section of the paragraph begins with the sentence, 'We must not, however, . . . '. The use of the 'we' is unusual and though not as rare in the *Wealth of Nations* as might be expected. Although the *Wealth of Nations* has been analysed by Brown as 'monological', there are, as there are bound to be, instances of small-scale dialogical episodes (Brown, 1994; Henderson, 2004, 65). There are choices open to Smith concerning the relationship with the reader at this point. A neutral possibility is something along the lines of 'It must not be imagined . . . ' though such a construct may not conform to late eighteenth-century usage.[3] 'You' is a distinct possibility and Smith, in fact, directly addresses the reader in this way later in the paragraph when conclusions are being drawn. In the light of the moves made at the end of the paragraph, Smith's choice of 'we' is a strategic one whose significance will only become clear when the analysis of the end of the paragraph is made. The 'we' is to be taken to be 'you and I working together', that is, it is a co-operative 'we'.

Here are the five sentences that form the second unit:

> We must not, however, upon this account imagine that the gain of the town is the loss of the country. [sentence 6][4] The gains are both mutual and reciprocal, and the division of labour is in this, as in all other cases, advantageous to all the different persons employed in the various occupations into which it is subdivided. [sentence 7] The inhabitants of the country purchase of the town a greater quantity of manufactured goods, with the produce of a much smaller quantity of their own labour, than they must have employed had they attempted to prepare them themselves. [sentence 8] The town affords a market for the surplus produce of the country, or what is over and above the maintenance of the cultivators, and it is there that the inhabitants of the country exchange it for something else which is in demand among them. [sentence 9] The greater the number and revenue of the inhabitants of the town, the more extensive is the market which it affords to those in the country; and the more extensive that market, it is always the more advantageous to a greater number. [sentence 10]
>
> (*WN*, III.i.1)

This cluster of sentences is constructed around the notion of the division of labour, a key concept in Smith's analysis and well familiarised for the reader in books one and two. The sentences are longer than in the first unit and the language more technical than that of the first unit. Sentence 6 signals that what is coming next will be an exploration of ways in which the town and the country both gain from the exchange. Sentence 7 serves to remind the reader of the relevance of the discussion and sentences 8, 9 and 10, develop using aspects of the arguments around the division of labour, that is specialisation and links to the size of the market. Sentence 7 reinforces earlier understandings, 'division of labour, is in this as in all other cases, advantageous . . . '. The 'as in all other cases' reminds readers that this is a general proposition applicable to numerous other examples and contexts. As concepts have been extensively familiarised in books one and two, there are within the sentences no attempts to define terms such as 'division of labour' and 'surplus produce' simply to use them. Readers are being given a prompt to recall previous knowledge and to integrate their developing understanding. However, the words used to refer to the size of the market are neither 'size' nor 'extent'. The phrase 'the more extensive is the market' is the preferred way by which Smith refers to market size. It becomes clear that this is to be taken to mean the geographical draw of the market. Whilst the content deals with the principles, backward links to earlier discussions are not specifically made. The general nature of the discussion (i.e. the lack of detailed exemplification of terms, thus far) suggests the assumption that the reader is now familiar with concepts.

Here are the sentences that form the third unit:

> The corn which grows within a mile of the town, sells there for the same price with that which comes from twenty miles distance. [sentence 11] But the price of the latter must generally, pay not only pay the expense of raising and bringing it to market, but afford too the ordinary profits of agriculture to the farmer. [sentence 12] The proprietors and cultivators of the country, therefore, which lies in the neighbourhood of the town, over and above the ordinary profits of agriculture, gain, in the price of what they sell, the whole value of the carriage of the like produce that is brought from more distant parts, and they save, besides, the whole value of this carriage in the price of what they buy. [sentence 13]
>
> (*WN*, III.i.1)

This is a detailed exemplification, but of what or for what? Does the unit illustrate the 'mutual and reciprocal' gains and the extensive influence of the market in a developed town or does it serve to introduce a later point? It seems rather to be preparing the reader for the next unit, highlighted later. The three sentences form a mini case study, illustrating, if we ignore issues of rent, the advantages to agricultural producers who cultivate the land near to a town. Whilst the sentence structures are complex, the case study is very short. A lot of information is packed into sentence 13, for example, including the double advantage of selling and buying that those close to town have. The sentence concretises and locates the advantages to those 'proprietors and cultivators' that live close to the town. There is no need at this stage in the writing to define terms such as the concept of the ordinary profits of agriculture and what these imply. These have already been set out in earlier chapters, so any example can be brief and to the point.

Here are the sentences in the fourth unit:

> Compare the cultivation of the lands in the neighbourhood of any considerable town, with that of those which lie at some distance from it, and you will easily satisfy yourself how much the country is benefited by the commerce of the town. [sentence 14] Among all the absurd speculations that have been propagated concerning the balance of trade, it has never been pretended that

either the country loses by its commerce with the town, or the town by that
with the country which maintains it. [sentence 15]

(WN, III.i.1)

Sentence 14 opens with an instruction to the reader: 'Compare the cultivation
of the lands...'. Smith's writings are often built around mini exercises in
observation and comparison. Here it is the reader's role as economic spectator, a
role first hinted at in book one, chapter one, where the 'spectator' is specifically
mentioned, that is being stressed. The request for reader-activity would be unreasonable as an excursion in the middle of reading, but possible as a reflection,
given the nature of Smith's target readers. Again, by this stage, the expectation is
that the reader is familiar with the type of observation/reflection that is required,
though there are hints in the preceding sentence. Smith spells out neither the
method nor the detail, the reader is constrained to look at 'any considerable town',
but he does indicate in very certain terms the conclusion that the reader is
expected to draw: '... and you will easily satisfy yourself how much the country
is benefited by the commerce of the town'.

The instruction does not lead to an open-ended exercise in consideration and
reflection. There is a right answer, clues as to how to look are contained in the
earlier section of the paragraph. Sentence 15 re-enforces the point. Balance of
trade discussions have involved many absurdities – a reference to mercantilist
literatures – but 'it has never been pretended that...'.[5] Smith, in using the notion
of absurdity, is making a very strong evaluation of ideas that differ from his. From
elsewhere in the paragraph we have a 'we' and a 'you' and now there is a kind of
implied 'them'. The reader has a strong incentive to agree with Smith: if others
have not made this error then neither should the reader. Smith has a strong
motivation for securing the agreement for the aim of the writing is to persuade the
reader that there is a 'natural order of things' and a natural sequence in the pattern
of economic development. This understanding will become one basis for his attack
on mercantilism in book four. There is a lot of effort invested in the first paragraph
for it is the foundation upon which the rest of the chapter is constructed.

The development of the argument

The next paragraph opens with a sentence constructed on Smith's version of
'if/then' language that is frequently used in modern positive economics and to
which I have drawn attention elsewhere:

> As subsistence is, in the nature of things, prior to conveniency and luxury, so
> the industry which procures the former must necessarily be prior to that
> which ministers to the latter.

(WN, III.i.2)

The sentence corresponds to the form of 'as it is/so it is' and is to be taken as
having a role like that of a predictive 'if/then' statement in modern economics. It

frames an implication from the preceding section. The implication is that in a natural order of development, the production of conveniences will come before that of items of luxury. This reflection upon the text could be put in another way: the first part could be taken as a 'given' and the implication as a statement of something 'new'. Here we see an example of Smith's text moving from something that is accepted as uncontroversial, ('subsistance is . . . prior to conveniency') to an implication that may have to be argued for. This notion also works for the 'if/then' and 'as it is/so it is' format, and serves to make a rhetorical link between the different ways of looking at the sentence. Smith's argument is carefully built in terms of the language though there is no other basis for the claim that he is making. In a modern economics textbook, such a statement would be hedged by the phrase 'other things being equal'. It is, on reflection, almost slipping a proposition past the reader. The notion of natural conditions ('subsistence' before 'conveniency') seems by implication to suggest a set of natural wants in exchange and hence carry a hint of Aristotelian thought. The phrase 'in the nature of things' is an insert, the sentence works almost as well without it. But it reinforces the notion of a natural order and prepares the way for further discussion of 'necessity' and of the 'natural inclinations of man'. It looks innocent but has a significant role in relation to the sentence as a whole and to what is to come. Smith has paid attention to the details of the writing. This 'prior' necessity becomes the main theme in the following sentence that matches the vocabulary of the first sentence in this respect. It is also a sentence that furthers the implications ('therefore'). The next sentence continues to develop the theme and works out a further implication (also signalled by 'therefore'). The paragraph ends with a reversal that is worth looking at in detail:

> The town, indeed, may not always derive its whole subsistence from the country in its neighbourhood, or even from the territory to which it belongs, but from very distant countries; and this, though it forms no exception from the general rule, has occasioned considerable variations in the progress of opulence in different ages and nations.

Book three as a whole is concerned with the 'different' progress of opulence in different nations and Smith is alluding to the bigger plan of the book as this point. However, the general rule is maintained, such a town still derives its subsistence from some other countryside. The general rule is given by necessity (subsistence comes first, even, it must be supposed, if this is somewhere else than in the locale) but variations are found for particular historical reasons ('the progress of opulence in different ages and nations'). This sentence, not untypical of sentence length and structure in the *Wealth of Nations* as a whole, packs a lot of information and analysis into its span.

The argument develops in the next paragraph, which opens thus:

> That order of things which necessity imposes in general, though not in every particular country, is, in every particular country, promoted by the natural inclinations of man. If human institutions had never thwarted those natural inclinations, the towns could nowhere have increased beyond what the

improvement and cultivation of the territory in which they were situated could support; till such time, at least, as the whole of the territory was compleatly cultivated and improved.

(*WN*, III.i.3)

The opening phrase here is 'The order of things which necessity imposes'. This is a textual variation but picks up and expands on the earlier phrase 'in the nature of things'. Human 'inclinations' promote the natural order, but human institutions may frustrate the achievement of this order, though this is an interpretation that is not entirely justified by what is actually written. There is nothing (strictly) in the second sentence that suggests a negative judgement, though the use of the verb 'thwarted' does not leave the issue entirely open. If Smith prefers balanced to unbalanced growth this is not an implication of the second sentence as it stands. Any further interpretation at this point requires reading back to the end of the previous book and reading forward to the conclusion of the present chapter. The full significance of the impact of human institutions is not introduced until the final paragraph of the chapter.

Smith spells out, in the rest of the paragraph, how 'human inclinations' working upon given economic circumstances to allocate resources first to agriculture and then to manufacturing in accordance with the predictions and implications of natural necessity. The 'natural inclinations' are exemplified in the contrast set up between the peace of mind and relative security that is involved in 'improvement in land' and the accidents to which those engaged in 'manufactures or in foreign trade' are prone. The narrative episodes that constitute the rest of the paragraph are typical of such passages in earlier books. Smith is capable of telling a good story. The first episode is about economic risk, as has already been illustrated, and the story is constructed on the assumption of 'equal or nearly equal profits'. As the rest of the chapter is focused on the natural order of the employment of capital, the episodes must link economic behaviour and natural inclination, that is through human sentiment. The second episode is about a 'predilection' for 'the original destination of man' or the charms of the country life, a 'predilection' that holds 'in every state of his existence'. But note, that part of the charms of such a life is the 'independency which it really affords'. Smith returns to this notion in a later paragraph when he is considering the development of the agricultural sector in North America. It is in detailed links such as this that Smith, like other writers, achieves coherence.[6] (Smith is careful to specify assumptions in country life.)

Smith's skill with language in portraying the human condition, is well in evidence:

The man who employs his capital in land, has it more under his view and command, and his fortune is much less liable to accidents than that of the trader, who is obliged frequently to commit it, not only to the winds and the waves, but to the more uncertain elements of human folly and injustice, by giving great credits in distant countries to men, with whose character and situation he can seldom be thoroughly acquainted.

(*WN*, III.i.3)

Whilst the construction of this sentence may not satisfy compositional rules in the twenty-first century, it is a very persuasive account of the risks of trade under eighteenth-century conditions. Some readers may see this as an example of Smith's prolixity. To me it is rather an example of his 'economy', evidencing Smith's capacity to pack a lot of ideas and information into a relatively small compass. It follows an established compare-and-contrast method. It derives emotional force from the range of experiences that are packed into one sentence. The internal balance of the sentence is carefully contrived. Compare the limited and unelaborated potential accidents of the 'man who employs his capital in the land' (and hence the hint of stability and order) with the mounting problems of the uncertainties faced by the trader. It would seem that considerable emotional effort has been invested in the writing at this point. There is an almost breath-lessness about the sentence (try reading it aloud) and an element of iconicity. The content and the form act together to reinforce the proposition that trade is a risky business. The variable elements, 'the winds and the waves' (an example of alliteration) and the exemplified, and double-phrased, 'human folly and injustice' contrast with the fixed idea of 'land' and the firm idea of 'command'. Smith's persuasive powers are exercised throughout the paragraph. Evidence such as this, would suggest that Rothschild is right to see in the *Wealth of Nations* a whole plethora of human sentiment (Rothschild, 2001). Notice too the role of the (partial rather than impartial) spectatorial eye in the phrase 'under his view' (an idea both suggested by common sense and by Xenophon in *Oeconomicus* where Ischomachus extends a commonplace proverb and claims that 'the master's eye produces beautiful and good work') and its consequences (Pomeroy, 1994, 175).

So if the natural inclination is towards life in the country, how do towns come about? Smith does not explicitly ask this question but this next paragraph is, in effect, an answer to it and it is necessary that he does so. To do this Smith tells an idealised and general story of initial development. Towns arise because of the need for services to agriculture supplied by 'artificers' that is carpenters, wheelwrights and so on (Smith's usual cast of independent artisans) and the need of such 'artificers' to draw upon each other. 'Artificers' supply the needs of those responsible for creating subsistence output if we read back to the sentence that makes the link between the need to support necessities before luxuries. They locate near one another for convenience but they serve the agricultural sector. In the course of the passage Smith makes explicitly a statement that links him through time with 'balanced growth' theories, developed in development economics in the 1950s:

> Neither their employment nor subsistence, therefore, can augment, but in proportion to the augmentation of the demand from the country for finished work; and this demand can augment only in proportion to the extension of improvement and cultivation.
>
> (*WN*, III.i.4)

Smith's next two paragraphs explore the situation with respect to 'our North American colonies' (where land is abundant) and in already developed countries ('where there is either no uncultivated land, or none that can be had on easy terms').

In America, the artificer prefers to take any surplus and acquire uncultivated land where he can be 'master, and independent of all the world'. In already agriculturally developed societies, the artificers turn to work 'for more distant sale' that is a reasoned approach to the development of larger scale manufactories. Smith is using devices over a sequence of paragraphs (compare and contrast) that he has used elsewhere whilst furthering a narrative about 'natural inclinations'. It is easy to see why North America is used as an example: it provides a laboratory of developmental conditions.

The next paragraph in the sequence furthers the argument. The opening sentence is:

> In seeking for employment to a capital, manufacturers are, upon equal or nearly equal profits, naturally preferred to foreign commerce, for the same reason that agriculture is naturally preferred to manufacturers.
>
> (*WN*, III.i.7)

The language used in this paragraph parallels that in the paragraph that introduced the notion of 'natural inclinations'. Parallel arguments are used to effect elsewhere in Smith and they are by a number of devices, including, as in this case, repetition of lexical elements. But what is less clear is whether the 'naturally preferred' has the same force as 'natural inclinations'. There is also a kind of 'chaining': agriculture and local trade; local trade and distant trade. Smith uses this kind of chain elsewhere.[7] The repeated sections are 'upon equal or nearly equal profits' (Smith is re-enforcing an economic argument) and the double-phrased 'view and command', the latter referring to the preferences of people to see their assets. Smith, in the details of the language of the first two sentences (i.e. the repetition of phrases) binds by backwards references the paragraph to the earlier one. The writing is carefully contrived in this way to secure cohesion. The rest of the paragraph explores the question of the employment of surplus product and the role of trade and reaches the conclusion that whoever finances the trade, that is a domestic or foreign national, is of 'very little importance'.

The dramatic denouement

The final two paragraphs form the conclusion to the chapter. The penultimate paragraph is as follows:

> According to the natural course of things, therefore, the greater part of the capital of every growing society is, first, directed to agriculture, afterwards to manufactures, and last of all to foreign commerce. [sentence 1] This order of things is so very natural, that in every society that had any territory, it has always, I believe, been in some degree observed. [sentence 2] Some of their lands must have been cultivated before any considerable towns could be established and some sort of coarse industry of the manufacturing kind must have been carried on in those towns, before they could well think of employing themselves in foreign commerce. [sentence 3][8]
>
> (*WN*, III.i.8)

[The numbering is consecutive within the paragraph and not within the chapter.]

The first sentence summarises what is meant by the 'natural course of things'. The 'natural course' is a (universal) theoretical concept and so the verbs are in the present tense. The 'natural course' suggests a progressive structural transformation in which resources gradually shift away from agriculture to manufacturing and services, an idea further developed in the fifties and sixties by Kuznets in the context of a wider set of characteristics of the process of economic development (Kuznets, 1966). Sentence 2 contains two tenses: the simple present tense is used to refer to the universal natural order but the second half of the sentence uses the present prefect. The author also intrudes directly into the writing: 'I believe'. Is the status of the knowledge claims being made in the chapter as a whole overtly addressed at this point? Is this rare direct intervention by Smith designed to bolster a case that it not wholly convincing when examined through the detail of its development, assuming that Smith as author was aware of the moves that he was making? 'I believe' is both a hedging device and an authorial intrusion that may be designed to back the appeal. Another feature of the sentence is the repetition, using textual variation, of the notion of 'the natural course of things'. In sentence 3, the use of modal forms 'must have been cultivated', 'must have been carried out': the combination of 'must' and 'could' in sentence 3 together with the 'I believe' in sentence 2 suggests that Smith is overtly showing his hand. The argument is conjectural and the elements in the writing here recognise it as such. Elsewhere in the narrative, the past tense and the conditional have been used but where description is used to further Smith's argument the verbs are usually in the present tense. This is not, in my view, an accidental feature of the writing. 'Is' and the present tense suggest a (conceptual) permanence that is not carried, and cannot be carried, by 'was' or the past tense. We will need to reflect upon why this recognition is made. But in terms of what it reveals by a close reading, this reflection can only be undertaken after the analysis of the final paragraph.

The last paragraph is as follows:

> But though this natural order of things must have taken place in some degree in every society, it has, in all the modern states of Europe, been, in many respects entirely inverted. [sentence 1] The foreign commerce of some of their cities has introduced all their finer manufactures, or such as were fit for distant sale; and manufactures and foreign commerce together have given birth to the principal improvements of agriculture. [sentence 2] The manners and customs which the nature of their original government introduced, and which remained after that government was greatly altered, necessarily forced them into this unnatural and retrograde order. [sentence 3]
>
> (*WN*, III.i.9)

The past tense is again in evidence in all three sentences. Sentence 1 starts with 'But' and dramatically reverses the pattern suggested by the conjectural history. Smith has to some extent prepared the reader for this shock by revealing the theoretical nature of the earlier discussion. Sentence 2 supplies the evidence needed to buttress sentence 1. Sentence 3 offers a possible historical explanation of this perverse pattern. Notice the language: 'necessarily forced them into this unnatural and retrograde order'. Smith's evaluations are, once again, robust. There is a sense that the opposite of 'natural' (at the start of the paragraph), 'unnatural', (at the end) is somehow highly distasteful. The explanation of this lack of optimality is to be found in the 'manners and customs... of their original government'. Smith does not use the term 'human institutions' at this stage but 'government', 'manners' and 'customs' are part of what it intended by this phrase when it was introduced in the second sentence of the second paragraph of the chapter.

The chapter is thus brought to a dramatic end. But although it is a conclusion to chapter one, it serves a double purpose. The final paragraph in chapter one serves as motivator for the content and organisation of chapter two. The ending predicts the content of the rest of the book: actual historical investigation of the origins of the retrograde order in terms of 'manners' and 'customs' and 'institutions'. In chapter two, these are taken to be the development of the laws of inheritance, and surrounding legal circumstances and consequences, together with the social attitudes that accompany the institution of primogeniture.

Reflections on the method and results

It is clear from the linguistically led, rather than discourse led, close reading that a sentence-by-sentence analysis can reveal the ways in which Smith furthers his argument through specific features of the writing. The method as applied here assumes that anything that qualifies as a text exhibits cohesion and coherence. It has also been assumed without reflection that passages from the *Wealth of Nations* constitute a text. Cohesion and coherence are features that are essentially textual though in the case of the meaning of a text, the external relationships and expectations will alter meanings. What can be traced out by a linguistically led close reading are those features that are found in the text itself and no external evidence or judgements or relationships are required to make an investigation of these features. If you re-read the analysis you will find that little external evidence has been called upon to investigate or explicate the textual features. The method has been adhered to as far as possible, consistent with maintaining the reader's interests, and has not been adulterated by combination with other methods or approaches such as those suggested by intertextuality. This has required authorial discipline as it restricts the scope of the analysis but adherence to the process makes the method and its strengths and weaknesses clear. Cohesion is that feature of writing that sustains 'text-syntactic' connectedness (Titscher *et al.*, 2000, 22). Coherence is that which is taken to be 'the meaning of the text' (Titscher *et al.*, 2000, 22). Reflection (see later) is not constrained in the same way and there is every reason to encourage a translation of insights from a linguistic-led to a discourse-led reflective context.

Cohesion or connectedness is exhibited linearly following 'grammatical rules and dependencies'. Smith in his explanation of the relationship between town and country, for example, repeats the same basic pattern 'town/country' over a number of sentences in a consistent pattern that becomes over a stretch of writing a basic text pattern. The socialization of 'natural' and its connection with 'necessary' and 'must' and the strong implications that Smith chooses to work with through the lexis chosen, 'invert', 'unnatural' and 'retrograde', at the level of words, are the result of syntactical implications (necessary/must) and decisions made about subordinate dependencies. The recurrence of phrases and words help bind the text together and increase its ability to convince the reader of the strength of the case that Smith is making. Recurrent vocabulary and repeated phrases used strategically to strengthen a case is likely to prove to be a significant feature of Smith's writing in the *Wealth of Nations*.

Not all aspects of coherence, in the sense of judgements about the text's meaning, can be traced linguistically. Smith does not spend time in the passages familiarising concepts that have been worked on earlier in the work as a whole. Similarly, in the passage dealing with assets in land and foreign trade, space is left for readers to fill in the implications of 'wind and waves', the destructive nature of which is within the readers' experience, but the exemplification of the 'follies of men', specifies the particular follies as not every reader will have previously reflected on the risks associated with distant trade under eighteenth-century conditions. Readers are left to fill out the meanings where previous reading or social experiences are thought to be relevant. Nonetheless, the theme is consistently developed and Smith's overall argument is clear and sustained by a worked out strucutre. If we wanted to catch the meaning of the writing in its totality, we would need to reintegrate the results of the close reading with other parts of the given text, that is, other passages in the *Wealth of Nations* or with similar passages in other texts. There will be an opportunity to link this close reading with that with a slightly different emphasis presented in Chapter 8 in order to reach a wider set of conclusions about aspects of Smith's writing.

What insights have been gained as a result of the exercise into Smith's writing as writing and as economics writing? It is assumed in this formulation that Smith's writing is economics writing in the sense that it has some family resemblance to later economics writing. There are several aspects that ought to be considered. First, there is the issue of reflection. Second, there is the relationship between the micro-level understanding and the work as a whole and third, there is the relationship between insight generated and the wider secondary literature. Undertaking the kind of reading that is likely to lead to understanding is normally taken to require some reflection and self-questioning. The published analysis was not arrived at in one go, even if the analysis is not reported on in a 'layered' or monitored way, in the sense of 'first I thought this and then I thought that'. As part of the thinking process and of what has been gained from this way of engaging in reading, an articulation of and reflection upon insights can be helpful. Indeed the object of reading is to increase understanding and that is in the first instance located within. In trying to understand the text as an object in itself, it is also possible to gain insight into our immediate experience of the text. The reflection that follows will incorporate the aspects articulated above.

An important consideration is that it has altered my relationship with the given text. 'Slowing down' the reading experience has heightened awareness of the text as an artefact, crafted in detail by an experienced writer. Impressions and intuitions about Smith as a writer have been tested against details of the text even if the analysis arose primarily out of the text rather than having been framed deliberately by such prior impressions and intuitions. It is clear that a close reading is capable of providing detailed evidence concerning the way in which the writing is constructed to persuade. If we view Smith as engaged as writer in making choices concerning the delivery of his argument then a linguistically led close reading can help illuminate the choices made and the implications. The notion of choice here is built on Suassure's distinction between *langue* and *parole*. *Langue* refers to the system of codes or rules in a language and *parole* refers to the individual selection from the available elements in the given language. What is envisaged is the possibility of an author making active choices with respect to the content of an argument and its linguistic expression (Leech and Short, 1980, 38–39). This has been demonstrated already for the way in which the treatment of what is 'natural' has developed in the writing. Of course, Smith may have become trapped in his own insight and led down a lexical path on which the opposite of 'natural' is 'unnatural', and all that the idea of unnatural is associated with carried along in its train. His follower, Dugald Stewart, held whilst reviewing the notion of conjectural history that 'the real progress is not always the most natural' (Stewart, 1980 [1794], 296). It may be worth recalling, when reflecting upon the significance of Smith's views on the 'natural order' of sectoral development, Viner's published lectures on 'The Role of Providence in the Social Order'. In the third lecture, Viner, in a passage that is not directly nor textually indirectly connected with Smith, uses two quotes from Aquinas (un-referenced) as follows:

> [T]he higher a thing is the more self-sufficient it is; since whatever needs another's help is by that fact proven inferior.
>
> A city which has an abundance of food from its own territory is more dignified than one which is provisioned by merchants.
>
> (Aquinas quoted in Viner, 1966, 39)

It is perhaps easy to see why Smith held the agricultural sector in esteem as the basis, historically and in the world in which Smith lived, for sustained development. Agriculture was significant in size as a sector and liable to fluctuating output. The expansion and contraction of agricultural output and the impact of this on food prices and demand more widely would have an impact on the level of economic activity as a whole. It would be prudent to secure the home base before building manufacturing on foreign food supplied. Elsewhere, Smith was very much impressed by the significance of inland trade to national well being. But an important part of Smith's arguments about foreign trade would be that there should be an international market in 'corn'. If domestic provision means domestic self-sufficiency at the level of the producer then what is traded is an annual surplus then the economy would look more like that of Aristotle – that is trade based on the 'natural needs' of the household – than the economy that Smith seems to be arguing for in the work as a whole. Is there a lingering presence of scholastic thinking in the way that Smith conceptualises the 'natural' in the context of sectoral development?

It has been assumed that writing a robust text calls for reflection, choice and a sense of purpose. Smith will take his conclusions forward to later sections of the book – it has already been shown how he links one chapter to another in a clear and consistent way through the closing and opening sections of each chapter – and use them as a basis for his argument against mercantilist economic policy so we can assume a strategic purpose in his writing.

The insights gained on the use of 'natural' in the passages analysed can be compared with Smith's use of 'natural' and related concepts such as 'nature' and 'human nature' in the development of arguments elsewhere in his writing. A proposition that can be made even with the evidence currently available is that 'nature' and 'natural' are likely to be used in different though related ways and that in some contexts the use will be problematic. Forbes, writing many years ago, put the process thus: 'The "Natural Order" accommodated progress and progress became "natural" ' (Forbes, 1953–1954, 645). There will be choices as to how the use can be investigated for example, through the words used in close association with the notion of 'nature' or 'natural' at the level of the phrase and through an analysis of the argumentation at a unit of analysis above the phrase. The methods chosen will depend upon the questions being asked or the purpose that is being pursued. Such an investigation is of significance for understating Smith's ideas on the stages of economic development and the nature of human motivation and agency. Smith locates agency in human nature and especially in the *Theory of Moral Sentiments* constructs humans as operating under a situational irony in which they are duped to carry on working and accumulating long after their basic needs for shelter, food and clothing have been met. 'Nature' in that context carries with it not only the sense of 'human nature' but 'Nature' itself that is something overarching and possibly God-like (see the chapter on 'Irony and Economic Agency'). In addition, Smith creates the world anew with his idea of 'the system of natural liberty'. Close investigation of what Smith takes 'nature' to be and how he employs the term in various textual or discourse contexts is of some importance for understanding.

In addition, noticing a phenomenon at the micro-level can lead to a bottom-up analysis in other areas as well. A number of examples from the reading can be provided. One such is the role of the 'eye' and 'the spectator', also revealed in the close reading, in the *Wealth of Nations*. The role of the spectator is a significant macro-level feature of *Moral Sentiments* but is less visible at the macro-level in the *Wealth of Nations*. The 'spectator', synechdochies of spectator and spectatorship and synonyms relating to 'seeing', may have, nevertheless, a micro-level and less transparent presence. Thus, in book one chapter one, Smith talks of the ways in which a small-scale manufacturing process can be seen and understood by 'the spectator' in a way that more roundabout methods of manufacturing can not. Whilst there may be an accumulation of instances, these may not be observed in routine reading. Close observation has the potential to raise the profile and to further questioning. Direct observation in economic management is recommended by Xenophon in his *Oeconomicus* in the already quoted phrase translated as 'the eye of the master's eye produces beautiful and good work'. In this phrase the 'eye' itself is an economic or managerial agent, appoint made even clearer in the originating proverb developed by Xenophon in which the response to the question 'What fattens a horse most quickly?' is 'his master's eye' (Pomeroy, 1994, 175). This respect, as in other respects, such as with the Platonic notion of the burden of wealth, Smith seems to be adapting aspects of an ancient discourse to modern circumstances. With additional details from a number of instances, elsewhere in the text, it would be possible to question how Smith constructs through the details of the writing, the act of spectatorship and how he transforms in detail spectatorship from an event into something almost metaphysical.

Another micro-level concern is Smith's handling of time and the difference between an historically constrained proposition (one that is transitory and evidences in a particular set of historical circumstances or modes of subsistence) and a time-less or analytical proposition. What is significant (here and elsewhere) is likely to be Smith's employment and manipulation of verb tenses and how he works with stretches of time or how he conceptualises for the reader time passing. A textual exploration of this has the potential to add to our understanding of the textual real-isation of conceptual history. Further evidence will be provided in the next chapter of how Smith manipulates language to collapse the passage of time and the working out of historical processes into a comparatively short span of writing.

Awareness has been altered in other respects. It is understood in the wider literature that Smith tells stories, that is that narration is a significant part of the way he constructs his writing and relays his message to his readers. What this close reading has revealed is that effective 'stories' can be one-sentence long, as is the case in his contrast between investment in land and investment in long-distance trade. Other examples can be found in the *Wealth of Nations*. A par-ticularly well-painted one-sentence story, an example of 'small-scale sentimental exchange' between, in this case, the writer and the reader, involves the fears of a mother: 'A tender mother, among the inferior ranks of people, is often afraid to send her son to school at a seaport town, lest the sight of the ships and the conversation and adventures of the sailors should entice him to go to sea' (*WN*, I.x.b.32). Whilst this 'mother' is not identified socially as of the same class as Crusoe's mother, the concerns of both mothers are similar. In context the story is effective in making Smith's point that risk, evaluated negatively by the mother, can sometimes be seen as attractive and so potentially evaluated positively by the son.[9] In both of the examples Smith is working on the relationship between human sentiments and economic activity and is moving the analysis close to real-ity through story telling. Readers are both instructed and entertained, engaged both intellectually and emotionally. It is perhaps as well to be aware that Saint-Fond, a contemporary of Smith, admired Rousseau's capacity to conduct 'the reader to reason and truth by the attraction of sentiment, and the force of conviction' (Force, 2003, 22). Smith's *Wealth of Nations* is an instructive text but as will be illustrated also in Chapter 8, bringing together reason and story is a characteristic method of engagement in it.

This analysis of risk in long distance trade is constructed as a narrative and located in human nature. It is also told in a way that helps readers identify sympathetically with the risks involved. The sentence-long story exhibits connectivity and internal contrasts. The elaborations are based on what a reader may be taken to understand without setting out implications ('wind and waves') and where the reader may need help to fill out the details (the explication of 'follies' in the less well-known context of trade). The close reading has highlighted micro-aspects of narrative as a textual possibility with smaller units of analysis than may otherwise have been expected. From this basis it is relatively easy to think of other examples, such as the mother, in a seaside town, worrying about her son choosing a life of risk at sea, and so build up a case for a text constructed along the 'sympathetic' response. Smith locates economic life in human nature and his understanding of human nature and the significance of the sympathetic response would suggest that a 'human interest' dimension to his economics writing would help draw readers into the world that he is creating through his writing. His primary aim is no doubt analytical but micro-story telling will keep readers involved in a sustained basis with the imagined world that he is shaping. The 'slowed down' approach reveals narrative details, sentimentally constructed, that can then be integrated with knowledge of Smith's argumentation derived from other readings such as Rothschild's *Economic Sentiments*.

8 Adam Smith's construction of 'History' and 'Story'

The analysis of primogeniture

The Wealth of Nations makes extensive use of historical evidence. As a result, Smith has been considered as the 'fountainhead', not just of formal economics, but also of economic history. Smith had a view about the construction of history, expressed in his *Lectures on Rhetoric and Belles Lettres*. History is a matter of both entertainment and instruction. Of interest are the actions of men, causes and effects. As to the ordering of the narrative, it is to follow the historical order. How does Smith construct history in writing, and how is history used in the *Wealth of Nations* to further his project?[1] By what means does Smith, with respect to history, lead his readers 'gently' by the hand (Brown, 1994, 10; Schumpeter, 1954, 185)?

In this chapter, linguistic evidence, drawn from book three, chapter two of the *Wealth of Nations* will be used to throw some light on the devices Smith uses to relate historical circumstances and conditions – or what will be shown to be a kind of historical sociology – to economic motivation and economic analysis.[2] The chapter is not primarily concerned with the veracity of Smith's historical understanding nor is it an exhaustive treatment of how Smith constructs and uses history. These are the concerns of historiography and have been explored, for eighteenth-century historical writing, by others (Braudy, 1970; O'Brien, 1997; Spafadora, 1990). Illustrating ways of reading Smith and of exploring how Smith constructs his text, continues to be the focus. Hence a selected text-based exploration of how Smith uses history, mediated through language and story, to further the development of his argument concerning the natural progression of economic development. The chapter is not heavily historical, in the way that his writing on the 'progress of the value of silver' is historical (*WN*, I.xi.e-j), rather it uses brief historical episodes to further an analysis.

The work presented here is based on selected passages from book three, chapter two. It uses discourse analysis techniques of mixed origin, sometimes drawn from linguistics, sometimes drawn from narratology, depending upon pragmatic opportunities created by inspecting the data. Such a pragmatic mixture of methods exemplifies the notion that any authentic reading experience is likely to be mixed (Czarniawska, 2004, 60–61). It aims to illustrate ways of carrying out a detailed reading prompted, in this case, by looking at how a story is told.

This chapter first introduces some notions concerning narrative. It then contextualises chapter two, in the context of book three of the *Wealth of Nations*, in order to locate the writing in a macro-context. A brief reflection on the uses of historical argument, drawing upon examples from elsewhere in Smith's writing, is then provided. An overview, of the content of book three, chapter two, follows. The results of the close analysis of the paragraphs on 'primogeniture' are then presented and this leads to a reflective conclusion. The constraints on close reading imposed in Chapter 7 have been removed, to some extent, and some attention is paid to the text as discourse, that is more attention is given to extra-textual aspects such as shared assumptions and understanding between the reader and the writer or the manner and tone of the passages as well as the existence of other texts, including the passages on primogeniture in *Lectures on Jurisprudence*. Exploration of how Smith gently moves his readers through his argument continues to be relevant.

Narrative and the *Wealth of Nations*

Smith's *Moral Sentiments* contains knowledge and insights that are narratively constructed. This has been illustrated in the chapter dealing with irony. The *Wealth of Nations* does not sit comfortably within a traditional genre category as it is divided between the development of abstract concepts deemed to exist through time (such as the principle of the division of labour) and narrative passages that deal with the substantive, located human condition. Such a divide is not now seen as clear cut as it was in the recent past and so, in this respect the application of literary techniques to the *Wealth of Nations* is no different from the developing understanding that arises out of the application of literary and rhetorical techniques to economics writing or scientific writing more generally. Challenges to genre categories in literary criticism made it possible 'to analyse numerous texts' which prior to the challenge 'would not have been considered works of literature at all' (Chamberlain and Thomson, 1998, 30). The fiction/non-fiction distinction is of less significance that was once the case and this blurring is exploited by Motooka in her work linking 'quixotism', rationality that is also a kind of madness, to Smith's notions of 'wonder' and 'imagination', by way of a reconsideration of the relationship of reason to sentiment. This is a realignment that was also explored, later and in a different way, by Rothschild (Motooka, 1998, 1; Rothschild, 2001). McCloskey's application of literary analysis to formal economics writing benefited, as did Henderson's notion of 'literary economics', from the changed understanding within literary criticism of the nature of writing (Henderson, 1995; McCloskey, 1985). In the previous chapter it was established that stories can exist in units as short as a sentence though a line between fictional example and sequenced story is difficult to draw. Paragraphs and spans of paragraphs are required for the detection and analysis of sustained stories. Sometimes a story is likely to be supporting an analysis. Sometimes the story will be a mixture of fact or analysis and fiction.

Although there are many approaches to the notion of narrative, of key significance is the ordering of events in a sequence (Fisher, 1987, 58). Sequence is not enough for in order for something to be narrated there has to be more than a mere list of events in chronological order (Todorov, 1990, 28). A text such as the *Wealth of Nations* is likely to be composite, made up of factual and fictitious elements. Fictitious elements project a 'world' such as the world of 'natural liberty'. Events in such a fictitious world need to be tied together in a way or ways that shape a meaning that is not available simply through the establishment of a sequence (Jasinski, 2000, 390; Todorov, 1990, 28). The expected linkages in a narrative are both with respect to chronological time and the causal linkages of discreet events (Todorov, 1990, 28). Plots supply the structure and these can be considered conventionally and actors carry the action. Jasinski, drawing upon Aristotle, outlines a conventional structure for a story in terms of the '. . . introduction of characters, rising action and introduction of complication, development of the complication, climax or discovery of how the complication can be overcome, and denouement or final resolution of the complication' (Jasinski, 2000, 390). The narrative should, in addition, move towards a 'satisfying conclusion'. The satisfactory nature of a conclusion to a story will depend in part on cultural assumptions. Sentiments and emotions will have a part to play in the ways by which stories are constructed and evaluated. Any application to the *Wealth of Nations* would require the identification of stories and other fictions (including examples) and then the exploration of narrative constructs within the stories told.

There is a cultural preference in modern-day stories for a disrupted time sequence and for stories in which there is no specified single act of closure. Such methods of telling stories are less relevant to the cultural context in which Smith himself was writing. Smith is aiming to persuade his readers of his analysis or of his point of view. There is business to be done and as this business is about furthering understanding of how an economy works or how wealth is created. There is an end point and this implies closure. In this sense Smith's writing is instrumental. His text is didactic. Stories create a world within the text. The stories may look like worlds beyond the text or they may not but the narrator must encourage the readers into the world that is textually created. But there is the added notion of transformation of the world beyond the text, and this is both an idea linked to story telling and to Smith's purpose as a writer. How that world is experienced over time and how the past influences the present are suitable subjects for narratives.

Although the analysis that follows uses a number of techniques, including that of text patterns, the passage will be used *primarily* to illustrate how concepts associated with narrative may help us deepen our understanding of Smith's writing.

Book three and the context of chapter two

An analysis has already been made of book three, chapter one. This was seen as a conceptual chapter that sets out the notion of a 'natural order' in the sequence of economic development. Smith is contextualising his work in the 'natural law' tradition. Smith uses this tradition to effect in his analysis in book three, chapter two. The 'natural order' of sectoral development supposes that agricultural improvements come first, followed by the growth of towns to serve the rural community, then the growth of towns for more distant trade and finally the robust development of foreign trade. Smith holds that this 'natural order of things' to have been 'entirely inverted' in European countries by the enduring influence of the 'manner and customs which the nature of their original government introduced'. The political order that came about after the fall of Rome led to feudalism and feudalism is the source of the institution of primogeniture. This is a theme first explored in the *Lectures on Jurisprudence* (*LJ* A, i.116). Smith is concerned with the exploration of why European countries were 'necessarily forced' into 'this unnatural and retrograde order'.

The three chapters that follow are ordered in line with the overall sequence of historical events as mediated through the sequences suggested by the model. Chapter two is concerned with the discouragement of agriculture after the fall of the Roman Empire. Chapter three outlines his theory of the growth of towns. Chapter four focuses on the interactions between the development of towns and the development of the countryside. In this respect Smith is making a consistent analysis that is in keeping with the notion of the progressive nature of towns, held by writers such as Voltaire, Hume and Robertson, as places that challenged the feudal economic and political order (O'Brien, 1997, 11). Smith's concerns are conceptual and analytical and these macro-concerns tend to be reflected in micro-aspects of the writing.

The uses of historical argument

Persuasion is likely to be at the heart of the matter, for Smith has only a limited range of objective evidence (i.e. various types of observations and exemplifications) to support his economic arguments. The range is: current, observable situations; situations in the present that have been observed by other writers and that can be checked, given time and resources, by observation; limited statistical data; other evidence from history. Historical evidence cannot be easily checked but, where the text points to (say) other texts or something generally accepted as historical evidence, it is of a different order of evidence than pure conjecture.

Smith uses the past imaginatively as, for example, in his story, *elsewhere*, of the evolution of the division of labour in a tribal society.[3] (See Chapter 2 of this work.) This society could be located, both, in the present (since different stages of development are experienced in different parts of the Smithian world) or in the past, but since he is dealing with an evolution, the past is the more likely location.[4] The story goes from low levels of division of labour to higher levels, but Smith is less interested in 'before' and 'after' (i.e. start point and end point) and more interested in illustrating the process of change. Conjecture, then, is one way in which the past is used. Whilst human nature is founded on certain propensities and predispositions, particular behaviours and values will be determined by economic conditions and historical circumstances (*MS*, V.1.4). The conjectures can be varied but a significant element is the development of notions that can be broadly labelled as the natural history of mankind. Thus in the story of the ways in which the division of labour could come about, he is presenting what he sees as a plausible account of a developmental process that can no longer be observed but can be imagined by the exercise of what he would have called 'the fancy' or the imagination (*WN*, I.ii.3). It is in the past but cannot easily be identified as history as it points to something other than a specific and retrievable historical event. This same drive to construct a plausible account is in evidence (see later) in the passages on primogeniture.

Chapter one of book three provides another and more extensive example of this, but with more significant historical narrative. Smith constructs, using a few simple propositions (at the core is the fact that subsistence production of food comes first in the production chain) a theory of development according to 'the natural order of things' (*WN*, III.i.3). This 'natural order of things' is used to develop a sectoral theory of growth and the evidence is based upon humankind's need for food. Out of a mixture of historical speculation, an examination of human inclinations and human nature and limited contemporary evidence, Smith constructs his theory of sectoral growth. Smith reaches the conclusion that the 'natural order of things' has not been the European developmental path.

We are faced with a situation in which the past leads to an unsatisfactory present. Smith has a means of undertaking an exploration of the past, but the comparisons are not likely to be based on a simple 'then and now', 'compare and contrast pattern'. His ideal model of development provides the means whereby the past can be analysed and evaluated. Thus he is not engaged in comparing and contrasting 'then' with 'now', for the 'retrograde' order is experienced 'now' as a result of 'then'. He is engaged in comparing what 'was' and 'is' with what could have been or ought to have been. By using theoretical constructs, Smith, in his historical explorations is, and remains, a social analyst of a scientific bent. Smith has set up a hypothesis in the form on an ideal and is using history as a means of showing why that ideal was not realised in Europe. Smith is not interested, here, in general history or history for its own sake. His aims are instrumental.

But how is all of this realised in writing? Smith in paragraph three of chapter one sets up a potential contrast between what is supported 'by the natural inclinations of man' and what happens as a result of 'human institutions' (*WN*, III.i.3). These human institutions are capable of thwarting the natural order. At this stage Smith does not tell us what these institutions are. At the end of the chapter, in the closing moves of the final paragraph, Smith makes his dramatic statement about the European pattern of development as 'unnatural and retrograde'. In the process he tells us that the developmental path was influenced by '[t]he manners and customs which the nature of their original government introduced, and which remained after that government was greatly altered...'. Smith is looking towards the development of a historical analysis that focuses on 'institutions', 'manners and customs'. Smith does not specifically say that this is what he is doing. By this stage in the reading, the target reader is likely to expect, given the signalling processes encountered in books one and two, that the end of one chapter can be used to set up the starting point for the next chapter.

Overview of chapter two: context and content

So what does Smith mean by 'institutions', 'manners and customs'? What Smith means by these terms is exemplified throughout chapter two. There is a range of specific and historically located examples. What follows, here, is a series of topics loosely organised along lines suggested by the terms used by Smith and presented as a list. 'Institutions' can be taken to be legal institutions though these are sometimes linked to 'origins'. 'Manners and customs' are taken here to refer to attitudes and behaviours. Attitudes are emotional or mental and would normally be, in a modern-day context, inferred or interpreted from behaviour. Present behaviours (an observable) can, in the method of 'conjectural history' pursued by the Scottish Historical School, be read backwards into past history, provided circumstances are similar.

Here, then, is the edited list. It is 'edited', because one of Smith's features as a writer is his economy. That his writing exhibits 'economy' of expression, may seem paradoxical to modern-day readers who no doubt find his work rather to exhibit prolixity. Nevertheless, Smith can pack a lot of analysis and discussion into a short account. It is drawn from book three, chapter two, with the individual items set out in the order that they appear in the chapter and then allocated, as the result of the reading, to one or other of the categories outlined above.[5]

> [T]he origins of the alienation of land after the fall of Rome or in Smith's terms '[t]his original engrossing of uncultivated lands' [institutions]; primogeniture and entails; the natural law of succession[institutions]; the nature of power [institutions/manners and customs]; the universal preference for the 'male sex'[manners and customs]; security of possession; [institutions]; 'the pride of family distinctions'[manners and customs]; noble birth as 'a necessary qualification' for 'the enjoyment either of civil or military honours' [manners and customs]; great proprietors and their desire for ornamentation; [manners and customs]; the occupiers of land (tenants; yeomanry) [institutions]; slaves, slavery and the attitude of slaves [institutions/manners and customs]; *metayers* [institutions]; *long leases*; [institutions]; rent; [institutions]; purveyance; [institutions]; tallage, the taille and taxation in general [institutions/manners and customs]; 'the general prohibition of the export of corn' and other 'absurd laws'[institutions/manners and customs].

Although this is a list of diverse topics, the chapter is coherent for the central theme is well developed and the sequence of paragraphs follows a discernable structure and builds to a clear outcome. Existing institutional arrangements, and the manners and customs that are implied by them, (including, e.g. the institutions of slavery and near slavery) do not lead to an efficient allocation of resources in the agricultural sector. Such institutions are inefficient. Smith's interest in improvement and commercialisation is founded on his notion that agricultural produce should be available the poor as cheaply as possible in line with natural justice. Unimproved estates do not contribute to this equitable outcome.

In order to explore Smith's writing in this chapter, two paragraphs within it will be subjected to close analysis. The passages deal with 'primogeniture'. This is a significant topic for it follows up his analysis of the development of the 'natural' progression of economic life explored in Chapter 7. This is not the first time that Smith considered primogeniture. He makes a more detailed and more fully historical analysis of it in *Lectures on Jurisprudence* (*LJ* B, 163–165). The passages on primogeniture, from the *Wealth of Nations*, will be analysed sentence by sentence. However, just as there is 'no complete list of the linguist properties of text; therefore we have to select the features of study', so the notion of selection is unavoidable (Leech and Short, 1980, 70).[6]

The passages on primogeniture

The introduction to the principal paragraph on primogeniture is found at paragraph two, and the main 'theoretical' passage is found at paragraph three. Paragraph two sets up the problem and details the causes:

> This original engrossing of uncultivated lands, though a great, might have been a transitory evil. [sentence 1] They might soon have been divided again, and broke into small parcels, either by succession or by alienation. [sentence 2] The law of primogeniture hindered them from being divided by succession: the introduction of entails prevented their being broke into small parcels by alienation. [sentence 3]
>
> (*WN*, II.i.2)

Sentence 1 is setting up a problem, that of the 'engrossing of uncultivated lands' and signals that the problem is significant, a 'great...evil'. Sentence 2 shows how the problem could have been eliminated. Sentence 3 sets out the causes of the problem. Sentences 2 and 3 together signal the structure of the sequence of paragraphs that follow. 'Primogeniture' and 'entailments' are fixed in the reader's mind as the source of 'evil'. There is some reinforcement in the reading in the play between 'natural' and 'unnatural' and 'good' and 'evil', given what was written at the end of the preceding chapter about 'unnatural and retrograde'.

The causes of the problem are subject to analysis, in subsequent paragraphs in the order signalled by sentence 3. One way to look at this is in terms of textual patterns. The pattern within this paragraph is 'problem – significance of the problem – causes of problem' rather than a fully developed 'problem–solution pattern'. A fully developed pattern, in a modern interventionist text would go something like 'problem, significance, causes, consequences, intervention, solution, evaluation'. The whole of this extended pattern is not found in the paragraph under review nor is it found in the chapter as a whole. The chapter consists of a discussion of the causes of the problem in terms of 'primogeniture' and 'entails' as well as of the social consequences in terms of 'customs and manners' that both lead to. Nonetheless there is enough to classify the rest of the chapter in terms of 'problem, significance, causes and consequences'. Not quite a 'problem–solution' pattern, then, but something close to it. The subsequent paragraphs evaluate the outcome of this section, 'primogeniture', as a new 'problem'.

A significant amount of attention has already been given to this kind of textual pattern in Smith's writing (see the chapter on 'Exemplification Strategy'). Another reading can be achieved through identification of the narrative elements in the passage. What do we see, in addition, if we also look at the passage with narratology (however simple and underdefined) in mind?

Here is the whole of the next paragraph:

> When land, like movables, is considered as the means only of subsistence and enjoyment, the natural law of succession divides it, like them, among all the children of the family; of all of whom the subsistence and enjoyment may be supposed equally dear to the father. [sentence 1] This natural law of succession, accordingly, took place among the Romans, who made no more distinction between elder and younger, between male and female, in the inheritance of lands, than we do in the distribution of movables. [sentence 2] But when land was considered as the means, not of subsistence merely, but of power and protection, it was thought better that it should descend undivided to one. [sentence 3] In those disorderly times, every great landlord was a sort of petty prince. [sentence 4] His tenants were his subjects. [sentence 5] He was their judge, and in some respects their legislator in peace, and their leader in war. [sentence 6] He made war according to his own discretion, frequently against his neighbours, and sometimes against his sovereign. [sentence 7] The security of a landed estate, therefore, the protection which its owner could afford to those who dwelt on it, depended upon its greatness. [sentence 8] To divide it was to ruin it, and to expose every part of it to be oppressed and swallowed up by the incursions of its neighbours. [sentence 9] The law of primogeniture, therefore, came to take place, not immediately, indeed, but in the process of time, in the succession of landed estates, for the same reason that it has generally taken place in that of monarchies, though not always at their first institution. [sentence 10] That the power, and consequently the security of the monarchy, may not be weakened by division, it must descend entire to one of the children. [sentence 11] To which of them so important a preference shall be given must be determined by some general rule, founded not upon the doubtful distinctions of personal merit, but upon some plain and evident difference which can admit of no dispute. [sentence 12] Among the children of the same family, there can be no indisputable difference but that of sex, and that of age. [sentence 13] The male sex is universally preferred to the female; and when all other things are equal, the elder everywhere takes place of the younger. [sentence 14] Hence the origin of the right of primogeniture, and what is called lineal succession. [sentence 15].

> (*WN*, III.ii.3)

Smith's writing is highly persuasive and the writing is reader-aware and reader-oriented. Sentence 1 illustrates this in a number of ways. The inheritance of land, which is in the reader's experience based upon primogeniture, is compared with the inheritance of moveables, which in the reader's experience is based upon a division among 'all the children of the family'. This is an argument that uses experience to make comparisons. The agent in the sentence is 'the natural law of succession'. The specific context is that of the wider tradition of 'natural law'. There is also a textual link, given the reader's previous reading, to the argument concerning the primacy of subsistence developed in the preceding chapter and to the notion of a 'natural order' of economic development. However there is a double phrase 'subsistence and enjoyment', and this double phrase, suggested by a passage in book three chapter one about 'predilections', is repeated later in the sentence. Another emotional context is added, 'may be supposed equally dear to the father' that is in the context of 'natural law', 'manners and customs'.[7] The sentence makes both a rational argument 'when land, . . . is considered as the means only of subsistence . . .' to which is added an emotional appeal, 'equally dear to the father'. The link to sentiment and human interest allows the reader to reflect on experience. The link is between the natural primacy of subsistence and justice represented by the sentiments of the father. The use of the present tense is forceful, for Smith will later suggest that given contemporary conditions of security of tenure then the 'natural law' of succession should apply.[8] The construction of sentence has a hint of 'as it is . . . so it is' or, perhaps it is more like 'if/then'. The timelessness implied by the 'is' is significant.

Sentence 2 moves from a timeless theoretical statement of sentence 1 to an active historical example, 'among the Romans'. The 'accordingly' points out the consistency of Roman practice with the natural law principle. In terms of 'story' this is the original condition, a good state in line with natural law and with cultural assumptions about the Romans, as a people to be admired. The potential inheritors are classified into 'elder and younger' and 'male and female': this spells out the understanding of what constitutes, 'all the children of the family' presumed 'equally dear' in the previous sentence. Attention is again drawn to the reader's own experience (shared): 'who made no more distinction . . . than we do in the distribution of moveables'. The Romans are approved of and the reader knows that in the earlier passages the state of Europe after the barbarian invasion is constructed as a kind of fall from grace. The 'we' and implied 'they' provide readers with an emotional link to past experience. Human behaviour is situated in a historical and a contemporary context.

The historical experience is reversed in sentence 3, 'But . . .'. The initial condition is disrupted. There is no specified agent who is considering the status of land, nor of reaching a conclusion concerning inheritance. The sentence has abstract elements and it is a theoretical proposition of, almost, the same order as that outlined in the first paragraph. The principal verb is in the past tense: the historical conditions are in the past, and so the principle is not an enduring one, even if the condition is. This will be seen in the first sentence of the next paragraph where Smith argues that laws continue long after their historical justification has gone. Another double phrase is used, 'power and protection' to describe the conditions that (theoretically) gave rise to primogeniture ('descend undivided to one'). However agency is implied. 'Considered' and 'thought' imply a thinking subject though this subject is not identified. Thomas Aquinas, who thought through the issue of property, both private and communal, in the context of natural law thinking and of Aristotelian thought, sees property as an extension to natural law by 'right reason'. In this sense Smith also sees human institutions as the product of human reason. Smith's sentence locates the development of a set of institutions in this way through the cognitive verbs, 'consider' and 'think'.

In sentences 4–7 the time period is not carefully delineated though in the context of the whole chapter it is clear that it refers to the 'disorderly times' after the fall of Rome. The disruption (the need to consider 'power and protection') gives rise to complications. A new agent is introduced: 'every great landlord' and the role equated with that of a 'petty prince'. 'Great lord' or 'great landlord' or 'landlord' are well-worked phrases in the *Wealth of Nations* thus far and the reader by this stage is aware of Smith's criticism of landlords as a class. Smith could have written the sentence otherwise or even omitted the sentences numbered from 3–8 without significant disruption to his argument, at this point. Reading forward, the characterisation of the 'petty prince' as one in possession of military and law-making powers makes Smith's switch from landed estate to monarchy easier. The detailed parallels have been made without specifying them as such. Its construction is also influenced by Smith's stance on landlords and the prejudices of his readers. This agent is part and parcel of 'those disorderly times' and the activities here exemplify the disorder and the need for protection and support the proposition put forward in sentence nine, rather than the thinking subject. In the sentences that follow it is the 'petty prince' that is carried by the repetition of 'He'.[9] Although the timeframe is vague, the agent is thus exemplified as concrete. A human actor is identified and readers can bring their own ideas to the text for example in deciding how to interpret 'petty prince'. This gives a tangible presence that passes, well enough, for an active and peopled version of authentic history.

In sentence 5 a move is made from 'tenant' to 'subject' (this is in parallel to the move from 'great lord' to 'petty prince') and in subsequent sentences, the 'petty prince' is reconstructed within the 'master–subject' role. This is in essence a small-scale biography of a life of action. In a sense the categories of the present are used to move the reader into the past. Although the phrases are not used, the sentences are dealing with both 'manners and customs' and 'institutions'. The set of sentences, from 5 up to 9, are concretised examples of 'those disorderly times' (a huge span of historical time dealt with in a few simple moves), mentioned in sentence 4. Sentences 4–9 exemplify 'power and protection' stated in sentence three.

The next set of sentences deals with the institutional outcomes or consequences of the unsettled conditions. Sentences 8 and 9 are the immediate conclusions of the sequence: that the landed estate should not be divided. Sentence 10 examines the institutionalisation of primogeniture, as the preferred method of maintaining an undivided estate. Is this the moral of the story thus far or a conceptual villain? The move from 'primogeniture' to 'monarchies' is quickly made.

The details of sentence 10 are also interesting. It is an implication of sentences 8 and 9 ('therefore'). There is a complex pattern of hedging and an element of vagueness in the phrase 'came to take place, not immediately, in deed but...'. Smith is not interested in the detailed evolutionary process, only in general principles. The sentence starts from a past location and works forward ('came to take place') and from the future and works backwards ('has generally taken place'). In addition, its construction has some similarities to that of sentence 1, for Smith moves the reader from the wider discussion of landed estates to the narrower discussion of 'monarchies' (one landed estate). It is an argument by analogy as well as a simplification, for there are problems in establishing a clear historical turning point. By substituting 'monarchies' for 'landed estates' (or real princes for 'petty princes') the principle can be illustrated in a concrete way without providing any precise historical detail. Readers are capable of creatively filling in the gaps or of reading on. Even the hedging, 'not immediately, indeed' (for primogeniture) and 'though not always at their first institution' (for monarchies), is impressive and, if anything, adds to the authenticity and validity of the move. The reader is as familiar with 'monarchies' as he or she is with the 'moveables' in the opening sentence, and so the question of detailed historical exemplification can be sidestepped. In making the move from 'landed estates' to 'monarchies', the verb shifts from the awkward and awkwardly located, but convenient, 'came to take place', to 'has generally taken place'. Smith seems to imply that the evidence at this level is more directly available though he again hedges 'generally' and 'not always at their first institution'. What Smith is interested in is the inheritance rule. In effect we have a micro-argument based on comparisons in which the language is closely worked to gain acceptance of the propositions offered.

Sentence 10 transfers the discussion to that of the institutionalisation of primogeniture and the focus shifts from a landed estate to a kingdom. The nouns 'power' and 'security' follow thought the 'power and protection' of sentence 3, adding to the unit of the paragraph. Sentence 11 repeats the arguments for undivided inheritance, now for monarchies. This is another example (already illustrated in Chapter 7 for the notion of what is 'natural') of the kind of parallelism that Smith is fond of. The tenses gradually switch to the present tense, as general principles (in this case of custom and manners) are discussed. Sentence 12, which should, perhaps, also be read ironically, for Smith's longer term aim is to secure a market in land open to 'personal merit', states the need for a simple 'general rule' founded upon 'some plain and evident difference which can admit of no dispute'. In this story, Smith omits any reference to Rome and the inheritance problem for one emperor to the next where latterly personal characteristics were important. The double phrase, something that Smith has a fondness for, is again in evidence. Sentence 13 establishes the principles of difference: 'sex and age' and, in a sense, refers back to the classification of family members found in sentence 2. Smith proceeds step-by-step. Sentence 14 establishes in 'manners and customs' (though this phrase is not used) why primogeniture and lineal succession is settled upon: '[t]he male sex is universally preferred to the female'. Smith does not seem to notice that he started the paragraph with a different set of 'manners and customs' under the 'natural law of succession'. It could be that contextually 'now' or 'under the circumstances' are implied. Smith is relying on general cultural knowledge for the validity of the claims or perhaps on a 'universal' aspect of human nature but this thwarts the opening claim about the 'father'. But then, what is written, is, otherwise, carefully hedged. The 'human interest' aspects of the story are maintained, though in a much modified form as the principle comes more into focus and the biographical elements gently dropped. Notice that in the case of sentence 14 this is accomplished by that essentially modern phrase, so much part and parcel of formal economic argument, 'when all other things are equal'.

Primogeniture in *Lectures on Jurisprudence B*

Smith drew upon earlier ideas in creating the *Wealth of Nations*. His *Lectures on Jurisprudence*, touch on primogeniture in a number of places. When it is first mentioned, primogeniture is described as a 'method of succession, so contrary to nature, to reason and to justice' (*LJ* A, i.116) and later, mixed in with an abundance of historical detail, Smith hints that 'the right of primogeniture and the power of making entails have been the causes or the almost total bad husbandry that prevails in those countrys where they are in use' (*LJ* A, i.167). The recency of primogeniture in the German 'principalities' is also noted (*LJ* A, v.137; *LJ* B, 96). Smith sees primogeniture as against natural justice. The case is two fold. All children ought to have a right to inherit so that there is equality of access to landed property. The argument, by interpolation, is that the poor have a right to the fruits of the earth and these are supplied more cheaply from well-run estates that is estates that are subject to good management brought about by the possibility of market-led transfers as opposed to neglected or unimproved estates that sustain only the 'vanity of families'(*LJ* A, ii.3).

Primogeniture is given sustained treatment in the student report on his lecture on 'Private Law' (1766) and it is convenient to use this report for comparative purposes because it is developed in a span of writing similar in content and length to that as published in the *Wealth of Nations*. The context is that of the legal arrangements for the acquisition of property and the historical contexts (guided by the stadial theory of development) in which legal arrangements emerge. The report shows, in a related passage, that Smith holds that primogeniture 'hinders agriculture' as well as being 'hurtfull to the family', except in the case of monarchy. Although the passages concerned with primogeniture have more direct historical examples 'France', 'Germany', Tartary and 'Rome' with respect to countries and 'Bruce' and 'Baliol' with respect to personalities – the central propositions are very similar but are expressed in less concise and focused ways. Primogeniture is located in feudal conditions and in the context of military service. The discussion is concerned largely with rights and procedures and details of legal arrangements, but historical circumstances are not lost sight of. Thus the opening sentence of the main paragraph:

> It appears from this that it must have been a very difficult matter to secure property, especially if it was small, in those early times, and therefore nothing could have a worse consequence than the division of estates.

The evolution of primogeniture is based on people's experience but this is also left vague. Thus the 'consequences of dividing the kingdom of France were sufficiently experienced' (161). The agents are deleted. The process of institutionalising the rights of primogeniture are both more specific than in the later version in the *Wealth of Nations* but remain vague: 'on account of the opposition from the rest of the sons it was long before the right of primogeniture or the indivisibility of estates could be introduced...'. Plausibility is therefore also an issue with respect to the account given in the lectures. Historical circumstances forced the issue and 'estates were at last made indivisible' and the 'oldest son' was selected as the natural inheritor. Smith's use of 'naturaly' in this context must be contextualised within the notion of an 'indisputable' attribute. He is clear about the unsuitability of the alternatives: 'If it were to be given to wisdom or valour there might be great disputes, but among brothers they can be no contest who is the oldest'. Women are already excluded, we are told earlier, because of the link between feudal property and military service.

Although there is content in common between the passages in the *Wealth of Nations* and in the *Lectures*, the structure of the passages that deal with primogeniture are very different. In the *Lectures*, Smith appears to make no effort to activate previous knowledge or experience on the part of his audience. His lectors were students rather than adult readers. The material is unidirectional, factual and comparatively empty of dramatic and human interest. In the *Wealth of Nations*, as has been shown above, the reader is given opportunities to activate existing knowledge and to develop an emotional relationship with the passage. The writing in the earlier work is much looser and the narrative more complex in the senses of more filled out by examples of principles and practice. This reflects the assumed lack of experience on the part of the intended audience. If we consider audience and macro-purpose, it is clear that the passages in the lectures could not be transferred directly into the *Wealth of Nations*. Smith's lectures were no doubt written down by Smith to be spoken. When it came to publication, revision and re-contextualising was necessary. Reconsideration of purpose, intended audience and macro-context was essential to the rhetorical success of the new text. It would seem, from the evidence presented above, that the passages taken down in 1766 represent a key stage in the transition from the passages in 1762–1763 and the final version as published in the *Wealth of Nations*.

Outcomes of the reading

Smith, in book three, chapter two, is not interested in the past for its own sake. He is interested, primarily, in the world of his day and of understanding that world in terms of the conceptual framework that he is developing. Smith is also concerned with bringing the reader to the same understanding. It is interesting to note, in this respect, that Mill, who set as his objective for his *Principles*, the same comprehensiveness as Smith did, chose to outline the historical development of society (in ways that Smith would have recognised) in the 'Preliminary Remarks' to his principal work on economics and specifically constructed the feudal period ('that age of violence and disorder') in similar terms to Smith's (Mill, [1848] 1929, 9–19). The past is a source of evidence both, depending upon circumstance, for understanding of that present and for a demonstration of the validity and power of the few simple propositions, in line with the Newtonian approach to explanation that is found elsewhere in the work. The philosophical context is that of natural law and of institutional formation.

Yet, Smith's writing gives the impression of historical authenticity. The reader is carefully manipulated into sympathy with Smith's point of view. Something akin to the process that he describes seems acceptable. It would be difficult and indeed unnecessary to specify a 'realistic' account of the historical changes and processes, though Smith had already set out at least the elements of such an account in his *Lectures on Jurisprudence*. A more detailed history, such as found in the 1762–1763 version of his lectures, would not be appropriate given the macro-context of the version in the *Wealth of Nations*. Instead, Smith constructs a story, an analytical and philosophically informed historical fiction that represents the processes that he is interested in. By situating an agent or actor, an illusion of reality is created whilst conforming to the expectation that history is the history of 'the actions of men'. There is also entertainment value as the reader is drawn into the account emotionally and experientially. The passage is structured along a time line that goes from the Romans, through feudalism, to modern times in accordance with Smith's own views that a historical narrative should be ordered by historical time. The impression of authenticity is created by the details of the writing. The switch from theoretical ideas (no human agent present) to concretisation (gendered agent present) is one detail that adds a sense of a historical narration and drama. Events are tied together in a small scale narrative through human agency.

The move from 'stative' to 'active' and the pattern 'non-story/story' is one that McCloskey has derived from Prince and used to illustrate story in economics (McCloskey, 1994, 331). Smith is operating in just such a manner, punctuating story with analysis, in a pattern of cause and effect. The small-scale pattern reflects Smith's analytical purpose and his views on historical narrative being concerned with cause and effect as well as his insight that to generate understanding on the part of the reader is more likely to be achieved through sentiment as well as reason. The moves from 'every great landlord' to 'He' are executed with skill. It is this capacity to relate historical and institutional conditions to human action (or to convince the reader that such a link has in fact been made) that enriches the persuasive power of the writing.[10] There are sustained hints of Smith's dislike of feudalism, an attitude shared with other historians of his time, such as Voltaire, whom Smith admired, (O'Brien, 1997, 11) and exemplified in passages in *Lectures on Jurisprudence*, in the characterisation. Indeed Smith's concern for the liberating effects of the rise of towns and the erosion of feudalism is a general theme in the historical works of Voltaire, Hume and Robertson. Although the 'petty prince' may well be self-interested, the interests of the estate and those who live on it mean that there is a group interest. There is however no hint of a 'social contract'. The original government is imposed. Smith is vague about the means, in detail, whereby the new arrangements emerge, that is, how group interests actually emerge or how a landed estate becomes a political community, either in itself or part of a kingdom, but the story suggests iterations and social adjustments. A similar vagueness is found in passages dealing with the transition in *Lectures on Jurisprudence*. The writing side-steps the notion, found in Robertson and Voltaire, that feudal society 'was really only an archaic set of local jurisdictions incapable of generating a political community' (O'Brien, 1997, 111). Whole stretches of time and periods of history are ordered into a very small space. Such economy is found elsewhere in the *Wealth of Nations*.

The persuasive nature of the text is amply illustrated, also, by the relationship between the experience created in the text and that of the expected or target reader. Thus the repeated pattern of close analogies (like 'movables' and 'monarchies') and the shared experience, between author and reader, to which these point, in an effort to link the past directly with the present and vice versa. Smith familiarises past possibilities in terms of the reader's experience of the present and allows the reader to participate in the process by working backwards, for example, from the known to the less known in keeping with the spirit of conjectural history. Such devices engage the reader directly and repetition adds to the unity and familiarity of the argument. Smith mixes theoretical analysis with a small-scale human interest story, producing a text that is subtle rather than forced. The repetition of textual elements gives the paragraph coherence and the use of double phrases ('power and protection'; 'oppressed and swallowed'; 'plain and evident') add to its dignity. The story is tightly constructed and analytically focused (in contrast with the account of primogeniture given in the *Lectures on Jurisprudence*) to fit with the wider strategic aims of the writing. Smith's vagueness, his manipulation of the verb tenses and hedges also add, paradoxically, to the authenticity of looking at the broad sweep. Readers are given vantage point from which to view the argument. These aspects help secure the integrity of the argument. The sociological speculation, typical of Smith's writing about hunter–gatherers and pastoralists in the context of the stadial theory of development, is in evidence in the details of the writing. The whole passage is carefully crafted to construct an acceptable 'situated rationality' (Lawson, 1997) as a means of illustrating how institutions emerge and of suggesting, by drawing attention to changed historical circumstances, how they can be altered. An altogether reasonable impression is created that 'it must have happened like this'.

As in most passages of Smith's writing there is both more and less there than meets the casual eye. By undertaking a close analysis there is a sense of detecting Smith at work in writing the *Wealth of Nations*. Smith uses the historical episode to instruct but is careful to introduce an emotional dimension to draw in the reader through shared experience of family life and cultural norms. The character and actions of the 'petty prince' helps paint a picture and adds an element of spectatorship and potential enjoyment. The passage, albeit in miniature, incorporates some of Smith's suggestions concerning the writing of history delivered up in his *Lectures on Rhetoric and Belles Lettres*. The mixture of historical and natural law arguments and contrasting republican and monarchical values, carried by or contested by, various characters – 'the father', 'the petty prince' – point out the extent of Smith's commitment to the realisation of conceptual thinking in a written format that makes it easy for the reader to engage. The concretisation and personification of change lowers the level of abstraction and gives the illusion of lived lives. McCloskey identifies just such narrative moves in discussions about economic models in the context of economics seminars and largely for similar reasons, to provide meaning by giving a sense of 'being there' (McCloskey, 1990, 15). Smith's passage on primogeniture, given its recurrent reference to male agents ('father', 'great landlord', 'petty prince', 'monarch' – not gendered in itself but associated with 'maleness' and the 'male sex') remains embedded in the context of primogeniture.

Smith's approach to argumentation has, in a sense, not changed from that of books one and two. The fact of their existence changes the context. Smith's target reader has already experienced those books.[11] The earlier process of socialising terms, making illustrations to particular contexts or building up arguments are all now givens. Readers by this stage are socialised in the role of spectator and at looking at ideas from the vantage points that Smith creates for them. The context of book three is the more demanding one of the broad sweep and of economic development as a whole. The expected reader is moving to bigger issues and Smith's writing is constructed to make this transition easy. The encoding of the message has been accompanied by attention to the details of the writing whilst keeping the bigger rhetorical purpose in mind. Only enough narrative is provided to fix the principles, unencumbered with country-specific or period specific detail, in contrast with the material delivered in his *Lectures on Jurisprudence*. History is used nevertheless to challenge contemporary institutional arrangements.

The basis of Smith's approach to history, institutions and social consequences in book three, chapter two, is rooted in the natural law tradition, in the widest sense that the good things of this world are to be made available to all of human kind. The force of the chapter is that the historical conditions that gave rise to primogeniture and entailments have passed and that the impact of the remnant institutions on contemporary society is detrimental to agricultural development, a proposition also put forward in *Lectures on Jurisprudence*. Smith is also demonstrating in the act of writing, a kind of 'situated rationality' that has many of the elements that Lawson identifies in his 'critical realist' approach to agency and choice (Lawson, 1997). Smith's account is both narratively and deductively constructed. Smith merges agency, historical conditions and narrative to generate an understating of significant institutions. Anything approaching significant historical evidence or detail is, in this chapter, lacking and the treatment of time is entirely fictional and subservient to the plot.

The overall story is that of a fall from republican grace where Roman republican virtues were in line with the natural law of inheritance. In this passage there is no final denouement, in the sense of no resolution of the conflict between primogeniture and the 'natural law of inheritance'. 'Primogeniture' is explained by the story (or the story thus far) so there is a stable outcome. But the message or moral of the story is still clear. The present is the outcome of a recent past in which monarchies emerged and found the basis for a stable social and economic order, but the distant past, republican Rome, did it better. The detailed analysis of this passage has revealed the effort that has gone to its construction and shows in miniature a much bigger and wider theme of that of republican and monarchical manners in the *Wealth of Nations*. It also shows that in the relatively small-scale passage subjected to close analysis, Smith has re-plotted book three, chapter one. An unsatisfactory present, in which land monopolisation and stability of monopolised holdings distort consumption and production patterns and the natural order of development, is the result of past historical experience.

Notes

1 Reading the *Wealth of Nations* and Smith's other writings

1 This needs to be glossed. Hume made it into political and economic discussion with respect to monetarism when this was a contentious policy option. Hume and Locke are likely to feature from time to time in political journalism in the quality press. I doubt if the frequency or potency is as great as that of Smith. This is essentially an empirical question and my statements are based on impressions only. *The Times* article under reference mentions Locke.

2 Smith's thumbnail sketch of the mother worrying about a son's potential to run away to sea has a cultural parallel in the description of the concerns of Crusoe's mother (*WN*, I.x.b.32). Smith drew on emotional images that readers of his day would have immediately identified with.

3 I am currently exploring the possibility of such a text-based project with Professor Susan Hunston, a colleague, in applied linguistics, at the University of Birmingham.

2 How does Smith achieve a synthesis in writing? Evidence from his analysis of the propensity to truck, barter and exchange

1 Thanks go to Warren Samuels and Roger Backhouse for comments on an earlier draft.

2 A similar charge was made, in the nineteenth century, against Locke whose philosophy was described as 'unoriginal and a mere unacknowledged plagiarism'.

3 Rothbard wrote later and claims that Smith 'originated nothing that was true, and whatever he originated was wrong; that [Smith] was a shameless plagiarist, acknowledging little or nothing and stealing large chunks, for example, from Cantillon' (Rothbard, 1995a, 435).

4 Hutcheson also stressed propensities in human nature to social action.

5 'Passion', as an eighteenth-century notion, suggests a range of phenomena: pain and pleasure, instincts, propensities, emotions and sentiments.

6 Smith can change perspectives as he does elsewhere, according to Ahiakpor, in looking at the whole subject from the point of view of the 'statesman or legislator' (Ahiakpor, 1999, 370).

7 Elsewhere Smith demonstrates an awareness of the contrasting ways (Mandeville versus Rousseau) of depicting the 'life of a savage': 'a life either of profound indolence, or of great and astonishing adventures' (*EPS*, p. 251).

8 Buckle also argues that Hume's Newtonianism is over-stated (Buckle, 2001).

3 Nature's dupes: irony and economic agency in Smith's writing

1 It should be noted that Smith uses the phrase 'ingenious and agreeable philosopher' to refer to David Hume in a sentence that sings Hume's praise as a writer (*MS*, IV.i.2).

This, when taken together with associated ways of talking that he has an authentic philosopher in mind when he writes of 'the splenetic philosopher'. Additional evidence supplied by the editors of the *Moral Sentiments* can be drawn in to suggest Rousseau.

4 The political economy of *Castle Rackrent*: Maria Edgeworth and Adam Smith

1 I thank Roger Backhouse, Dinah Birch, Vivienne Brown, Tricia Cusack, Kevin Down, Sebastian Mitchell and Andrew Skinner for their valuable comments made on an earlier draft.
2 Irony, as a rhetorical concept, merges at the margins with sarcasm, mocking, banter and satire.
3 Whether with the same mocking tone has not been investigated here.
4 Smith had an impact on subsequent economics writing. Ricardo (1817) thought out some of the details of his principles as a critique of Smith and Mill (1848) still refers directly to some of Smith's views. Ricardo was also critical of landlords. Mill views 'Great landowners as everywhere an idle class' (1848 book two, chapter five, para. 2) and draws attention to the inefficiencies of agriculture under conditions of monopoly.
5 Smith's knowledge of the Scottish economy should not be exaggerated. He probably knew less about Scotland that did Sir James Steuart, a writer that Smith makes no reference to in the *Wealth of Nations*. The *Wealth of Nations* is not a parochial work, references to America are almost as extensive as references to Scotland.

5 Exemplification strategy in Adam Smith's *Wealth of Nations*

1 I thank Vivienne Brown, Ann Hewings, Warren Samuels and Sebastian Mitchell for comments on earlier drafts of this paper.
2 Contemporary judgements were not always favourable. Walpole, no great lover of Scottish philosophers, found the work, according to Ross, badly written and repetitive (Ross, 1995, 250).
3 There is a very special quality to Smith's use of examples. It is the business of the rest of this paper to make that quality explicit. But there is nothing to match it in, say, the economics writings of Hume, another very clear writer. Hume was engaged, however, in writing essays on economic topics and not a complete discourse. Smith pays the same attention to examples in his *The Theory of Moral Sentiments* where he is concerned with the relationship between philosophy 'and ordinary life' (Griswold, 1999, 22).
4 This use of examples is complex and may be developed within a framework that is referred to in the wider literature on Smith as the method of 'conjectural history'. This method is one in which 'principles established on the basis of observed facts' are used to explore 'events where facts were not readily available' (Skinner, 1972, 308). However, 'hypothetical examples', in the sense used here, can be contrived out of direct evidence; that is they can have an iconic quality.
5 Most of Smith's readers will never have seen a highland village so in this respect he is providing a substitute experience of 'observation' (Brown, 1994, chapter seven).
6 Both Deleyre and Diderot had already published on the 'Pin' in the *Encyclopèdie* (Still, 1997, 71).
7 Indeed the notion of social life as a 'spectacle' and the individual as both 'spectator and spectacle' has been seen as a significant metaphor in Smith's other major work, *The Theory of Moral Sentiments* (Brown, 1997, 286; Griswold, 1999, passim). In the passages analysed here from the *Wealth of Nations*, the notion of economic life as a wondrous spectacle can also be found, so that once again, 'spectator and spectacle' are brought together.
8 'Compare and contrast' is to be taken as a general descriptor of a repeated textual pattern. However, each occurrence is adapted to the specific context or argument being made.

9 Smith in his *Philosophical Essays* points to the role of 'wonder' and its temporary consequence of 'giddiness and confusion' in exciting philosophical investigation (Skinner, 1972, 309; Skinner, 1983, passim). The long last paragraph of chapter one with its exclamations and quick-fire list of examples suggests a rhetoric of wonder, excitement and perhaps even giddiness.

10 Smith's formal text influenced a number of creative writers. Harriet Martineau produced in 1832 her first tale illustrating political economy, *Life in the Wilds*, in which the theme of 'economic progress' is considered from the perspective of a 'modern' group that has fallen on hard times in 'the south of Africa'. One of the manufacturing processes that helps the group discover the significance of specialisation and the division of labour is the making of arrows. This is both an example, and a developmental context, suggested by her reading of Smith on the division of labour, chapter two paragraph two in particular. This is further evidence of the forcefulness of Smith's examples for his initial readers.

11 Keynes, in 1936, used the language of natural propensities, in the form of psychological propensities to set up a relationship between increases in income and increases in consumption. The meaning of Smith's 'propensity to truck, barter and exchange' is open.

12 Smith's example points up the significance of rhetoric for economic life in a specific context of exchange (i.e. the language of buying and selling, though in modern-day capitalism the emphasis is on the language of selling) but the idea is perfectly general. The division of labour and the emergence of specialist roles implies the emergence of specialist languages, for example think of the consequences of the application of the division of labour to the work of 'philosophers'. The English language expanded its vocabulary during the eighteenth century as a result of international trade.

6 A very cautious, or a very polite, Dr Smith? Hedging in the *Wealth of Nations*

1 West notices one aspect of the hedging (if this is the correct interpretation of italicisation of 'greatest' and 'greater') but does not notice the 'seems'. He does not otherwise draw any attention to the hedging (West, 1964, 24). Rosenberg notices Smith's hedging with respect to his view of slaves: 'Slaves...are very seldom inventive; and all the most important improvements, either in machinery, or in the arrangement and distribution of work which facilitate and abridge labour, have been the discoveries of freemen' (Rosenberg, 1965, 131; *WN*, IV.ix.47). Rosenberg also notices a link between hedging and conjectural history (Rosenberg, 1965, 133). Rosenberg does not explore the issue of hedging more widely.

2 Stewart states that Smith's conversational style differed from his writing style. The full passage is: 'But, in the society of his friends, he had no disposition to form those qualified conclusions that we admire in his writings; and he generally contented himself with a bold and masterly sketch of the object, from the first point of view in which his temper, or his fancy, presented it' (Stewart, 1980, 331). This extra-textual evidence suggests that Smith was a reflective writer.

3 A similar instance can be drawn from Hume's 'Of the Jealousy of Trade'. This opens with the following sentence: 'Having endeavoured to remove one species of ill-founded jealousy, which is so prevalent among commercial nations, it may not be amiss to mention another, which seems equally groundless' (Hume; Rotwein, 1955, 78). Hume suggests that it 'seems' groundless to look upon trading neighbours as necessarily rivals, but uses the rest of the essay to show that it is, in fact, groundless.

4 This pattern is found for chapters as a whole, see for example chapters one, two and three in book one where the pattern is very clear (though there are other textual patterns within each). It can also be found within paragraphs where a hedged proposition, developed as part of a wider argument, is stated and then justified by evidence.

5 In book one, chapter two, the opening sentence assumes that the case has already been argued: 'This division of labour, from which so many advantages are derived...' (*WN*, I.ii.1). This is an example of the link between didactic writing and hedging.

6 Details of Smith's writing, for example, the use of the phrase 'if one may say so' and closely related varieties of it, have been explored by Rommel who reaches the conclusion that Smith is concerned with building a sense of 'trustworthy narrator' (Rommel, 1997). Rommel does not investigate knowledge claims but, rather, Smith's use of vivid images.

7 Smith's authorial comments can be provocative and far from polite (see Brown, 1994, 192–193).

8 Boyle also recommended a 'naked way of writing' that avoided being trapped by preconceived ideas founded on other texts (Shapin, 1984, 496–7). The experiment was more important than references to other systematic texts. Could such views have influenced Smith, given the scarcity of citations in the *WN*?

9 A collected edition of Boyle's *Works*, edited by T. Birch, was published in London in 1772 (Shapin, 1984, 511).

10 Stewart refers to Smith's interest in 'polite literature both of ancient and modern times' (Stewart, 1980, 305).

11 Smith found Shaftesbury to be a shallow thinker (*LRBL*, i.136,140). Smith is scathing about Shaftesbury's style: 'Polite dignity is the character he aimed at, and as this seems to be best supported by a grand and pompous diction that was the Stile he made choice of' (*LRBL*, i.146).

12 Such small-scale examples of dialogism are likely to be found in other places in the *WN*.

13 The concept of decorum is one explored in Cicero's *Orator*, a work that Smith refers to in his *LRBL*. According to Jasinski, decorum is difficult to define but it can carry the idea of appropriateness to subject matter, audience and occasion (Jasinski, 2001, 147). Ethos is another concept that seems simple but can become complex. It is a notion 'used by Aristotle to refer to the ways in which the perceived attributes of a speaker, manifest in discourse, are persuasive' (Jasinski, 2001, 229). Thus Rommel's view of Smith's stance can be integrated with both notions. Smith's use of 'we' suggests that he, too, modestly shares in the potential failure to understand the significance of the observation. The 'we', in the passage cited, creates a community between himself and the reader and does not then put the reader at a disadvantage. There are other ways of creating such a community. For a detailed analysis of passages in *WN* and TMS containing 'I' and 'we' see Brown (Brown, 1994, 28–45). Smith accepts in *LRBL* that Cicero's 'character' is able to 'shine out...thro all his writings', so although 'ethos' does not seem to be directly mentioned by Smith in the passage on Cicero, the author's 'spirit and mind' shines through (Brown, 1994, 10; *LRBL*, ii.2334).

14 A factive verb commits a speaker to the truth of a proposition contained in a subordinate clause. Some verbs are factive ('show', 'know') and others not ('think').

15 When the statement is repeated later in the chapter 'probably' is replaced by 'seems': 'I shall only observe, therefore, that the invention of all those machines by which labour is so much facilitated and abridged, seems to have been originally owing to the division of labour' (*WN*, I.i.8). The recurrence of hedging increases the sense of cautious claims.

16 The link between conjectural history and 'hedged' language use (though the term is not used nor the point made generically) is made by Dugald Stewart: 'In examining the history of mankind, as well as in examining the phenomena of the material world, when we cannot trace the process by which an event *has been* produced, it is often of importance to be able to show how it *may have been* produced by natural causes' (Stewart, 1980, 293; original emphasis).

17 There is another hedged sentence at the start of chapter two: 'Whether this propensity be one of those original principles in human nature, of which no further account can

be given; or whether, as seems more probable, it be the necessary consequence of the faculties of reason and speech, it belongs not to our present subject to enquire' (*WN*, I.ii.2).

18 Here is a sustained example from the introduction to book two:

> In the following book I have endeavoured to explain the nature of stock, the effects of its accumulation into capitals of different kinds, and the effects of the different employments of those capitals. This book is divided into five chapters. In the first chapter, I have endeavoured to show what are the different parts or branches into which the stock, either of an individual, or of a great society, naturally divides itself. In the second, I have endeavoured to explain the nature and operation of money considered as a particular branch of the general stock of the society. The stock which is accumulated into a capital, may either be employed by the person to whom it belongs, or it may be lent to some other person. In the third and fourth chapters, I have endeavoured to examine the manner in which it operates in both these situations. The fifth and last chapter treats of the different effects which the different employments of capital immediately produce upon the quantity both of national industry, and of the annual produce of land and labour.
>
> (*WN*, II.Intro.6)

Factive verbs are here modified by the use of 'endeavoured'. Smith modifies 'explain' and 'examine' similarly. There are few counter-examples but there are some, for example, 'This rate is naturally regulated, as I shall show hereafter, partly by the general circumstances...' (*WN*, I.vii.1).

19 In *LRBL* Smith sets out his delight in Addison as a writer who exhibits 'modesty', a trait that leads Addison to express his sentiments 'in the least assuming manner' (*LRBL*, i.126–8).

20 Smith hedges the following statement: 'Live cattle are, perhaps, the only commodity of which the transportation is more expensive by sea than by land' (*WN*, IV.ii.17). This is followed by an analysis and justification, including a reflection on the importation by sea of Irish cattle. The hedge itself, if readers notice it, invites investigation of other exceptions such as horses, geese and other livestock. There is a potential here for the hedge to undercut the main point. The hedged proposition is then explored and so provides a paragraph-level example of textual organisation following didactic rules established by Smith in *LRBL*.

21 A good example of a conjecture hedged as prediction is found in Smith's discussion of the 'freest importation of foreign goods': 'The silk, perhaps, is the manufacture which would suffer the most by this freedom of trade, and after it the linen, though the latter much less than the former' (*WN*, IV.ii.41).

22 Thus, for example, the chapter on Colonies is relatively unhedged as it is descriptive and factual, though there are exceptions: 'Plenty of good land, and liberty to manage their own affairs their own way, seem to be the two great causes of the prosperity of all new colonies'(*WN*, IV.vii.b.16). This example is consistent with the use of hedging of knowledge claims elsewhere in the work.

7 Natural and human institutions: reading for argumentation in book three of the *Wealth of Nations*

1 There is a very minor use of the list within the penultimate paragraph of chapter one. It is used within the opening sentence to refer to the natural order of 'every growing society' that is 'capital' is 'first, directed to agriculture, afterwards to manufactures, and last of all to foreign commerce'. This is a sentence-level feature and the list is not used to organise larger units of text.

2 The general aim is similar to that of McCloskey's 'How to do a rhetorical analysis and why' but the methods and data are substantially different (McCloskey, 1994).

3 This is something that I am not sure about.

4 The final sentence of the final chapter of book two needs to be kept in mind for it is the key signal concerning the aim of the new book. It reads:

> What circumstances in the policy of Europe have given the trades which are carried on in towns so great an advantage over that which is carried on in the country, that private persons frequently find it more to their advantage to employ their capitals in the most distant carrying trades of Asia and America, than in the improvement and cultivation of the most fertile fields in their own neighbourhood, I shall endeavour to explain at full length in the two following books.
>
> (*WN*, II.V.37)

5 The whole of book three is leading up to the attack on mercantilist policies found in book four.

6 Although 'enjoyment' is not used in this passage it is implied ('predilection') as are the origins of rural life in 'subsistence'. If we look into chapter two, Smith refers a period when land is viewed 'as the means only of subsistence and enjoyment'.

7 The term is mine. See chapter ten, book two for a set of linked propositions concerning the remuneration of labour in different types of trade.

8 The numbering of sentences in this section is consecutive within the paragraph and not within the chapter.

9 It is hard not to read Smith's stock figure of the mother and the potentially wayward son, against the ambition of the young Robinson Crusoe to run away to sea (Defoe, 1965, 30–31).

8 Adam Smith's construction of 'History' and 'Story': the analysis of primogeniture

1 The paper is concerned with evaluating Smith's writing rather than with connecting what is said to the wider field of Smithian interpretation. However, where such connections can be made easily, they will be normally made in the notes.

2 The paper cannot make claims about all of Smith's uses and construction of history in the *Wealth of Nations*. That would be a big project. It can, nevertheless, initiate a discussion.

3 Smith's imaginative use of the story of how the division of labour develops in tribal society had a strong impact on two other writers on economic themes, Jane Marcet and Harriet Martineau. One of Smith's examples is the making of 'bows and arrows'. Jane Marcet gives the making of 'bows and arrows' a significant role in her discussion of the division of labour (Marcet, [1816] 1821, 71). Harriet Martineau's 'Life in the Wilds', is a story cantilevered on Smith's tale of the evolution of the division of labour, in a tribal society. There is a twist for the society is a group of stranded Europeans in the interior of Southern Africa. The community discovers the principles of the division of labour in the process of making items such as bows and arrows (Martineau, 1832). Both Marcet and Martineau take Smith's *Wealth of Nations* to be a work in which the nature of historical progress from the savage to the civilised is a central proposition.

4 Smith was very aware that he lived in a world, both international and national, in which communities were at different stages of development, as he, and the Scottish Historical School as a whole, would have classified them.

5 The list is edited because the chapter deals with institutions and 'customs and manners' in an integrated and cohesive way. There are lots of examples.

6 There is no attempt made here to analyse all the passages on primogeniture in the *Lectures on Rhetoric and Belles Lettres*. However my impression is that the earlier passages are more fully historical but less focused analytically than the passages analysed here. There are shared ideas across the two works but the passages in the *Wealth of Nations* are tighter and more sharply focused. The macro-contexts are also different.

7   The relationship between legal institutions, social and psychological dynamics, has been noted by Muller (1993, 128).

8   Grotius and Pufendorf are cited by Brown as the 'initiators of modern natural law' theories (Brown, 1994, 103).

9   The skillful use of the male pronoun to help the reader visualise or bring an activity into the mind in a concrete form is used elsewhere by Smith (e.g. in the passage in chapter ten of book one that deals with a comparison of different occupations).

10   The purpose of this article is to analyse Smith's writing rather than to compare it with the work of others. However, Smith's approach can be compared to that of Sir James Steuart. Steuart, in dealing 'Of Population in Agriculture' presents elaborated historical detail, albeit of a generalised kind. It is my impression that the interplay of theory and actuality, past and present is less skillfully handled than in Smith's writing. This is an impression, only, for an analysis has not yet been made though the conclusion is in accordance with other judgements on Steuart's work (Steuart [1767] 1966, Introduction, lviii).

11   Elsewhere I have posed the question 'What do we see in the *Wealth of Nations* when we treat it as a textbook?' One of the things that we see is the idea of a progression and change in the reader's experience or, from the point of view of Smith's writing, what can be taken as given and what needs to be familiarised. In other words issues around 'given' and 'new'.

Bibliography

Ahiakpor, J. C. W. (1992) 'Rashid on Adam Smith: in need of proof'. *Journal of Libertarian Studies*. Vol. 10: 171–180 (1999).

Ahiakpor, J. C. W. (1999) 'Did Adam Smith retard the development of economic analysis? A critique of Murray Rothbard's interpretation'. *Independent Review*, 3 (Winter): 353–383.

Belanger, J. (1998) 'Educating the reading public: British critical reception of Maria Edgeworth's early Irish writing'. *Irish University Review*. Vol. 28(2): 240–255.

Bloor, M. and Bloor, T. (1993) 'How economists modify propositions' in Henderson, W., Dudley-Evans, T. and Backhouse, R. E. (eds) *Economics and Language*. London: Routledge.

Booth, W. C. (1983) [1961] *The Rhetoric of Fiction*. London: Penguin.

Braudy, L. (1970) *Narratives in History and Fiction: Hume, Fielding and Gibbon*. Princeton, NJ: Princeton University Press.

Brown, S. (1996) (ed.) *British Philosophy and the Age of Enlightenment*. London: Routledge.

Brown, V. (1993) *Decanonizing Discourses: Textual Analysis and the History of Economic Thought*. London: Routledge.

Brown, V. (1994) *Adam Smith's Discourse: Canonicity, Commerce and Conscience*. London: Routledge.

Brown, V. (1995) 'The moral self and ethical dialogism: three genres'. *Philosophy and Rhetoric*. Vol. 28: 276–299.

Brown, V. (1997) ' "Mere inventions of the imagination": a survey of recent literature on Adam Smith'. *Economics and Philosophy*. Vol. 13: 281–312.

Buckle, S. (1991) *Natural Law and the Theory of Property*. Oxford: Clarendon Press.

Burke, K. (1969) *A Rhetoric of Motives*. Berkeley, CA: University of California Press.

Butler, M. (1972) *Maria Edgeworth: A Literary Biography*. Oxford: Clarendon Press.

Butler, M. (ed.) (1992) 'Introduction' in Maria Edgeworth's *Castle Rackrent and Ennui*. Harmondsworth, MD and London: Penguin, 1–54.

Campbell, T. D. (1971) *Adam Smith's Science of Morals*. London: Routledge.

Chitnis, A. (1986) *The Scottish Enlightenment and Early Victorian English Society* London: Croom Helm.

Cicero, [55 BC] *De Oratore* translated into English and with an introduction by E. N. P. Moor (1892) London: Methuen and Co.

Chamberlain, M. and Thompson, P. (eds) (1998) *Narrative and Genre*. London: Routledge.

Compact Edition of the Oxford English Dictionary (1971) Vol. ii, P–Z, Oxford: Clarendon Press.

Cooper, D. E. (1986) *Metaphor*. Oxford: Blackwell.

Cope, K. L. (1990) *Criteria of Certainty: Truth and Judgment in the English Enlightenment*. Lexington, KY: University of Kentucky Press.

Copley, S. (1995) 'Introduction', in Copley, S. and Sutherland, K. (eds) *Adam Smith's Wealth of Nations: New Interdisciplinary Essays*. Manchester: Manchester University Press.

Corbett, M. J. (1994) 'Another tale to tell: postcolonial theory and the case of *Castle Rackrent*'. *Criticism*. Vol. 35(3): 383–400.

Coulthard, M. (1994) 'On analysing and evaluating written text' in Coulthard, M. (ed.) *Advances in Written Text Analysis*. London: Routledge.

Coulthard, M. (1994) *Advances in Written Text Analysis*. London: Routledge.

Crabbe, G. [1783] (1850) *The Village* with notes by Sale, A. London: University Tutorial Press.

Czarniawska, B. (2004) *Narratives in Social Science Research*. London: Sage Publications.

Danford, J. W. (1990) *David Hume and the Problem of Reason, Recovering the Human Sciences*. New Haven, CT: Yale University Press.

Davie, G. E. (1973) 'The social significance of the Scottish philosophy of common sense'. *The Dow Lecture*. University of Aberdeen, 30 November 1972.

Defoe, D. (1965) [1719] *The Life and Adventures of Robinson Crusoe*. Harmondsworth: Penguin Books.

Dooley, P. C. (2003) 'Francis Hutcheson and the division of labour'. Manuscript.

Dudley-Evans, T. (1993) 'The debate over Milton Friedman's theoretical framework: an applied linguist's view' in Henderson, W., Dudley-Evans, T. and Backhouse, R. E. (eds) *Economics and Language*. London: Routledge.

Dwyer, J. (1998) *The Age of Passions: An Interpretation of Adam Smith and Scottish Enlightenment Culture*. East Lothian: Tuckwell Press.

Edgeworth, M. (1895) [1800] *Castle Rackrent*. London: Macmillan.

Edgeworth, M. (1991, reprint) [1800] *Castle Rackrent*. George Watson (ed.). Oxford: Oxford University Press.

Emerson, R. L. (1990) 'Science and moral philosophy in the Scottish Enlightenment' in Stewart, M. A. (ed.) *Studies in the Philosophy of the Scottish Enlightenment*. Oxford: Clarendon Press, 11–36.

Endres, A. M. (1991) 'Adam Smith's rhetoric of economics: an illustration using Smithian compositional rules'. *Scottish Journal of Political Economy*. Vol. 38: 76–95.

Endres, A. M. (1992) 'Adam Smith's treatment of historical evidence as illustrated from the theory of investment priorities'. *Journal of European Economic History*. Vol. 21: 217–249.

Endres, A. M. (1995) 'Adam Smith's advisory style as illustrated by his trade policy prescriptions'. *Journal of the History of Economic Thought*. Vol. 17: 86–105.

Evensky, J. (2003) ' "An inquiry into the nature and causes of the *Wealth of Nations*", Book 1: its relationship to Adam Smith's full moral philosophical vision'. *Research in the History of Economic Thought and Methodology*. Vol. 21(A): 1–47.

Fiori, S. (2001) 'Visible and invisible order: the theoretical duality of Smith's political economy'. *European Journal of the History of Economic Thought*. Vol. 8(4): 429–448.

Fish, S. (1972) *Self-consuming Artifact*. Berkeley, CA: University of California Press.

Fisher, W. R. (1987) *Human Communication and Narration: Toward a Philosophy or Reason, Value and Action*. Columbia, MO: University of South Carolina Press.

Flanagan, T. (1966) 'The big house of Ross-Drishane'. *Kenyon Review*. Vol. 28(1): 77.

Forbes, D. (1953–1954) ' "Scientific Whigism": Adam Smith and John Millar'. *The Cambridge Journal*. Vol. 7: 643–670.

Forbes, D. (1953–1954) 'The rationalism of Sir Walter Scott'. *The Cambridge Journal*. Vol. 7: 20–35.

Force, P. (2003) *Self-interest before Adam Smith, a Genealogy of Economic Science*. Cambridge: Cambridge University Press.

Fowler, H. W. (1966) *Modern English Usage*. Oxford: Oxford University Press.

Geertz, C. (1988) *Works and Lives: The Anthropologist as Author*. Stanford, CA: Stanford University Press.

Goldsmith, O. (1770) *The Deserted Village: A Poem*. London: W. Griffin.

Griswold Jr, C. L. (1999) *Adam Smith and the Virtues of Enlightenment*. Cambridge: Cambridge University Press.

Groenewegen, P. (2002) 'Adam Smith and the division of labour'. *Eighteenth-century Economics: Turgot, Beccaria and Smith and their Contemporaries*. London: Routledge.

Grotius, H. (1964) [1625]. F. W. Kelsey (trans.) *De Jure Belli ac Pacis Libri Tres*. New York: Ocean Publications.

Haakonssen, K. (1990) 'Natural law and moral realism: the Scottish synthesis' in Stewart, M. A. (ed.) *Studies in the Philosophy of the Scottish Enlightenment*. Oxford: Clarendon Press, 61–85.

Hack, D. (1996) 'Inter-nationalism: *Castle Rackrent* and Anglo-Irish Union'. *Novel – A Forum on Fiction*. Vol. 29(1): 145–164.

Harrison, J. R. (1995) 'Imagination and aesthetics in Adam Smith's epistemology and moral philosophy'. *Contributions to Political Economy*. Vol. 14: 91–112.

Henderson, W. (1995) 'Child's play: Maria Edgeworth and economics education'. *Economics as Literature*. London: Routledge, 21–42.

Henderson, W. (1995) *Economics as Literature*. London: Routledge.

Henderson, W. (2000) *John Ruskin's Political Economy*. London: Routledge.

Henderson, W. (2001) 'Natural and human institutions: argumentation and history in book three of the *Wealth of Nations*'. Unpublished paper, University of Birmingham.

Henderson, W. (2002) 'Exemplification strategy in Adam Smith's *Wealth of Nations*' in Hewings, M. (ed.) Academic Writing in Context: Implications and Applications. *Essays in Honour of Tony Dudley-Evans*. Birmingham: University of Birmingham Press.

Henderson, W. (2004) 'How does Smith achieve a Synthesis in writing? Evidence from his analysis of the propensity to truck, barter and exchange' in Samuels, W. J., Henderson, W., Johnson, K. D. and Johnson, M. (eds) *Essays on the History of Economics*. London: Routledge, 72–89.

Henderson, W. (2004) 'Of wages and profit in the different employments of labour: patterns of exposition and exemplification in Adam Smith's *Wealth of Nations*'. *Research in the History and Methodology of Economics*. Vol. 20-A: 1–15.

Henderson, W. and Hewings, A. (1986) 'Entering the hypothetical world: "assume", "suppose", "consider", and "take" as signals in economics texts'. Unpublished paper, University of Birmingham.

Henderson, W. and Hewings, A. (1987) 'Economics terminology: the problem of vocabulary'. *Economics*. Vol. 24: 113–127.

Herman, A. (2002) *The Scottish Enlightenment: The Scots' Invention of the Modern World*. London: Fourth Estate.

Hume, D. (1975) [1748, 1751] *Enquiries Concerning Human Understanding and Concerning the Principles of Morals*, in Selby-Bigge, L. A. (ed.). Textual revisions by P. H. Nidditch, 3rd edn. Oxford: Clarendon Press.

Hume, D. (2002) *Treatise of Human Nature,* edited by Selby-Bigge, L. A. Oxford: Clarendon Press.

Hutcheon, L. (1994) *Irony's Edge: The Theory and Politics of Irony*. London: Routledge.

Hyland, K. (1998) *Hedging in Scientific Research Articles.* Amsterdam/Philadelphia: John Benjamins Publishing Company.

Jasinski, J. (2001) 'Close reading'. *Sourcebook on Rhetoric: Key Concepts in Contemporary Rhetorical Studies.* London and Thousand Oaks, CA: Sage Publications.

Jensen, H. (1997) *Motivation and the Moral Sense in Francis Hutcheson's Ethical Theory,* The Hague: Nijhoff.

Jones, P. (1983) 'The Scottish professoriate and the polite academy' in Hont, I. and Ignatieff, M. (eds) *Wealth and Virtue: The Shaping of Political Economy in the Scottish Enlightenment.* Cambridge: Cambridge University Press.

Kaye (1924) (see entry for Mandeville).

Klein, L. E. (1994) *Shaftsbury and the Culture of Politeness, Moral Discourse and Cultural Politics in Early Eighteenth-century England.* Cambridge: Cambridge University Press.

Kuznets, S. (1966) *Modern Economic Growth: Rate, Structure and Spread.* New Haven, CT: Yale University Press.

Lakoff, G. (1972) 'Hedges: a study in meaning criteria and the logic of fuzzy concepts'. *Chicago Linguistics Society Papers,* 8: 183–228.

Lawson, T. (1997) *Economics and Reality.* London: Routledge.

Leech, G. N. and Short, M. H. (1981) *Style in Fiction: A Linguistic Introduction to English Fictional Prose.* Harlow: Longman.

Leff, M. (1997) 'Hermeneutical rhetoric', in Jost, W. and Hyde, M. J. (eds) *Rhetoric and Hermeneutics in Our Time.* New Haven, CT: Yale University Press.

Lodge, D. (1988) *Nice Work.* London: Secker and Warburg.

Lubasz, H. (1995) 'Adam Smith and the "Free Market" ' in Copley, S. and Sutherland, K. (eds) *Adam Smith's Wealth of Nations.* Manchester: Manchester University Press, 45–69.

McCloskey, D. N. (1985) *The Rhetoric of Economics.* Madison, WI: University of Wisconsin Press.

McCloskey, D. N. (1990) *If You Are So Smart: The Narrative of Economic Expertise.* Chicago, IL: Chicago University Press.

McCloskey, D. N. (1994) 'How to do a rhetorical analysis and why' in Backhouse, R. E. (ed.) *New Directions in Economic Methodology.* London: Routledge.

MaQueen, J. (1989) *Rise of the Historical Novel.* Edinburgh: Scottish Academic Press.

Mandeville, B. (1924) [1729, 1732] *The Fable of the Bees.* 2 vols. Kaye, F. B. (ed.). Oxford: Clarendon Press.

Marcet, J. (1816) *Conversations on Political Economy.* London: Longman, Hurst, Rees, Orme and Brown.

Markkanen, R. and Schröder, H. (eds) (1997) *Hedging and Discourse: Approaches to the Analysis of a Pragmatic Phenomenon in Academic Texts.* Berlin: de Gruyter.

Martineau, H. (1832) 'Life in the wilds' in *Illustrations of Political Economy.* London: Charles Fox.

Martineau, H. (1832) *Life in the Wilds: A Tale.* London: Charles Fox.

Mercier, V. (1962) *The Irish Comic Tradition.* Oxford: Clarendon Press.

Mill, J. S. [1848] (1929) 'Preface [1848]' in Ashley, W. J. (ed.) *Principles of Political Economy.* London: Longmans, Green and Co.

Mill, J. S. [1848] (1929) *Principles of Political Economy.* Ashley, W. J. (ed.) London: Longmans, Green and Co.

Miller, T. P. (1995) 'Francis Hutchison and the civic humanist tradition', in Hook, A. and Sher, R. B. (eds) *The Glasgow Enlightenment.* East Lothian: Tuckwell Press.

Mingay, G. E. (1963) *English Landed Society in the Eighteenth Century.* London: Routledge and Kegan Paul.

Moore, J. (1990) 'The two systems of Francis Hutcheson: on the origins of the Scottish Enlightenment' in Stewart, M. A. (ed.) *Studies in the Philosophy of the Scottish Enlightenment*. Oxford: Clarendon Press, 37–59.

Moore, J. and Silverthorne, M. (1983) 'Gershom Carmichael and the natural jurisprudence tradition in eighteenth-century Scotland' in Hont, I. and Ignatieff, M. (eds) *Wealth and Virtue: The Shaping of Political Economy in the Scottish Enlightenment*. Cambridge: Cambridge University Press.

Morgenstern, M. (1996) *Rousseau and the Politics of Ambiguity*. University Park, PA: Pennsylvanian State University Press.

Mortimer, A. (1984) ' "Castle Rackrent" and its Historical Contexts'. *Etudes Irlandaises*. No. 9: 107–123.

Motooka, W. (1998) *The Age of Reasons*. London: Routledge.

Muecke, D. C. (1969) *The Compass of Irony*. London: Methuen and Co.

Muller, J. Z. (1993) *Adam Smith in His Time and Ours*. Princeton, NJ: Princeton University Press.

Murray, P. (1971) *Maria Edgeworth: A Study of the Novelist*. Cork: Mercier Press.

Myers, G. (1985) 'Texts as knowledge claims: the social construction of two biology articles'. *Social Studies of Science*. Vol. 15: 593–630.

Myers, G. (1989) 'The pragmatics of politeness in scientific articles'. *Applied Linguistics*. Vol. 10: 1–35.

Oakley, A. (1994) *Classical Economic Man*, Brookfield, VT: Edward Elgar.

O'Banion, J. D. (1992) *Reorienting Rhetoric: The Dialectic of List and Story*. University Park, PA: Pennsylvania State University Press.

O'Brien, K. (1997) *Narratives of Enlightenment*. Cambridge: Cambridge University Press.

Omori, I. (2003) 'The "Scottish triangle" in the shaping of political economy: David Hume, Sir James Steuart, and Adam Smith' in Sakamoto, T. and Tanaka, H. (eds) *The Rise of Political Economy in the Scottish Enlightenment*. London: Routledge.

Phillipson, N. (1988) *Hume*. London: Weidenfeld & Nicolson.

Polkinghorn, B. and Thomson, D. L. (1998) *Adam Smith's Daughters: Eight Prominent Women Economists from the Eighteenth Century to the Present*. Cheltenham: Edward Elgar.

Pomeroy, S. B. (1995) *Xenophon Oeconomicus: A Social and Historical Commentary*. Oxford: Clarendon Press.

Price, J. V. (1992) *The Ironic Hume*. Bristol: Thoemmes Press. Reprint of 1965 edition, Austin, TX: University of Texas Press.

Prince, E. F., Frader, J. and Bosk, C. (1982) 'On hedging in physician–physician discourse' in di Pietro, R. J. (ed.) *Linguistics and the Professions*. Hillsdale, NJ: Ablex.

Pufendorf, S. (1927) [1673] *De Officio Hominis et Civis Juxta Legen Naturalem Libri Duo*. F. G. Moore (trans.) New York and Oxford: Oxford University Press.

Rashid, S. (1982) 'Adam Smith's rise to fame: a re-examination of the evidence'. *The Eighteenth Century: Theory and Interpretation*, 23, 64–85.

Rashid, S. (1990) 'Adam Smith's acknowledgements: neo-plagiarism and the *Wealth of Nations'*. *Journal of Libertarian Studies*. Vol. 9(2): 1–24.

Rashid, S. (1992) 'Adam Smith and neo-plagiarism: a reply'. *Journal of Libertarian Studies*. Vol. 10(Fall): 81–87.

Rees-Mogg, W. (2005) 'Before you take your new job, your holiness, read a little Adam Smith'. *The Times*. Monday, April 11: 21.

Ricardo, D. [1817] *Principles of Political Economy and Taxation*. London.

Richards, I. (1991) 'How to read a page' in Berthoff, A. E. (ed.) *Richards on Rhetoric, I. A. Richards: Selected Essays (1929–1974)*. Oxford: Oxford University Press.

Ricoeur, P. (1976) *Interpretation Theory: Discourse and the Surplus of Meaning*. Fort Worth, TX: Texas Christian University Press.

Ricoeur, P. (1981) *Hermeneutics and the Human Sciences*, edited and translated by John B. Thompson. Cambridge: Cambridge University Press.

Robbins, L. (1981) 'Economics and political economy'. *American Economic Review*. Papers and Proceedings, 71: 1–10.

Roll, E. (1942) *A History of Economic Thought*. Revised and enlarged 2nd edn. New York: Prentice Hall.

Rommel, T. (1997) 'A reliable narrator? Adam Smith may say so'. Available online at: http://www.cs.queensu.ca/achallc97/papers/pO32.html (accessed 2 July 2002).

Rosenberg, N. (1965) 'Adam Smith on the division of labour: two views or one?' *Economica*. Vol. 32: 127–139.

Ross, I. S. (1995) *The Life of Adam Smith*. Oxford: Clarendon Press.

Rothbard, M. N. (1995) *Economic Thought Before Adam Smith: An Austrian Perspective on the History of Economic Thought*. Vol. 1. Brookfield, VT: Edward Elgar.

Rothschild, E. (2001) *Economic Sentiments, Adam Smith, Condorcet and the Enlightenment*. Cambridge, MA: Harvard University Press.

Rotwein, E. (ed.) (1955) *David Hume: Writings on Economics*. Madison, WI: University of Wisconsin Press.

Saguaro, S. (1998) 'Maria Edgeworth and the politics of commerce'. *Moderna Sprak*. Vol. 92(2): 147–159.

Samuels, W. J., Henderson, W., Johnson, K. D. and Johnson, M. (eds) (2004) *Essays on the History of Economics*. London: Routledge.

Samuelson, R. J. (1996) 'The spirit of Adam Smith'. *Newsweek*. 2 December 1996. Vol. 128(23): 63.

Schneller, B. (1989) 'Maria Edgeworth, George Crabbe, and Oliver Goldsmith: a reassessment of *Castle Rackrent*'. Vol. 24(3): 126–131.

Schumpeter, J. A. (1954) *History of Economic Analysis*, London: Allen & Unwin.

Shaftesbury, A. A. (1964) *Characteristics of Men, Manners, Opinions and Times*. Annotated by J. M. Robertson (ed.), Indianapolis, NY: Bobbs-Morrell and Co.

Shapin, S. (1984) 'Pump and circumstance: Robert Boyle's literary technology'. *Social Studies of Science*. Vol. 14: 481–520.

Sher, R. B. (2004) 'New light on the publication of the *Wealth of Nations*'. *The Adam Smith Review*. Vol. 1: 3–29.

Silverman, D. and Torode, B. (1980) *The Material World: Some Theories about Language and their Limits*. London: Routledge and Kegan Paul.

Skinner, A. (1980) 'Introduction' in Smith, Adam, *The Wealth of Nations*. Harmondsworth: Penguin.

Skinner, A. (1993) 'Adam Smith: the origins of the exchange economy'. *European Journal of the History of Economic Thought*. Vol. 1(1): 21–46.

Skinner, A. S. (1972) 'Adam Smith, rhetoric and the communication of ideas'. *Scottish Journal of Political Economy*. Vol. 19: 307–319.

Skinner, A. S. (1979) *A System of Social Science*. Oxford: Clarendon Press.

Skinner, A. S. (1993) 'David Hume: principles of political economy' in Horton, D. F. (ed.) *The Cambridge Companion to Hume*. Cambridge: Cambridge University Press.

Smith, A. [1759] (1974) *The Theory of Moral Sentiments*, The Glasgow Edition of the Works and Correspondence of Adam Smith, edited by D. D. Raphael, A. L. Macfie. Oxford: Clarendon Press.

Smith, A. [1776] (1976) *An Inquiry into the Nature and Causes of the Wealth of Nations*, The Glasgow Edition of the Works and Correspondence of Adam Smith, edited by W. B. Todd. Oxford: Calrendon Press.

Smith, A. (1978) *Lectures on Jurisprudence*, The Glasgow Edition of the Works and Correspondence of Adam Smith, edited by R. L. Meek, D. D. Raphael and P. G. Stein, Oxford: Clarendon Press.

Smith, A. (1980) *Essays on Philosophical Subjects*, The Glasgow Edition of the Works and Correspondence of Adam Smith, edited by W. P. D. Wightman. Oxford: Clarendon Press.

Smith, A. (1983) *Lectures on Rhetoric and Belles Lettres*, The Glasgow Edition of the Works and Correspondence of Adam Smith, edited by J. C. Bryce. Oxford: Clarendon Press.

Spafadora, D. (1990) *The Idea of Progress in Eighteenth-century Britain*. New Haven, CT: Yale University Press.

Spiegel, H. W. (1971) *The Growth of Economic Thought*. Durham, NC: Duke University Press.

Steuart, Sir J. [1767] (1966) *An Inquiry into the Principles of Political Economy*. Vols 1 and 2, Andrew Skinner (ed.). Edinburgh: Oliver and Boyd.

Stewart, D. (1980) [1794] 'Account of the life and writings of Adam Smith LL. D.' in Smith, A. *Essays on Philosophical Subjects*. Wightman, W. P. D. and Bryce, J. C. (eds), The Glasgow Edition of the works and Correspondence of Adam Smith. Oxford: Clarendon Press.

Stewart, M. A. (1990) 'Introduction' in Stewart M. A. (ed.) *Studies in the Philosophy of the Scottish Enlightenment*. Oxford: Clarendon Press.

Stewart, M. A. (1996) 'The Scottish Enlightenment' in Brown, S. (ed.) *British Philosophy in the Age of Enlightenment*. Oxford: Clarendon Press, 274–308.

Still, J. and Warton, M. (1990) 'Introduction' in Warton, M. and Still, J. (eds) The Glasgow Edition of the Works and Correspondence of Adam Smith. *Intertextuality: Theories and Practices*. Manchester: Manchester University Press.

Stigler, G. J. (1982) *The Economist as Preacher and other Essays.* Chicago, IL: University of Chicago Press.

Stroud, B. (1977) *Hume*. London: Routledge.

Swailes, J. (1993) 'The paradox of value: six treatments in search of the reader' in Henderson, W., Dudley-Evans, T. and Backhouse, R. E. (eds) *Economics and Language*. London: Routledge.

Swift, J. (1744) 'On mutual subjection'. Available online at: www.readbookonline.net/read/3613/13471 (accessed)

Teichgraeber III, R. F. (1987) ' "Less abused than I had reason to expect": the reception of *The Wealth of Nations* in Britain, 1176–90' *The Historical Journal*. Vol. 30(2): 337–366.

Tenger, Z. and Trolander, P. (1994) 'Genius versus capital: eighteenth-century theories of genius and Adam Smith's *Wealth of Nations*'. *Modern Language Quarterly*. Vol. 55: 169–189.

Titscher, S., Meyer, M., Wodak, R. and Vetter, E. (eds) (2000) *Methods of Text and Discourse Analysis*. London and Thousand Oaks, CA: Sage Publications.

Todorov, T. (1990) [1978] in Porter, C. (trans.) *Genres in Discourse*. Cambridge: Cambridge University Press.

Tribe, K. (1995) 'Natural liberty and *laissez faire*: how Adam Smith became a free trade ideologue' in Copley, S. and Sutherland, K. (eds) *Adam Smith's Wealth of Nations: New Interdisciplinary Essays*. Manchester: University of Manchester Press, 23–44.

Viner, J. (1972) [1966] *The Role of Providence in the Social Order, an Essay in Intellectual History*. Jayne Lectures for 1966, Philadelphia: American Philosophical Society.

Watkins, F. (ed.) (1951) 'Introduction'. *Hume: Theory of Politics*. London: Nelson, vii–xxvii.

Watson, G. (1964) 'Introduction' in Maria Edgeworth's *Castle Rackrent*. Oxford: Oxford University Press, vii–xxv.

Weinscheimer, J. C. (1993) *Eighteenth-century Hermeneutics: Philosophy of Interpretation in England from Locke to Burke*. New Haven, CT: Yale University Press.

West, E. G. (1964) 'Adam Smith's two views of the division of labour'. *Economica*. Vol. 31: 23–32.

Westerman, P. C. (1994) 'Hume and the natural lawyers: a change of landscape' in Stewart, M. A. and Wright, J. P. (eds) *Hume and Hume's Connexions*. University Park, PA: Pennsylvanian State University Press, 1–22.

Whatmore, R. (2000) *Republicanism and the French Revolution: An Intellectual History of Jean-Baptise Say's Political Economy*. Oxford: Oxford University Press.

Whelan, F. (1985) *Order and Artifice in Hume's Political Philosophy*. Princeton, NJ: Princeton University Press.

Winch, D. (1973) 'Introduction' to David Ricardo's *The Principles of Political Economy*. London: Dent.

Winch, D. (1978) *Adam Smith's Politics: An Essay in Historiographic Revision*. Cambridge: Cambridge University Press.

Wood, P. B. (1994) 'Hume, Reid and the Science of Mind' in Stewart, M. A. and Wright J. P. (eds) *Hume and Hume's Connexions*. University Park, PA: Pennsylvanian State University Press, 119–139.

Woodmansee, M. and Osteen, M. (eds) (1999) *The New Economic Criticism: Studies at the Intersection of Literature and Economics*. London: Routledge.

Wolf, M. (2004) 'One economy, many states: the political economy of globalisation'. Thirteenth Annual IEA Hayek Memorial Lecture, July 2004.

Yamamoto, K. (2003) 'Acquisition of lexical phrases from text'. Unpublished paper, ATYR Spoken Language Translation Research Laboratories, Kyoto, Japan.

Young, A. (1780) *A Tour in Ireland with General Observations on the Present State of that Kingdom*. London: T. Cadell.

Index

Printed in Great Britain
by Amazon